The Counselor's Guide for Facilitating the Interpretation of Dreams

The Counselor's Guide for Facilitating the Interpretation of Dreams

Family and Other Relationship Systems Perspectives

Evelyn M. Duesbury

EVELYN M. DUESBURY

Routledge
Taylor & Francis Group
New York London

Routledge
Taylor & Francis Group
270 Madison Avenue
New York, NY 10016

Routledge
Taylor & Francis Group
27 Church Road
Hove, East Sussex BN3 2FA

Routledge is an imprint of Taylor & Francis Group, an Informa business

Printed in the United States of America on acid-free paper
10 9 8 7 6 5 4 3 2 1

International Standard Book Number: 978-0-415-88341-2 (Hardback) 978-0-415-88342-9 (Paperback)

Library of Congress Cataloging-in-Publication Data

Duesbury, Evelyn M., 1935-
The counselor's guide for facilitating the interpretation of dreams : a family and other relationship systems perspectives / Evelyn M. Duesbury.
p. cm.
Includes bibliographical references and index.
ISBN 978-0-415-88341-2 (hbk. : alk. paper) -- ISBN 978-0-415-88342-9 (pbk. : alk. paper)
1. Dream interpretation. 2. Counseling. 3. Psychoanalysis. I. Title.

BF1078.D767 2010
154.6'3--dc22 2010019521

Visit the Taylor & Francis Web site at
http://www.taylorandfrancis.com

and the Routledge Web site at
http://www.routledgementalhealth.com

Contents

Foreword

This book fills a major gap in training practicing counselors and students for the personal counseling and mental health professions. Although several texts on the theory and practice of counseling and psychotherapy emphasize the critical role that dream reports can play in helping people to live more effective, enjoyable lives, there are few books that teach current and prospective practitioners how to assist people who bring dream reports to their counseling and psychotherapy sessions.

In a study reported in the work of Rosner, Lyddon, and Freeman (2004), 43% of cognitive therapists reported no training in dream interpretation. Most theory and practice sections of counseling books—while they may describe the importance of dream interpretation—often devote only a few pages to working with dreams. *The Counselor's Guide for Facilitating the Interpretation of Dreams: Family and Other Relationship Systems Perspectives* is a comprehensive resource for counselors, psychotherapists, and educators seeking to fill this knowledge gap.

People come to counseling and psychotherapy looking for solutions to perplexing life problems. Because a predominant feature of dreams is problem solving, I have emphasized the use of dreams for creative problem solving for many years. This is not the only function of dreams, but many contemporary research studies indicate that cognition in dreams resembles waking cognition, especially insofar as problem solving is concerned (Foulkes, 1999). However, dream cognition may be more bizarre and unrealistic, yet may also be more creative and more insightful than waking cognition. Several years ago, a colleague and I addressed this issue: "By using your dreams for creative problem-solving you may also be able to increase your options and encounter new ways of thinking, feeling, and behaving that will enrich your life and actualize your potentials" (Krippner & Dillard, 1988, p. 248).

A foremost problem brought to counselors and psychotherapists is stress and anxiety stemming from relationship experiences. This book is uniquely sculptured for helping people, as well as their mental health providers, to utilize dreams to alleviate emotional stress from difficulty in their interpersonal relationships. Successful interpretation and use of dreams about relationships may not only alleviate stress but also provide the potential to catapult the dreamer into personal growth, including spiritual growth (Ullman, 1999).

Another unique feature of this book is its focus on the contemporary trend of the dreamer to become the interpreter of personal dreams and move away from the therapist as the interpreter. In this approach, the counselor or therapist facilitates the process but does not dictate the outcome (Rochlen & Hill, 1999; Ullman,

1999). In the case of children's dreams, parents' caring discussions with their children about scary dreams often comfort and contribute to the resolution of their children's fears.

This book has the advantage of being appropriate in various settings and for various populations. The table of contents indicates a splendid synopsis of the many populations touched in this book—adults, children, individuals, groups, and intercultural populations. This book can be used

- As a training tool for practicing professional counselors
- In courses in counseling, psychology, sociology, and social work as well as theological and seminary programs
- As a general education elective course in which all students, whatever their major, have opportunities to learn how to find meanings in their dreams.

Although the focus in this book is on relationship dreams, the model presented is useful in finding dream guidance for everyday activities, including events related to work, career, education, and health. Because dreams address waking-life experiences, the ability of counselors and psychotherapists to teach people how to interpret their own dreams has the potential of providing people with ongoing self-help for use after counseling or active psychotherapy sessions.

Because all people dream, and because dreams often reflect residual stress from waking-life events, the facilitation of people's interpretation of their dreams could become one of the most universally used and universally beneficial counseling techniques available. Indeed, there are now data indicating that the inclusion of dreams in counseling and psychotherapy enhances client satisfaction and is time efficient, reducing the number of sessions required to resolve the client's problem (Hill, 2004). I offer my congratulations to Evelyn Duesbury for compiling this useful text and hope that it receives the attention it deserves. It goes without saying that I have a similar hope for dream reports themselves.

Stanley Krippner, PhD
Professor of Psychology
Saybrook Graduate School and Research Center

Acknowledgments

To all who contributed their dreams and interpretations for our research and exploration projects. Their dedication to learning their dreaming language, their amazement at the solutions in their dreams, and also their frustrations—all these gave life to this book.

To the contributing authors. Their chapters fill unique needs in the dream interpretation world and unique needs in this book.

Kimberly Tuescher, PhD, and Brenda O'Beirne, PhD. (See Chapter 3, Overview of the Personalized Method for Interpreting Dreams [PMID].)

Montague Ullman, MD (1916–June 07, 2008). (See Chapter 13, Group Approach.)

Rosalind Cartwright, PhD and co-author Lynne Lamberg. (See Chapter 14, Cartwright's RISC Model.)

To the University of Wisconsin–Platteville:

Steven Becker, UWP, retired accounting department chair, for his confidence in my abilities and for giving me the latitude to develop my personal teaching style. This latitude helped me develop styles that not only blend with teaching accounting, but also blend with teaching how to facilitate the interpretation of dreams.

Mittie Nimocks, PhD, former dean of the college of liberal arts & education, current provost and vice chancellor, for her early scholarly edits of *The Counselors Guide for Facilitating the Interpretation of Dreams*.

The Karrmann Library and interlibrary staffs for providing numerous reference materials during my lengthy writing of this book.

The late James King, PhD, counselor education faculty, for helping me with research methods.

Steven Benish, PhD, counselor education faculty, for his experienced-based counseling support.

Students in my accounting classes. Their participation in my interactive teaching style and their dedication to learning nurtured my love for teaching.

To the University of Wisconsin–Whitewater:

David Van Doren, EdD, for his idea to research use of the Personalized Method for Interpreting Dreams (PMID) beyond the thesis that produced the model. That suggestion has been a huge benefit in refining the model. Practicing counselors, students in training, and the general public are the benefactors.

Aneneosa Okocha, PhD, for her knowledge of research reporting and for her dedication as co-investigator with me of a general population's ability to use the PMID model. Results of that general population's abilities to use the PMID model are similar to results of the populations (practicing counselors and students in training) that David Van Doren and I investigated.

Brenda O'Beirne, PhD, who also co-authored Chapter 3, for reviewing the quantitative results from colleagues and my research and exploration projects. Her experience in business administration and in counselor education benefits all who work with her.

Donald Norman, PhD, counselor education faculty, for his gentle nature and dynamic understanding of people, characteristics that were valuable influences during my early days as a counselor.

Denise Ehlen, director of research and sponsored programs, for a wide range of helping activities during our research projects.

Kathy Gibbs, retired distance education coordinator, for her personalized attention to my unique course in the interpretation of dreams.

To the American Counseling Association (ACA), with special thanks to David Kaplan, PhD, chief professional officer, for his foresightful recommendation to target this book primarily to practicing counselors.

To members of the International Association for the Study of Dreams (IASD) for their intellectual and scholarly appreciation of dreams. Several IASD professionals are quoted and referenced in this book.

To the Wisconsin Counseling Association (WCA) members whose ongoing encouragement inspired me along this journey to publication.

To Mary Katherine Nieponski, retired managing editor and book review editor of *The Family Journal*, for her support during my offerings to the journal. I will always remember Mary Katherine's uncommon inspirational rapport.

To Edward Bruce Bynum, PhD, clinical psychologist and writer, for sharing his time and talents on my journey toward teaching counselors how to help people who come to them with their dreams.

To Barbara Ardinger, PhD, writer and freelance editor, for her expertise, her wide-ranging knowledge, her attention to detail, and her thorough, prompt editing throughout my preparation of this book's manuscript.

To other editors, including Deirdre Barrett, Roberta Ossana, and Marian Sandmaier.

To Routledge staff for their attentive guidance:

> Dana Bliss, editor, for noticing opportunities that the facilitation of the interpretation of dreams has for practitioners and students within the counseling and therapy fields and for his ongoing inspiration.
>
> Chris Tominich, senior editorial assistant, for guidance during the journey from proposal to publication.
>
> Marsha Hecht, project editor, for her skillful to-the-point suggestions and prompt, positive feedback.
>
> Jane Harris, editor in the London office, for sharing my book proposal with her New York colleague, Dana Bliss. I now believe that Dana Bliss was the young man in my August 30, 2004 dream, which came the very night after I had finally begun in earnest to write this book. In the dream, I am walking with a young man and he says to me, "I bet you will be in New York."

To my own dreaming mind for being my primary writer's guide.

To my family and other relationships, both past and current: My reactions to experiences with them, both stressful and stressless, have given me opportunities to write, to research, and to teach.

To my in-house consultant and husband, John Duesbury, for his conscientious attention to details as he reviewed major parts of this book, for his spontaneous humor that keeps me chuckling, and for his companionship that makes our house a home and our marriage a partnership.

To my son, Steven Duesbury, for creating the venue for research projects, distance education classes, and book promotions (see http://www.yourguidingdreams.com), for creating the outline plus comprehensive suggestions for each chapter in this book. His suggestions continued as the master plan throughout. Also for inspiring John and me to pursue our common and our uncommon dreams.

To all others who have chanced to travel with me along this dream book trail.

Ethics Statement*

We celebrate the many benefits of dreamwork, yet we recognize that there are potential risks. We agree with the ethical position taken by the International Association for the Study of Dreams (http://www.asdreams.org) in that we support an approach to dreamwork and dream sharing that respects the dreamer's dignity and integrity and that recognizes the dreamer as the decision maker regarding the significance of the dream. Systems of dreamwork that assign authority or knowledge of the dream's meanings to someone other than the dreamer can be misleading, incorrect, and harmful. Ethical dreamwork helps the dreamer work with his or her dream images, feelings, and associations and guides the dreamer to experience, appreciate, and understand the dream more fully.

A dreamer's decision to share or discontinue sharing a dream should always be respected and honored. The dreamer should be forewarned that unexpected issues or emotions might arise in the course of the dreamwork. Information and mutual agreement about the degree of privacy and confidentiality are essential ingredients in creating a safe atmosphere for dream sharing.

Dreamwork outside a clinical setting is not a substitute for professional counseling or other professional treatment and should not be used as such.

All dreams and interpretations in this book are reprinted with the permission of the dreamers.

* Adapted from IASD Dreamworks Ethics Statement, Spring 1997, http://www.asdreams.org/idxaboutus.htm

Section I

Preliminaries of Dream Interpretation

PERSONAL NATURE OF DREAMS

Research shows that all people dream, so it is obvious that all reports of recalled dreams must originate from the dreamer. What is the dreamer to learn from his or her personal communication that is the dream? Let us begin by learning what dreams are.

Dreams are nighttime counselors. Although this definition fits with the context of this book, the idea of dreams as nighttime counselors may seem strange to people who have yet to use their dreams for problem solving. A straightforward definition of *dream* is "a series of thoughts, images, or emotions occurring during sleep" (Merriam-Webster's OnLine, http://www.merriam-webster.com/dictionary/).

Dreams that reflect problem solving and connect to our reactions to experiences with people in our lives are relationship dreams. Relationship dreams are the focus of this book. A great percentage of the images, thoughts, and emotions that pass through our minds while we are sleeping are about the people we have talked with, listened to, or thought about during the day before we go to sleep and dream. Those dreams may be about our reactions, both pleasant and unpleasant, to people from our past. Counselors find that a large percentage of people who come to us come for help in alleviating the stress from their reactions to major relationships in their lives.

Family systems and relationship systems perspectives are words I use in this text to describe reactions in relationship experiences. *Systems theory* is the term used by Bowen (1978), initiator of a family systems theory of human behavior. Family is the major system that is the focus of this book. In addition, people we work with, socialize with, or react to in any way are part of the systems perspectives presented in this book.

INDIVIDUAL CHANGE INITIATES SYSTEM CHANGES

A significant topic addressed in this book is the relief from stress that results when the person who feels the stress changes his or her reactions, which are new thoughts, attitudes (emotions), and behaviors adopted to relieve the stress. When the individual changes, the system eventually changes (Allen, 1994) with no need for the dreamer to approach other people about their behaviors.

It often is difficult, however, for us to change our reactions to others. It is difficult to change when we do not understand what initiates our stress. It is also difficult to change when it seems that others are either totally to blame or at least major sources of our stressful reactions to them. Researchers find that the dreams passing through our minds contain connections and associations to help us understand and change. Hartmann (1995) says there is "little question [that] … we appear to make distant connections or associations more easily during dreaming than during waking [thought]" (p. 215). Ullman (1996) declares that in dreams "we look at ourselves with greater honesty and in greater depth" (p. 250) than in waking life. Krippner states, "During our waking hours, we often feel frustrated that our rational attempts to solve life challenges are unsuccessful. It is then our dreams often provide innovative and unexpected answers" (personal communication, March 2, 2001).

One of the most frequent themes brought by adults to counseling is relationships. Listen again to Hartmann (1995): "Dreams often seem to be dealing with interpersonal problems, with the dreamer's current concerns about family, friends, [and] lovers" and dreams "appear to make connections with other persons or experiences in the past" (p. 215). Bulkeley (2000) wrote, "Perhaps the most commonly experienced form of problem solving through dreams comes in the context of personal relationships" (p. 190).

When dreams reveal that the dreamer's past reactions to other people or experiences affect his or her current reactions, at least in part, interpretation of those dreams yields clues for alleviating stress. Because systems effects can and do pass from generation to generation, when the dreamer removes stress from relationship concerns, current and subsequent generations will benefit. Delving into dreams thus has the potential to benefit coming generations of a family.

Our children's ability to react healthfully to relationship experiences is extremely important. Parents, counselors, and other caretakers can help children deal with stressful relationship experiences.

Since ancient times, many cultures have used dream guidance. Various roots of dream interpretation are given in Chapter 1, "Historical and Cultural Uses of Dreams." Included are summaries of both ancient and modern models for working with dreams. These models set the stage for the work of this book, which is dream interpretation.

Chapter 2 is an overview of how all people dream—children, adolescents, and adults. Although all people dream, not all recall their dreams. Further, not all people want to work with their dreams. Those who do and who bring dreams to counselors expect to receive guidance on how to find meanings in their dreams. Prominent in this book is the principle that the dreamer is the primary interpreter of his or her own dreams. Accordingly, all readers are encouraged to become familiar with their own personalized dreaming language.

Major groups of readers and learners include practicing counselors, students in training, clients in counseling settings, and self-study individuals. Counselors can glean information from their own dreams and from their clients' dreams on how to facilitate their clients' use of dreams to reduce stress.

Dedication at the beginning of any worthwhile venture is critical. Begin your study by applying the techniques presented in this section. Devote yourselves to developing a feel for uncovering the vast territory of the abundant accumulations of your psyche, accumulations that are immensely connected to your waking-life experiences.

1

Historical and Cultural Uses of Dreams

INTRODUCTION

The dream is a major self-discovery resource for everyone, everywhere, in whatever culture. Further, dream scenarios are exclusive to the individual dreamer. Moreover, dream contents reach beyond cognitive awareness. Cognitive behavior therapies concentrate on events, thoughts, and emotions. Dreams connect to events, thoughts, and emotions. The strengths of cognitive behavior therapies and the strengths of the facilitation of clients' dream interpretations can be combined.

DREAM GUIDANCE FROM ANCIENT TIMES

The most universally experienced nighttime activity is dreaming. Can we and do we use our dreams? We can, and we do. This chapter explores dream use by cultures around the world. We will become aware that some dream guidance practices were uprooted and fell into disuse, but in contemporary times, they are finding their way back to common usage.

People of primal cultures—those from the earliest known times—used their dreams to guide their waking lives. For instance, Native Americans often acted on dream guidance from their guardian spirits (Garfield, 1995; Kilbourne, as cited in Bynum, 2003; Wolff, 1952). Australian Aborigines developed a method of working with dreams based on the belief that the dreamer takes a journey and in the process receives guidance for specific purposes, such as healing, finding food, or spiritual enrichment (Bynum). Ritual prayers were developed by ancient cultures to stimulate dreams and receive answers to questions (Garfield). Incubation, a focusing process used to invite dreams about specific topics, was a common practice in several ancient cultures.

According to Wolff (1952), the ancient Babylonians and Egyptians are credited as the first cultures to develop dream theories. The Babylonians stressed the demoniac character of dreams, whereas the Egyptians stressed the divine character of dreams. Later, the Hebrews, Greeks, and Romans developed "a more specific elaboration" (Wolff, p. 9) of dream theories. The Hebrew prophets looked to their dreams to guide their people and to occasionally interpret the dreams of their Gentile rulers. Jewish people were freed from slavery in Egypt and Babylon, for example, as a result of Joseph and Daniel's interpretations of rulers' dreams. Whereas the Egyptians attributed the source of their dreams to their many gods, the Hebrew tribes attributed the source of their dreams to their one god. Early Greek appreciation for the power of dreams is reflected in Homer's heroes and in Hippocrates's medical discoveries. Although Greek dreamwork practices spread to the Romans, Cicero rejected the idea of dream credibility (Van de Castle, 1994).

Across the globe, the ancient Chinese connected their dreams to their daytime words and thoughts and used dreams for diagnostic purposes (Bynum, 2003; Garfield, 1991), a practice that continues in modern times. The Japanese tradition of dream interpretation is based on Japanese Buddhism and Shinto and, like several other early religions, "focuses on the worship of and devotion to deities of natural forces" (Bynum, p. 33). The Hindu Upanishads connect early childhood dreams to the dreamer's previous lives and later adulthood dreams to future lives (Van de Castle, 1994). The yogis of India believe that dreaming is a higher form of consciousness than waking life. Africa likewise has a "long cultural, clinical, and psychospiritual history" (Bynum, p. 30) of family dreaming that extends to contemporary times. Many Africans believe that both living and deceased family members, as well as the gods, appear in dreams and give guidance (Bynum).

Although most Christians in the Greek-speaking cultures "maintained the original dream tradition" (Savary, Berne, & Williams, 1984, p. 53), the Western church tradition of honoring dreams degenerated between the fourth and fifth centuries, when "teachers and theologians turned against the practice of observing dreams" (p. 50).

Jacob and Daniel's dreams are examples of how early Hebrew people honored their dreams. Dreams continued to hold a central place with the appearance of Jesus's birth. Although there appear to be no records of dreams that Jesus may have had, others' dreams (e.g., those of Joseph, Peter, Paul, and Stephen) are recorded in the New Testament. "Up to the beginnings of the fifth century, we can discern a well-integrated tradition of dreams" (Savary, Berne & Williams, 1984, p. 38).

According to Kelsey (1974/1991), many of the Christian writers who followed the New Testament authors were "some of the finest minds of those centuries" (p. 102). Kelsey cites Justin Martyr, Irenaeus, Tertullian, Clement, Origen, Athanasius, Augustine, Gregory of Nyssa, Synesius, and Chrysostom as intellectuals who were "educated in the world" (p. 103). All these authors wrote about dreams and visions in positive terms.

Jerome (347–490), a well-educated scholar, often shared his dreams with others and obviously valued them. For example, a major dream convinced Jerome to turn from studying classical literature to biblical studies. Yet it is, "among other things, because of him that dreams and dreamwork in the Church were held in disfavor for the next fifteen centuries" (Savary et al., 1984, p. 51). The pope persuaded Jerome to translate the Bible into Latin. Jerome mistranslated the word *anan* three of the ten times that the word occurs in the Bible. The word *anan* means "witchcraft," but Jerome mistranslated it three times as "observing dreams" (p. 51). Almost all translations of the Bible in use until the mid-20th century were made from Jerome's Vulgate and perpetuated the false condemnation of dreamwork (p. 52). Kelsey (1974/1991), an Episcopalian minister, discovered the mistranslation.

Savary et al. (1984), as well as other writers, found it startling that a person like Jerome, who was so dedicated to dreams, would make such a devastating mistake. "Perhaps," they wrote, "the mistranslation was a deliberate decision made by the religious authorities of Jerome's day" (p. 52).

One social idea that put dreams in disfavor was a shift in Christian thought after the Christians were no longer identified with the Holy Roman Empire. According to Savary et al. (1984), "For the most part, dreamwork in popular use had become a tool of magic and superstition. As such, it could not receive the support of the Church and its leaders" (p. 53). In that sense, perhaps Jerome was correct in "condemning the dreamwork of his day as a superstitious practice" (p. 53).

According to the philosophy of Aristotle (384–322 BC), "The only two ways humans can know or experience reality are by sense experience and rational thought" (Savary et al., 1984, p. 54). His conclusion that "dreams are not to be treated as gifts from the divine, but simply as natural phenomena" (p. 54) influenced later scholars. One of those scholars was the brilliant Thomas Aquinas, who deeply valued Aristotle's teachings. According to Kelsey (1974/1991), Aristotle was not trying to downplay dreams or the interpretation of dreams. Rather, the Greek philosopher was concerned, as were others of his time, about the "superstition and quackery that so often surrounded the consideration of dreams" (p. 72).

Thomas Aquinas (1225–1274) "made a synthesis of biblical tradition and the philosophy of Aristotle" (Kelsey, 1974/1991, p. 152). The result was "one of the most comprehensive theological and philosophical systems the world has seen" (p. 152). In the process, Aquinas faced a dilemma of how to address dreams. "With the rediscovery of the Greek language came also the rediscovery of the Greek-writing doctors of the early Church, who deeply valued dreams" (Savary et al., 1984, p. 55). Aristotle had said that "dreams had no divine significance." Aquinas handled his dilemma by avoiding the topic of dreams except for a few words. It is significant that during one of Aquinas's impasses in writing his great work, the *Summa Theologica*, he had a dream in which he "entered into a dialogue with the apostles Peter and Paul, and they had instructed him how to deal with the theological issue in question" (p. 56). When nearing the end of the *Summa*, Aquinas is said to have protested, "I can do no more. Such things have been revealed to me that all I have written seems like straw, and I now await the end of my life" (*Great Books of the Western World*, 1952, as cited in Savary et al., 1984, p. 56).

"In the end, despite what his books said, he [Aquinas] personally chose to follow his dream and the vision. However, it was his books that people read" (Savary et al., 1984, p. 56). This "one-sided interpretation of Thomas Aquinas" (Kelsey, 1974/1991, p. 8) further contributed to the devaluation of dreams.

In the 20th century, several writers (including Holowchak, 2002; Kelsey, 1974/1991; Savary et al., 1984; Van de Castle, 1994) have recognized some significant dream workers from the past. One of the ancient authorities on dreams was Synesius of Cyrene (ca. 373–414), who "was a fervent proponent of the many practical applications to be derived from cultivating dreams" (Van de Castle, p. 76). Among the practical applications of Synesius's philosophy was his conviction that people should explore the personal meanings of their dream symbols—a practice that is gaining momentum in current times—instead of consulting dream books for interpretations.

Alas, no one continued Synesius's pioneering work in the West through the Middle Ages. It was not until the 20th century that Kelsey (1974/1991) discovered the omission of Synesius's works from English texts. That omission, and other philosophers' pejorative assertions about dreams, had diminished respect for dreams.

Another significant interruption in the appreciation for dreams occurred during the middle and later parts of the 19th century, when the scientific method of discovery revolutionized the civilized world. Scientific emphasis on objective evidence and mistrust of anything subjective diminished credibility for working with dreams as guides (Kelsey, 1981), particularly in the Western world.

Even so, extraordinary advocates for the use of dreams arose in the 19th century. Alexander Grant, who wrote under the pseudonym Frank Seafield, gave extensive detailed reviews of the properties of dreams. A few of Seafield's findings are his recognition of the problem-solving aspects of dreams, of the power of thoughts and emotions on dream contents, and of the potential that dream insights have to balance the personality (Seafield, 1865).

Possibly the most famous 20th-century advocate for use of dreams was Sigmund Freud, who intentionally waited until the turn of the century to publish *The Interpretation of Dreams* (1900/1955). Freud's book set a precedent for the return of the Western World to the use of dreams in psychology. The gradual acceptance of qualitative data (dream reports) by the research world as credible evidence plus the dreamers' amplified involvement in working with their dreams is giving the dreamers of today expanded opportunities to use dreams for self-discovery.

DREAM INTERPRETATION MODELS IN THE 20TH CENTURY

Sigmund Freud (1856–1938) was born in Austria. Two of his closest colleagues were Carl Gustav Jung (1875–1961, Switzerland) and Alfred Adler (1870–1937, Austria). Jung and Adler left Freud to develop their own theories. Medard Boss (1903–1990, Switzerland) was analyzed by Freud but later developed a method for interpreting dreams based on existential psychology. Frederick (Fritz) Perls (1893–1970, Germany) was trained in Freudian therapy and later abandoned Freudian principles to develop the Gestalt method with his wife, Laura Posner Perls (1905–1990, Germany). The following paragraphs summarize the dream interpretation models of these five men.

Sigmund Freud

Freud based his techniques of dream interpretation on his observation that the images and feelings we experience in our dreams come from day residue, the experience of the preceding day. Freud wrote, "[A] dream is a (disguised) fulfillment of a (suppressed or repressed) wish" (1955, p. 160). For Freud, our dreams go through a process of condensation, displacement, representation, symbolism, and finally secondary revision. Underlying these mechanisms are Freud's (1900/1955) assertions that dreams are reactions to the day residue, as feelings, memories, and conflicting emotions appearing to the dreamer in disguised forms.

Condensation is the concept that the dream is a compressed version of all our dream-thoughts that arise about a particular theme. *Displacement* refers to differences in the obvious or manifest dream content from our deeper, hidden, and often forbidden dream-thoughts ("latent content"). *Representation* is the concept that dreams are predominantly visual and sensory. *Symbolism* refers to images found more often in folklore and myths than in dreams, although consideration of dream symbolism is necessary, as is some consideration of the dreamer's associations. *Secondary revision* refers to the "secondary" efforts of the mind to temper dream contents when a dream escapes the censoring mind and arouses distressing feelings (Freud, 1900/1955).

Carl G. Jung

In contrast to Freud, Jung (1954) saw dreams as revelatory of the dreamer's desires instead of hiding those desires by disguising them. Regarding a dream interpretation model, Jung wrote, "I have no theory about dreams. … And I am not sure that my way of handling dreams deserves the name of a 'method.' … On the other hand, I know that if we meditate on a dream sufficiently long and thoroughly something almost always comes of it" (p. 42).

Mattoon (1984), a Jungian analyst, presented Jung's "method" in steps, writing that the steps of interpretation are to

1. State the dream text with a structure (setting, plot, and lysis [solution or result]).
2. Establish the context of the dream.
3. Bring appropriate attitudes to the dream interpretation. Nothing can be assumed about the meanings or the images.
4. Consider the differences in personality of the dreamer and the interpreter and realize that the dream is not a disguise but a set of psychic facts.
5. Interpret the dream images as either objective or subjective.
6. Explore the dream for compensatory functions.
7. Consider the influence of the dreamer's conscious situation on the dream.
8. Verify the interpretation by confirmation with the dreamer and by comparison to subsequent dreams and subsequent events.

Alfred Adler

According to Adler, "very courageous people dream rarely, for they deal adequately with their situation in the daytime" (Ansbacher & Ansbacher, 1956, p. 360). Shafton (1995) suggests that Adler probably made that and similar statements to "accommodate the fact that at some point he personally stopped remembering his dreams" (p. 138). Adler is included, however, as one of our predecessors in dream theory because of his monumental influences on three major approaches to dreams:

1. Existential–phenomenological. The "best-known proponent is Medard Boss" (Shafton, p. 131).
2. Culturalist. One proponent is W. Bonime.
3. Gestalt, as developed by F. and L. Perls.

Adler's method of interpreting dreams is based on his theory of individual psychology, which posits that all humans are spurred by their feelings of inferiority to strive for perfection. The primary environment in which the individual's striving for perfection and avoidance of feeling inferior occurs is the social realm.

Adler taught that the conscious life and the unconscious life are inseparable. "[T]he methods used in interpreting the 'conscious' life may be used in interpreting the 'unconscious' or 'semi-conscious' life of our dreams" (Ansbacher & Ansbacher, 1956, pp. 358–359). The interpretation of dreams can only be successful when the dream is considered to be one aspect of the dreamer's lifestyle. According to Adler, while dreams move the dreamer toward solving a problem, they do so by metaphors that can deceive or fool the dreamer.

Medard Boss

For Boss (1958), who developed a form of existentialist interpretation of dreams, waking life is presupposed in all dream interpretation, no matter if dreams sometimes appear in symbolic and unrecalled form. Dreaming and waking life are plainly interdependent, so that without connections to waking life there would be no dreaming.

> Again and again it happens that a dreamer purposefully decides to intervene in the dream events, [and] then carries out his decision to the letter. Even people who don't quite know what is happening to them in their waking lives, allowing themselves to be driven by their momentary moods, often show an astounding strength of will while dreaming. (Boss, 1977, p. 184)

Boss (1977) further wrote that the "waking and dreaming existence of a given human being belongs fundamentally together in a unique, human Da-sein [Being-in-the-world] and selfhood that endures uninterruptedly lifelong" (p. 185). Dreams are thus personal to the dreamer. Further, dreams are repetitious until the dreamer resolves them or at least develops a resolution of them in waking life. Boss (1958) saw dream experiences as more valuable than waking-life experiences:

> How often does a dreamer not prize the reality of dream events beyond that of waking experience? The poet Franz Grillparzer, for instance, thought that the waking world compared with a recent dream of his was like a drawing compared with a painting, or a foggy day compared with a sunny one. (p. 82)

Frederick (Fritz) Perls

Although Perls (1969) had significant assistance from others (including his wife, Laura) in advancing his intuitive creation, Gestalt therapy, he seems to have been the one most dedicated to the Gestalt dream interpretation model. This was because he especially liked to work with dreams.

> [I]n a dream we have a clear existential message of what is missing in our lives, what we avoid doing and how we avoid living fully; we have plenty of material to reassemble and to help us re-own the alienated parts of ourselves. (p. 76)

Perls's original technique assumed that every element of the dream represents a part of the dreamer's personality and is a projection of the dreamer's self. Longtime Gestalt therapists E. and M. Polster (1973) honored Perls's projection perspective but also extended their work to include the dreamer's reactions to others: The dreamer's interactions with and reactions to other people are aspects of the dreamer's existence that dreams reflect.

AMERICAN DEVELOPERS OF DREAM INTERPRETATION MODELS

This segment turns from dream interpretation models developed by European researchers to those of American researchers. Brief descriptions of some dream models developed by Americans are given.

Calvin Hall

Calvin Hall (1909–1985) studied thousands of common people's dreams and became convinced "any clear-headed person should be able to interpret dreams" (Hall, 1953, p. 93). Hall wrote that "a dream is a creation of the dreamer's mind" (p. 93) and not a mysterious supernatural creation. He gave four rules for understanding dreams:

> 1. The dream is a creation of the dreamer's mind. The dreamer is playwright, producer, director, scenery designer, stage manager, prompter, principal actor, and audience all at the same time.
> 2. Nothing appears in dreams which the dreamer does not put there himself.
> 3. A dreamer may reveal more than one conception of himself or of another person in a single dream or in a series of dreams.
> 4. The dream should be interpreted as a whole because it reflects an interconnected network of ideas in the mind of the dreamer. [Further,] a dream ought never to be analyzed…without consulting other dreams of

> a series in order to see how thoughts of a person are tied together. (pp. 93–96)

Hall, assisted by R. A. Van de Castle, also developed a method of "classifying dream content so that it could be evaluated in an objective and quantitative fashion" (Van de Castle, 1994, p. 296). This method is Hall–Van de Castle content analysis. Instead of being a way to interpret dreams, it is a standardized way to assess significance to the most common dream symbols.

Montague Ullman

American psychiatrist and parapsychologist Montague Ullman (1916–2008) opened one of the first sleep laboratories (1961) at the Maimonides Medical Center in New York City.

> [This] laboratory [was] devoted to the experimental study of dreams and telepathy. In more recent years Dr. Ullman had been in the forefront of the movement to stimulate public interest in dreams and to encourage the development of dream sharing groups. Working with a small group process that he felt was both safe and effective he had spent the past three decades leading such groups both here and abroad, especially in Sweden. (Siivola, par. 2 and 3, retrieved February 1, 2010 from http://www.siivola.org/monte/biographical_note.htm)

Ullman's group approach to working with dreams has four stages:

1. The group elicits and clarifies the dream.
2. The group makes the dream its own.
3. The dreamer responds and works toward closure.
4. The dreamer reviews the dream.

Chapter 13 of this book presents Ullman's explanations and demonstrations of his group approach to working with dreams.

Rosalind Cartwright

The work of Rosalind Cartwright, for psychotherapist Carl Rogers, beginning in approximately 1950, sparked Cartwright's curiosity about whether dreams reveal people's fears, which they hesitate to talk about in waking life but obviously bother them. In 1978, Cartwright founded the Sleep Disorder Service and Research Center at Rush University Medical Center in Chicago. Her first work was the "study of dreams of people in crises" (Cartwright & Lamberg, 1992/2000, p. xi). Cartwright's personal experiences during her own earlier crisis inspired her to find ways to help other people in crisis.

Cartwright's RISC model has four steps. The first letter of each step forms the acronym RISC, which helps dreamers remember that the idea is to "risk" stepping in to change the endings of their dreams and work toward a more positive self-image.

R—Recognize when you are having a bad dream, the kind that leaves you feeling helpless, guilty, or upset the next morning
I—Identify what it is about the dream that makes you feel bad
S—Stop having bad dreams
C—Change negative dream dimensions into their opposite, positive values

Chapter 14 of this book presents Cartwright and Lamberg's work and demonstrates Cartwright's RISC model.

Gayle Delaney

Gayle Delaney developed a model aimed at general readers. She explained her dream interview method as follows:

> I have developed an unusual career as a dream psychologist who does not practice psychotherapy but devotes her entire practice to teaching people to teach themselves and others how to understand dreams and how to target them for specific problem solving. (Delaney, 1988, p. ix)

In Delaney's dream interview method, the interviewer, either a dreamwork specialist or the dreamer himself or herself, conducts an interview to elicit the meanings of the dream. A crucial part of this method is that the interviewer pretends to come from another planet. This fiction forces the dreamer to give his or her own specific associations to the dream. The goal is for the dreamer to interpret the dream from personal knowledge, opinions, and beliefs with as few interpretations or explanations from the interviewer as possible (Delaney, 1988, 1996).

Clara Hill

Clara Hill, professor of psychology at the University of Maryland, developed the cognitive experiential model with help from her students. She and her students and colleagues have conducted extensive research on this model.

The cognitive experiential model has three stages (Hill, 2004, p. 230):

1. Exploration. The goal of this stage is to "stimulate the client's cognitive schemas so that the experiences, memories, thoughts, and feelings that propelled the dream are activated."
2. Insight. The goal of this stage is to "understand the meaning of the dream at one of a number of levels (e.g., experience, waking life, and inner personality dynamics)."
3. Action. In this stage, the therapist "helps the client translate insights gained from working on the dream into exploring changes in waking life."

Alan Siegel and Kelly Bulkeley

Psychotherapists Alan Siegel and Kelly Bulkeley developed a parents' guide for understanding children's dreams and nightmares (Siegel & Bulkeley, 1998). Siegel and Bulkeley each have children who began sharing dreams with their parents as early as age 2. Their experiences as parents provided them with a wealth of inspiration for their work with preschoolers, elementary-age children, and teens, as well as undergraduate and graduate students.

Siegel and Bulkeley developed various models for parents to use in guiding their children's work with dreams. Their 1998 book, *Dreamcatching, Every Parent's Guide to Exploring and Understanding Children's Dreams and Nightmares*, is an excellent resource that contains explanations and illustrations of their various models. In addition, Siegel (1998) published "Nighttime Remedies, Helping Your Child Tame the Demons of the Night," in *Dream Time.*

THE NEUROLOGY OF DREAMING AND THE COGNITIVE CENSOR

In the first paragraph of this chapter, I stated, "dream contents reach beyond cognitive awareness." Stated another way, during dreaming the cognitive sensor is locked away from bowdlerizing the dreaming mind's creative explorations into the vast, vast territory of the psyche's rich accumulations. By *cognitive sensor* I mean brain structures that somewhat maintain our attention on directed thought during waking life but are relatively inactive or blocked during sleep and dreaming. Consequently, associations and memories (often in symbolism) are frequently far more extensive during dreaming than during waking life.

Now, we are talking about the neurology of dreaming. The activities of our brain during sleep and dreaming differ in various respects from the activities of our brain during waking life.

Next is a brief exploration of what occurs in our brains during sleep and dreaming that opens our inward view to wide vistas. See Appendix A: The PMID Model Researched and Explored to support statements that I make about individual PMID (Personalized Method for Interpreting Dreams) steps.

On the one hand, some brain structures are either completely or partially deactivated during sleep and dreaming. For instance, the dorsolateral prefrontal and parietal cortex that somewhat confines thinking in waking life to directed thought and voluntary control is shut down during dreaming (Braun et al., 1998). Material entering the dream can thus extend beyond waking-life thoughts. Waking-life thoughts frequently prompt dreams (PMID Step 2). Earlier experiences (memories) are reflected in dreams, often in the same dreams that connect to similar current waking-life experiences (PMID Step 6).

On the other hand, some brain structures are reactivated during sleep and dreaming, for instance, the limbic and paralimbic systems, seat of our emotions (Braun et al., 1997; Maquet et al., 1996; Nofzinger, Mintun, Wiseman, Kupfer, & Moore, 1997). Emotions felt in a dream reflect the dreamer's emotional responses to waking-life issues symbolized in the dream (PMID Step 4).

The anterior cingulate is also reactivated during dreaming (Nofzinger et al., 1997). Results include connections to waking-life concerns and even possible suggestions for waking-life actions. PMID Step 5 supports finding suggestions and solutions in dreams.

The flow of natural chemicals (neurotransmitters) through the brain structures also affects dreaming. Brain chemicals reported to be active during dreaming, their pathways through the brain, and to what extent each affects dream contents are the subjects of research with interesting results.

On the topic of pathways and resultant dream contents, Bynum (2003) wrote that some researchers believe neuromelanin passing through the locus coeruleus of the brain initiates "the flow of dream images of a personal, familiar, and collective nature" (p. 68). For Bynum and others, this suggests that there is a constant exchange between both the subjective intrapsychic and the collective unconscious transconscious currents in our intimate dream life. The PMID model (primary dream interpretation model in this book) traces effects from the dreamer's reactions to family and other major relationships to dream content.

Obviously, there is much more involved in the neurology, chemistry, and functions of the brain during dreaming than presented in this short segment. For further information, turn to the resources cited here.

In the next segment, we return to the function of dreams that my research and exploration colleagues, the participants in our projects, and I consider significant: Dreams provide personal guidance for the varied activities of waking life. An added plus of helping clients find guidance in their dreams is the potential for the client-dreamer's ongoing self-discovery after the counseling sessions conclude.

THE VALUE OF SELF-DISCOVERY FROM WORKING WITH DREAMS

Mahrer (1989), a psychotherapist, wrote, "If you want to undergo profound personal change, probably the best way is to work with your own dreams" (p. 10). Radha (1994), a swami and dream studies teacher, held steadfastly to the belief that when the conscious mind is asleep, the dreamer's higher thoughts guide him or her. Can "undergoing profound personal change" be coupled with accessing "higher thoughts"? Which comes first? Or, do personal change and access to higher thoughts conjoin? What is involved in "undergoing profound personal change"? Radha uses the analogy of "opening an old water pipe," explaining that before we are able to achieve higher consciousness, we must first clear out the clogs; that is, identify emotional stressors that stop us from opening up to higher consciousness.

According to Jung (1966), emotions are dominant dream themes. Moreover, the dreaming mind often gives a more accurate reflection of the person's emotions than the person outwardly expresses or knows (Freud, 1900/1955; Jung, 1966; Mahrer, 1989; Seafield, 1865; Ullman, 1996). When I began to work with my dreams, one of the first shocks I had was seeing the stark honesty of my dreaming emotions, which were often more accurate than I consciously realized. Later, I discovered a consensus among several other writers and researchers.

Dreams not only identify emotional stressors but also give suggestions for resolving problems (Hill, 1996; Jung, 1960; Krippner & Dillard, 1988). If the dreamer's emotions lead to dream suggestions for resolving problems, who, then, is the most reliable interpreter of dreams? Many cultures, both ancient and modern, depend on specialists to interpret dreams for individuals. However, in Faraday's (1997) view, "There are millions of intelligent and basically 'normal' people who are perfectly capable of exploring their own dreams for greater self-knowledge" (p. 17).

Mahrer (1989) pointed out that he works with his own dreams "because of [their] effects on the very person that I am and can be, not because I am a psychotherapist" (p. 12). He encouraged all people to work with their own dreams for personality development. Mattoon (1984), a Jungian therapist, wrote that Jung encouraged all people, including those who do not consult professional counselors, to work with their dreams because dreams encompass the unconscious as well as conscious thoughts and consequently promote "development of their personalities" (p. 4).

The approach of the American Counseling Association is that the counselor facilitates the client's alleviation of his or her own stress. This approach agrees well with the interpretation of dreams. When the counselor facilitates the client's interpretation of his or her dreams in the counseling session, the client-dreamer has the potential for ongoing self-discovery after the counseling sessions conclude. "The aim of all help is self-help and eventual self-sufficiency" (Brammer & MacDonald, 2003, p. 6).

Work with dreams augments the aim of eventual self-sufficiency and blends with our recognition that the dreamer is the ultimate authority on his or her dream meanings. The dreamer is the ultimate authority because many parts of the dream are derived from his or her pre-dream experiences. Because all people dream, self-discovery dream interpretation is a commonly available technique. Do other counseling approaches incorporate self-discovery features?

FACILITATION OF CLIENTS' DREAM INTERPRETATIONS AS COMPLEMENTARY TO CONTEMPORARY COGNITIVE BEHAVIOR THERAPIES

Cognitive behavior techniques—for example, thought control and self-talk—are currently predominant counseling techniques, especially in the United States. Are these techniques commonly available? Thoughts are generated through the mind. Since all humans think, thoughts are commonly available. Self-talk is generated through the mind. Since all humans are able to do some form of self-talk, self-talk is commonly available.

Two cognitive models that encourage self-discovery are Beck's cognitive therapy and Meichenbaum's cognitive behavior modification. Beck's cognitive therapy (Beck, Rush, Shaw, & Emery, 1979) is a collaborative technique in which therapists teach their clients how to monitor their thoughts, especially their automatic thoughts. Meichenbaum's (1977) cognitive behavior modification is a self-instructional therapy that focuses on helping clients listen to their "internal dialog or inner speech" (p. 201), which is their self-talk.

Albert Ellis (2001), the creator of the forerunner of the cognitive behavior therapies, developed rational emotive behavior therapy (REBT), an approach to changing "irrational" (Ellis's word to replace "distorted") thoughts. Ellis's approach is more therapist directed and less empathetic in nature than Beck and Mechenbaum's approaches, so there is naturally less self-discovery potential in his method than in the other two approaches. Still, the client is motivated to discover his or her irrational thoughts.

When using Beck's method (Beck et al., 1979), the therapist asks the client to search for distorted thought patterns, even following such patterns back to earlier experiences in his or her life. Then, the therapist asks the client to explore whether these distorted thought patterns either lack support or stem from distorted impressions from the past.

When using Meichenbaum's method (1977), clients observe their "thoughts, feelings and physiological reactions, and or interpersonal behaviors" (p. 219) to recognize maladaptive behaviors and move toward changing their incompatible internal dialogues. When clients use inner dialogue to assess others' reactions to their changed behaviors, this assessment often determines the client's continuance of his or her new behaviors.

Cognitive behavioral approaches to counseling give excellent support to the PMID model. With the PMID approach, dreamers, either alone or facilitated by a counselor, record and study their before-the-dream events (behaviors), thoughts, and emotions for connections to their dreams.

> Dreaming and waking mental activity both involve the making of connections in the networks of the mind. However, in dreaming connections are made more loosely and broadly than in waking. (Hartmann, Zborowski, Rosen, & Grace, 2001, p. 116)

Using our dreams is an excellent way not only to discover broader connections than we find in our waking-life cognitions but also to discover (detect) which thoughts, which behaviors, and which emotions precede distorted or irrational thoughts, illogical self-talk, cognitions, and behaviors.

On the one hand, the strengths of cognitive techniques are that waking thought is more accessible than dream content, and cognitive techniques are often easier to learn than dream interpretation techniques. On the other hand, "Dreaming makes connections more broadly and more 'peripherally' than does typical waking thought" (Hartmann, 1995, p. 213). In addition, "The dream gives a true picture of the subjective state, while the conscious mind denies that this state exists, or recognizes it only grudgingly" (Jung, 1933, p. 5). Because the cognitive mind is at rest during sleep, cognitive control is almost eliminated during dreaming. An exception is lucid dreaming, in which the dreamer is aware of the dreaming state.

A weakness of the cognitive behavior approaches is that they have limited acceptance in some cultures. For instance, in some Mediterranean and Middle Eastern cultures, there are values in religion, marriage and family, and child-rearing practices

(Dattilio, 1995, as cited in Corey, 2008, p. 301) that strictly forbid cognitive behavior-type interventions that require people to question their root cultural principles.

The greatest weakness in the use of dreams in counseling is probably the counselor's lack of training. Yet, dreams incorporate experiential information beyond what we grasp in our waking thoughts. Dreams make broader connections to our past experiences than our waking cognitions make. Consequently, the facilitation of clients' interpretation of their dreams may be the *most encompassing* universal counseling approach available since during sleep the cognitive censor is locked away from bowdlerizing the dreaming mind's creative explorations into the vast territory of the rich accumulations of the psyche.

Strengths of cognitive behavior therapies and strengths of the facilitation of clients' dream interpretations can be combined. Cognitive behavior therapies concentrate on events, thoughts, and emotions. Dreams connect to events, thoughts, and emotions. Counselors whose skills include the facilitation of clients' dream interpretation naturally extend their services in helping their clients alleviate stress.

SUMMARY

This chapter traces the use of dreams from ancient times to today. Many lands and cultures provide examples of work with dreams, including those of Native Americans, Australian Aborigines, Hebrews, Greeks, Romans, Africans, Chinese, Indians, Egyptians, and Japanese.

Although use of dreams was disparaged and uprooted in Western Christian cultures, credibility began to reemerge during the 19th and 20th centuries. Freud's psychoanalytic emphasis on the use of dreams influenced his colleagues, Jung and Adler, although both developed dream interpretation styles that deviated from Freud's. Adler's influence resulted in Boss's development of an existentialist approach to dream interpretation. Perls developed the Gestalt dream interpretation approach. More recent developers of dream interpretation models include Hall, Ullman, Cartwright, Delaney, Hill, and Siegel and Bulkeley.

A brief discussion of the neurology of dreaming is included to help us understand a few of the "whys" that dream scenarios vary from waking-life cognitions. Increased acceptance of qualitative data and dreamers' amplified involvement in working with their dreams is giving today's dreamers expanded opportunities to use their dreams for self-discovery. Dreams incorporate experiential information beyond what dreamers grasp in waking thoughts. Thus, practicing counselors who know how to facilitate their clients' interpretation of dreams yield expanded opportunities for them to help their clients who bring dreams to counseling sessions.

SELF-STUDY QUIZ: CHAPTER 1

1. What proportion of people dream?
2. Dreams have been used for guidance since ancient times.
   True _____
   False _____
3. List at least one specific result claimed from use of dreams. List the culture, country, or leader identified with the result you identify.
4. How is dream content affected by deactivation of dorsolateral prefrontal and parietal cortex brain structure?
5. Give two strengths presented in Chapter 1 for the use of dreams in counseling settings.

2

Preliminaries to Working With Dreams

I would be running as hard as I could, trying to escape the devil and get to Mother and Dad in the distance.

—Harry, a dreamer

IMPORTANCE OF WORKING WITH EARLY LIFE DREAMS: CHILDREN'S DREAMS

The most important help that parents can give when their children awaken from dreams, whether happy or scary, is to patiently listen as their children relate their dreams. In this way, the children's feelings and reactions are valued. It is also possible that waking-life activities that might have prompted the dreams may be revealed as the children talk about their dreams.

As Siegel and Bulkeley (1998) wrote, "Although the world's religious traditions differ in many important ways, one thing they do agree on is that dreams can be a valuable source of spiritual experience, insight, and understanding" (p. 165). Sometimes, however, parents' early learnings cause them to wonder about the safety of dreams.

As the dream fragment given at the beginning of this chapter indicates, children do dream about religious teachings. Harry's recall of a childhood nightmare shows what can happen when parents are unaware of how to help their children who are having scary dreams. His parents had either faint or no realization of what was happening in Harry's life that may have brought his nightmare. Harry (now an adult) wrote about his childhood nightmare (which may have continued into adolescence):

Harry's Reflections on His Childhood Nightmare

I am not able to recall everything that Mother told me about the dream, but … I recall her trying to soothe me, holding me. … The nightmares came frequently when I was a child, and they terrified me. One of those that most terrified me was a recurring nightmare. In it, I would be running as hard as I could, trying to escape the devil and get to Mother and Dad in the distance. The devil was the classic red devil, complete with tail and pitchfork. Occasionally, Mother would wake me up because I was screaming in my sleep. One time, she took me to her and Dad's bed and let me lie between them. She told me the devil couldn't get me there. However, the dream started up again, and now the devil was under the bed with his pitchfork aimed up at me! As a child, I was often ill with asthma attacks and occasionally ran a high temperature that produced hallucinations. This nightmare would haunt me at such times.

[In retrospect] these nightmares and other anomalies of my personality were most certainly a result of lessons taught by our church. We often had a lay minister deliver the message. One particular lay minister was extremely vociferous and preached mostly about sin and its consequences. I was very impressed by this individual. He would parade back and forth, loudly proclaiming damnation. … He said that if you even thought ill of someone, you had committed a grievous sin, like murder, in the eyes of the lord.

As to whether or not the dream continued into adolescence, I'm not certain when it started, when it stopped, or why it stopped. I think I had stopped sleeping in Mother and Dad's bedroom. At least I was old enough to understand what the preacher was saying and understood exactly what he was trying to put across. I only remember that particular dream was extremely terrifying to me. I believe it continued until I was old enough to understand that perhaps preachers sometimes said things to emphasize a point, and perhaps I was beginning to realize I wasn't going to burn in hell for eternity just because I thought ill of someone.

As an adult, Harry has become a searcher into the soul. Perhaps his spiritual searching now has been prompted at least somewhat by his childhood terrors. Adult teachers have sacred responsibilities to the adults to whom they preach and, perhaps more importantly, to the children who hear them. Had Harry's mother been aware of the dynamic impact of the lay minister's hellfire sermons on her child's dream life, she would certainly have been better able to help him stop having these nightmares. They would not have lasted into Harry's adolescence.

FROM CHILDHOOD DREAMING INTO ADOLESCENT DREAMING

Siegel's wisdom on counseling adolescents comes from over 25 years of specializing in adult and child psychology. Siegel (2002) found that children entering into adulthood commonly and frequently have "coming-of-age" dreams.

> The most common contents of adolescent coming-of-age dreams revolve around interactions with friends, siblings, parents, and teachers. In these dreams, adolescents reflect on their waking-life efforts to form mature personal relationships of various kinds. Because these life events are so often filled with tension and conflict, adolescents' dreams frequently have an anxious, frightening quality.
>
> Teenagers on the verge of leaving home are often convinced that they are fully equipped to handle any problem and all the responsibilities of young adulthood. When they get their college acceptance or go through the exciting high school graduation parties and rituals, they may have exhilarating dreams of flying, finding money, or playing star roles in movies or performances. These are not just adolescent dreams but occur during peak experiences and positive life passages throughout adulthood. They may symbolize a sense of creative power and the joy of accomplishment and new maturity.
>
> When the moment of departure grows near, the adolescent may still deny any anxiety, but the steps he or she will take reverberate deeply. As clearly as anything else, this is the end of childhood, the end of being able to depend fully on parents, and the beginning of what for many is a more rocky road into early adulthood than they anticipated in their fantasies about independence.
>
> For the young adult who is open to his or her feelings, there is a mixture of excitement about the new horizons of independence, and simultaneously there is grief about leaving the safety of their parents' home and maybe even a bit of terror about the responsibilities ahead of them.
>
> When dreams are taken seriously and discussed in the family, children [and adolescents] will remember more dreams, often throughout their lives, and will recall a mixture of both upsetting and positive dreams. Sharing dreams helps to increase a child's emotional IQ by helping them identify and express important issues. Family dream sharing can also promote quality time by giving both parents and children a focus for talking about their feelings.
>
> At life passages and times of stress, repetitive nightmares are a clear signal that some deeper conflict has not been resolved. … Telling dreams to a parent or teacher or mental health professional may provide the child with a vehicle for expressing unresolved feelings that they have no other way to talk about. (Siegel, 2002, pp. 37, 39)

Strauch (2005), a researcher living in Switzerland, studied Swiss children's dreams from ages 9 through 15. She found that there are "notable increases over time on inventiveness, self-involvement, and the inclusion of speech" (pp. 166–167), findings that were similar "to those reported by Foulkes [1982] with American children 20 years earlier" (Strauch, p. 168). Strauch wrote that Foulkes had concluded that "dreaming is, for the most part, adult-like by ages 9–11" (p. 166). Strauch also wrote that her findings "fit with Foulkes' further claim that there are subtle changes in dreaming cognition that manifest themselves throughout adolescence" (p. 167). These similar results suggest "that the developmental changes in dreaming from ages 9 to 15 years are mostly independent of time and national differences, at least within the context of Western culture" (p. 168).

OPPORTUNITY FOR SCHOOL COUNSELORS

Here is an opportunity for school counselors to first become at ease with the Personalized Method for Interpreting Dreams (PMID) model to interpret your own dreams. Then, consider using the PMID to help your students who bring dreams to you. Siegel and Strauch strongly supported the helpfulness to adolescents of sharing their dreams with knowledgeable adults. I and my colleagues have yet to explore use of the PMID model for working with adolescents' dreams. We welcome your observations and comments about its applicability for facilitating 7th- through 12th-grade students' interpretation of their dreams.

FROM ADOLESCENCE INTO ADULT LIFE DREAMING

Adult life dreaming is the primary topic of the present book, which focuses on the principle that the adult dreamer is the primary interpreter of his or her own dreams. When a counselor is involved, the counselor facilitates the client-dreamer's exploration of his or her dreams for solutions or suggestions on how to alleviate waking-life concerns. In the process, the dreamers are often helped to understand and better know themselves. Although interpreting dreams is a potent way for people from all walks of life to know themselves better, in America and much of the Western world, people often overlook dreams as resources. One reason is the historical belief that only professionally trained people can interpret dreams.

However, several contemporary dream interpretation models look at the dreamer himself or herself as the best authority on the meanings of his or her dreams. Among those models are Delaney's dream interview model (Delaney, 1996); Cartwright's RISC (recognize, investigate, stop, change) model (Cartwright & Lamberg, 1992/2000); Ullman's group dreaming model (Ullman, 1996); and my PMID (Duesbury, 2000). The dreamer is the best authority because most dreams arise from his or her personal experiences, thoughts, and emotions.

Another reason that the Western world places little emphasis on dreams is that Westerners have become acculturated to quick fixes. Ironically, in our culture of highly skilled practitioners of the arts, sciences, entertainment, and athletics who dedicate themselves every day of their lives to developing skills in specialized fields, it seems amazing that so many people look for quick fixes for something as vital as understanding themselves.

DREAMING DURING LATER ADULTHOOD

Shortly after I began to research dreams, I met Rose. I was beginning a career in counseling after being in the business and academic worlds for many years. Rose and her husband were also making a transition. With their children grown and away from home, Rose and her husband were alone for the first time in several years. Although Rose's husband seemed to make the transition with ease, Rose had difficulty. Her dreams reflected the stress she felt.

Then, I invited Rose to be a case participant in my thesis research. (See Table A1 for details of the thesis research.) During our research, Rose reviewed her dream journals from 7 years. She discovered several relationships to which she was currently reacting based on her unresolved stressful reactions from earlier experiences.

Other beginnings for people in later adulthood include retirement and transitions to various relaxing activities after many years of work in and out of the home. Included for several people are moves to retirement homes and to assisted care centers. Our U.S. society and the societies of other countries devote enormous time and resources to showing senior citizens how to live fulfilled lives.

Change often brings guidance through dreams. One of the most productive resources that people build over the years is a library of personal experiences. Later adulthood is a time when our library of experiences is brimming with histories of our interactions with other people. Dreams access those earlier experiences to guide us in living fulfilled current lives.

FIRST STEPS IN DREAM INTERPRETATION

For the first steps in dream interpretation, start cold. That is, let go of your preconceived ideas on how to work with dreams. Whether you are a counselor, a client, or a self-study individual, some procedures presented in this book will be new to you. Procedures that are common to other dream interpretation models include dream recall, dream recording, and learning your own dreaming language.

Although all people dream, not all of us recall our dreams. Further, not all people want to work with their dreams. Those who do, and who bring their dreams to counselors, expect to receive guidance on how to find meanings in their dreams. A major objective of this book is to teach counselors how to help their clients work with dreams. We begin by assuming that all readers are beginners. The first steps in most dream interpretation models are to recall and record your dreams.

Dream Recall

1. Tell yourself before you go to sleep that you will recall your dreams. Say to yourself several times, "I will remember a dream when I wake up." This affirmation will help you recall spontaneous dreams. *Spontaneous*, as the word implies, means that dreams respond naturally to the events, thoughts, and emotions of the previous day. Waking-life events, thoughts, and emotions are major prompters of spontaneous dreams. Dependence on spontaneous dreams for encouraging dream recall is the foremost approach given in this book.

   An alternative approach is to ask for help or incubate a request for help on a specific issue before you go to sleep. Delaney (1996) emphasized dream incubation. When asking for help on a specific issue, be alert for whether spontaneous dreams override pre-dream queries.
2. When you wake in the morning, lie very still. Keep yourself in a relaxed, almost drowsy state, and wait for dream recall to emerge into your mind.
3. If no recall comes after you have been lying still for a while, turn slowly to another position and keep waiting for recall. When you have recall, while continuing to lie still, rehearse or describe the dream in your mind.

4. Also, be alert for dream recall during the day, especially during relaxed moments.
5. Trust the process. Be confident in your ability to remember dreams. All people dream. It is a matter of biological necessity.

Dream Recording

Many people are unaware that dedicated dream recording can lead to productive use of dreams for the rest of their lives. Dedication begins with recording the dream when the dream is still fresh in your mind.

1. Keep a pad and pencil, or a tape recorder if you prefer, near your bed. These will remind you to recall your dreams and record them as soon as you awaken.
2. Record your dreams in first person and present tense to foster the immediate and intimate feelings of the dream.
3. Include your dreaming emotions in your dream narrative. Emotions are integral parts of the dreaming experience.
4. Record every recalled detail of the dream, regardless of its apparent relevance or importance. Details that seem insignificant are often keys to later insights.

Learn Your Personal Dreaming Language

Every dreamer's dreams are unique because dreaming language varies based on the dreamer's experiences, current and past. But, dreams are usually symbolic of something that is happening in waking life or a combination of symbolic and straightforward form, *straightforward* meaning the message is clear without further interpretation. Thus, learning dream language is similar to learning a new spoken language. The good news is that once the dreamer becomes acquainted with his or her own dream code, meanings will be "neither mysterious nor inaccessible" (Cartwright & Lamberg, 1992/2000, p. 5).

When counselors recognize that their clients' dreams often stem from the clients' experiences, this provides valuable information to counselors for how to use a specific client's dreams to guide that client. Anecdotal summaries of clients' dreams that helped their counselors guide them are presented next.

CLIENTS' DREAMS THAT HELPED THEIR COUNSELORS GUIDE THEM

Letting Go of the Past

A client's dreams about his earlier challenge of handling the tragedies in his children's lives gave him insights into how to let go of the past. The same client understood a later dream about "moving on to a life of sunshine" as an affirmation of the fact that he had succeeded in releasing his stressful emotions and actions.

The client's definitions of major phrases from his dreams helped his counselor understand that the client was reacting to systems effects that had happened many years earlier. Three groups of words (phrases) and the client's definitions of them are as follows:

1. **Hiding in the unlighted barn:** Hiding my feelings and fears from others (like from my grown sons)
2. **Lighted house:** Place where I keep my children safe, secure, and warm
3. **Letting the air out of my ex-wife:** Getting rid of the "power" of that relationship as well as the fears from the past

The client's dream of moving on to a life of sunshine gave confidence to the counselor that the client had succeeded in moving past the earlier fears and assurance that the client had settled that long-standing concern.

Courage and Patience to Wait

A client's series of dreams about choices gave her the courage and the patience to wait until a major decision felt right for her instead of relying on others to make an important choice for her. She had been selected by a local committee, composed primarily of her relatives, to represent the committee on a 2-year assignment in a foreign country. Although she supported the goals of the committee and willingly did volunteer work in her local area, she was unprepared to accept their decision that she would be the one to make this long-term commitment.

The counselor, who was aware that emotions in dreams are often more accurate than waking-life appraisals of the same emotions, understood the intense pressure the client was feeling. That understanding helped the counselor also understand the factors that compounded the client's decision. For instance, some emotions the client felt in one dream, which she titled "Which Door Shall I Choose?" included "*Angry* about being asked to do something I am not ready do (pick a door)" and "*confused* about why I am pushing myself and pressuring myself to make a choice."

The woman reported emotions in a later dream, in which she first talked with some family members, then made her own choice. In her dream language, "I open the door and walk through it." The emotions she felt during that dream went from feeling "confused, upset, anxious, annoyed, hesitant," [and] "afraid" [to feeling] "relieved." She wrote, "The relief that I felt at the end of this dream is different from any that I felt in any other of the dreams in this series."

Facing a Long-Term Pattern

A client's dream helped him realize that his advice to a teammate on how the teammate could better conduct himself was futile. The athlete-dreamer-client stopped "painting pictures" of how his teammate could improve his life.

The client's connections of his day-before-the-dream events, thoughts, and emotions about having confronted the teammate's questionable sportsmanship were clearly symbolized in the dream. For instance, his emotions of how he really felt about having decided to confront his teammate were shown by these two statements: "I open the door to the basement [the teammate's inner depths]," and "I feel a little nervous and scared."

The young client's pre-dream thoughts were not only about his teammate's current actions but also about how he, the dreamer, had for the first time taken a stand against his long-time friend and teammate's actions. He recognized that his dream scenario was saying, "I cannot force my teammate to look at things in a deeper way," and "I can continue to express how I feel, but I can't expect him to be on the same level if he's not ready to be."

From this dream and earlier dreams, the client saw a pattern in his life. He had repeatedly carried "the burden of feeling like I need to make people feel a certain way" instead of saying how he really feels when he did not support what others close to him were doing.

With the client gleaning so much information from his dream, there was little more the counselor needed to do beyond what he had already done—facilitate the client's use of a dream interpretation model to understand his dream. The counselor commended her client for his courage to explore this long-term pattern.

Hidden Substance Abuse

A client's interpretation of her dreams about substance abuse in the family helped her move from fear to anger to love and then to peace in her relationship with her husband. The process began when the client, Dolly, had difficulty gathering the courage to visit with her husband, Carlton, about his increasing dependence on an addictive substance. Dolly went to a counselor for help. The counselor facilitated Dolly's interpretation of her dreams that related to her concern for her husband. Definitions that Dolly developed for phrases taken from her dreams helped the counselor recognize that the first issue area he needed to help Dolly with was fear of "coming out of hiding" about Carlton's use of an addictive substance. Only then could she gather her courage to visit with Carlton about the addiction.

Following is a selection of client Dolly's definitions of phrases from her dreams that helped the counselor better recognize Dolly's initial need.

1. **Cave room:** A hidden place no one knows about. It's dirty like the dirty little secret I keep by not speaking about the addictive substance.
2. **Pillow over the head:** A place to hide or be hidden.
3. **Face down:** Unable to respond to see what's happening.
4. **Can just blow the fire out, so I do:** I think I create a smoke screen to hide what I really feel.
5. **Dead battery:** Having nothing left to give. Without energy.
6. **Dead man:** Represents me in the dream, a person who is lifeless and empty.

Dolly also defined phrases from her dreams that helped her counselor corroborate her affirmations that she was indeed moving beyond fear and beyond anger. For example,

7. **Carlton lying on the bed without covers, exposed:** This is a place where Carlton and I are most comfortable and like ourselves. We are okay with the exposure of talking about what his addiction brings into our lives.
8. **Deerdog:** A faithful, but fragile friend. My husband.

Difficulty with Family Traditions

A client's work with dreams about family traditions gave her the courage to confront the truth around a serious family difficulty instead of hiding behind façades that insisted there were no family problems.

When the teacher-client brought dreams that reflected her growing up years, the counselor not only facilitated her interpretation of these dreams but also learned a great deal about how the teacher had reacted to and continued to react to family traditions. One major tradition was, "We must never let any one believe there are difficulties in the family." One of the last dreams that the teacher discussed with her counselor was about an elaborate, many-storied house. The client's ability to connect her reactions to her previous day's visit with her grandparents and her parents was extremely instrumental in helping her better understand the issues faced and emotions involved with the stress that she felt.

COUNSELORS' DREAMS THAT GAVE INSIGHTS INTO HOW TO HELP CLIENTS

There are times when counselors dream about the challenges they are facing in helping a client. Those dreams may contain suggestions for the counselor. A few examples in anecdotal form follow.

On-Target Quotation

Tim, the client, lamented that although his girlfriend, Anne, is attentive to him, she is also seeking other friends. Tim wants to be with Anne all the time. During the counseling session with Tim the day before he dreamed about Tim, the counselor had spontaneously quoted Kahlil Gibran—"Let there be spaces in your togetherness" (Gibran, 1984, p. 15). After the session, the counselor continued to think about Tim and his difficulty in being apart from Anne.

Counselor's dream: *I am sitting on a piano bench playing the piano. Anne first stands behind me, then sits behind me on the piano bench and pushes me in a friendly way. It is a good friendly way, as if she thinks I'm a fine teacher.*

Insight from dream: "Yes, my music and Anne's music are the same." Her sitting so close to me signifies that Anne agrees with the "music" I play. "Let there be spaces in your togetherness" speaks to the closeness that caused the couple's breakup for now. Tim wanted to be too close.

Further Efforts Needed

A counselor had concerns about whether she was reaching a client named Gretchen.

Counselor's dream: *I am reaching out, stretching my arm toward a young woman who is reaching her hand out to me. Our hands are almost touching. She is a bright, alert young woman.*

Insight from dream: "I am almost touching Gretchen." The dream helped the counselor extend her efforts a bit further to understand Gretchen's circumstances.

Recommended Book

This counselor is working with Dorothy, a client who experiences numerous anxious thoughts and emotions about every little thing. One night after Dorothy had missed her appointment, the counselor gave much thought to this client and wondered how she could better counsel her. Then, the counselor asked herself, "Why am I running this over and over in my mind? Dorothy didn't come for her appointment. She just may not be coming back at all." The counselor's thoughts continued, anyway.

Counselor's dream: *Dorothy arrives at her appointment. She says she is reading a really good book. When she tells me the title, I realize that it is a book I have in my library.*

Insight from dream: I should recommend the book from my dream to Dorothy. The counselor was surprised because the content of the book seemed contrary to Dorothy's belief system. Yet, when Dorothy arrived at her next appointment and the counselor recommended the book, Dorothy readily related to it.

Unwise to Interface

A counselor was strongly thinking about suggesting family counseling to a young client's parents because their daughter was threatening to quit school.

Counselor's dream: *A male relative of my husband comes and speaks excitedly to him, saying we had better do something because the female child of one of our relatives isn't going back to school. After the man is gone, my husband says to me, "No, we're not going to do anything. This is not a place where we should interfere."*

Insight from dream: Take your dream husband's sage advice. Suggesting family counseling to the client's parents would be unwise interference.

Countertransference

A client tells his counselor about intense stress in his marriage. The counselor thinks about possible countertransference arising from earlier stress in his own marriage, but then he decides that there can be no possible countertransference because he and his wife worked through their stress. That night the counselor had a dream about the circumstance.

Counselor's dream: *I am walking in a woody area and see animals that look like deer. I am not afraid of them. Next I hear a low sort of bellowing noise, but I don't see anything. I am still not afraid. Then I hear the people ahead of me cautioning against staying here because of this wild animal, which I assume is a stag in the herd. I feel afraid now, and I run. But I have difficulty running. I see the large man ahead of me stumbling as he runs, but he is making it okay. As my dream ends, I am still laboring to run, and I still do not see the bellowing animal.*

Insight from dream: The counselor was perplexed about what the stag he could not see represented until it came to him in a flash of intuition as he was standing under the shower the morning after the dream. "When I thought about my own stuff," he said, "I knew in a flash that the countertransference was about my emotions over my parents' marriage. My mother's offensive treatment of my dad caused great distress to me. During my youth, I often wished my dad would leave her, that he would escape from her shameful treatment of him."

QUESTIONS AND ANSWERS REGARDING MY DREAMS ABOUT MY CLIENTS

Question: How do you recognize that you have interpreted your dreams about clients accurately?

Answer: The recognition is the same as with other dreams—I have an intuitive feel. It is almost a feeling in my body that my interpretation is accurate. Krippner and Dillard (1988) suggested that the best way to interpret dreams is to integrate logical reasoning with intuition; the two go together and maintain a balance. I agree. My clients' reactions when I use my dream suggestions corroborate the accuracy of my interpretations. I am always concerned that I might misinterpret my dreams about my clients, just as I am always concerned that my waking thoughts and strategies about how to facilitate my clients' work may be inaccurate. I have on occasion had "correcting" dreams that have helped me realize I had misinterpreted an earlier dream.

Question: Do you tell your clients when you dream about them?

Answer: I nearly always refrain from sharing my dreams about clients with them. My clients' abilities to achieve understanding and reliance on their best thoughts and on their own dreams are far more useful to them than depending on me or on my dreams.

Whether you are a practicing counselor, a student in training, or a reader interested in using dreams for self-discovery, keep in mind that dedication at the beginning of any worthwhile venture is critical. Devote yourself to developing a feel for uncovering the vast territory of the abundant accumulations of your psyche, which are intimately connected to your waking-life experiences. Learn from your own dreams before facilitating your clients' work with dreams.

SUMMARY

The purpose of this chapter, which presents elementary instructions for working with dreams, is to ensure that all readers are prepared for the work of this book. Topics covered are the dreaming of children, adolescents, and adults. The best help a parent can give his or her child is to be present when the child awakens from dreams and to patiently listen to the child, to value the child's dreams, and to become aware of the child's reactions and feelings and any waking-life activities that may have prompted the dreams. Sharing dreams with parents, teachers, and counselors may be the only way (or only one of a few ways) an adolescent can find relief from the stress of teenage transitions. Adults can learn to recall and record their dreams as they embark on a course of dream interpretation. The chapter concludes with anecdotes that tell how clients' and counselors' dreams can be helpful to the counselors' work with clients.

SELF-STUDY QUIZ: CHAPTER 2

1. What is a major way that parents can help their children when they wake from a dream?
2. What is a "coming-of-age" dream, and who most often has such dreams?
3. List one procedure for dream recall that most strikes you as productive.
4. List one procedure for dream recording that most strikes you as productive.
5. Circle the best ending to the following sentence: Counselors can find guidance for counseling their clients from
   a. Their own dreams
   b. Their clients' dreams
   c. Neither a nor b
   d. Both a and b

Section *II*

Personalized Method for Interpreting Dreams (PMID)

In a few years, after you have interpreted many of your dreams, who will you be then?

Tonight, after you have interpreted this morning's dream, who will you be then?

INTRODUCTION

Not only has my own use of the Personalized Method for Interpreting Dreams (PMID) model helped me far beyond my greatest expectations, but also, as shown throughout this book, when others have used the PMID model, it has benefited them beyond their expectations. In addition to using the model to alleviate stress arising from relationship issues, we use it to find guidance in most circumstances of our waking lives.

Will the PMID model work for you? Will it work for each person who comes to you for counseling? Only you and your clients as individuals can answer that question. To expand your horizons on the value of dream guidance, I summarize several other dream models (Section I) and explain and demonstrate two other dream interpretation models (Section III).

The PMID model was developed during my thesis research. My thesis achieved recognition as the thesis of the year in 2000 at the University of Wisconsin–Whitewater.

My colleagues and I refined the PMID model during three additional research projects (Okocha & Duesbury, 2005–2006; Van Doren & Duesbury, 2000, 2005–2006) and four explorations (Duesbury, Bynum, & Van Doren, 2002, 2003, 2004; Van Doren & Duesbury, 2001). (See Appendix A for results of those projects.) It is significant that the PMID model was used as a stand-alone process in all these projects. It is also significant that information obtained in all projects shows that the model has potential for use with most psychotherapy approaches.

A unique feature of the PMID model is its attention to influences arising from reactions to family and other major relationships in relationship experiences. The systems approach to dream interpretation considers influences, both past and current, arising from our reactions to other people. That is, each member of a family (or other major group) affects and is affected by others to the extent it makes no sense to attempt to understand the individual in isolation. With the PMID model, the dreamer, either facilitated by a counselor or working alone, studies his or her dreams about major relationships instead of meeting with others in the system of relationships to discuss concerns.

Another unique feature in the PMID model is that the dreamer himself or herself selects major phrases from the dream and defines them in the context of the dream. The general definition for *phrases* as used here is "a string of words." Strings of words can be phrases, clauses, or whole sentences. The dreamer's ability to define dream phrases from personal experiences is a significant key to finding meanings in the dream. A combination of intuitive insights and logical reasoning is often needed to develop these meanings.

Each step in the PMID model builds on previous steps. That is, ability to do each step blends with performing the succeeding steps. Each step also has a unique purpose.

PERSONALIZED METHOD FOR INTERPRETING DREAMS (PMID)

PMID Step 1: Connect your **previous-day** (often the day before) **events** to the dream to discover the theme of this dream. The events may appear in either symbolic or literal terms in your dream. Write down the appropriate events and record when they occurred. (Chapter 4 explains this step.)

PMID Step 2: Connect your **previous-day** (often the day before) **thoughts** to your dream to detect which thoughts may have prompted this dream's responses. Like events, your thoughts may appear in your dream in either literal or symbolic terms. Write "I thought" statements and record when you thought them. (Chapter 5 explains this step.)

PMID Step 3: Select and define **major dream phrases** and symbols from your write-up of this dream to discover the dream's personalized meanings. Consider effects of your events and thoughts of the day before your dream and earlier experiences on the meaning of each major dream phrase and symbol. The general definition for phrases as used in this step is "a string of words." The strings of words can be phrases, clauses, or whole sentences. (Chapter 6 explains this step.)

PMID Step 4: Compare your **emotions in your dream** with your **pre-dream, waking-life emotions** to discover whether your waking-life emotions accurately reflect how you feel about the issue in this dream. Note that the issue may be a relationship issue. What differences, if any, do you find between your emotions in your dream and your waking-life emotions? It is useful to periodically review your emotions in your dreams regarding the main issue or relationship at hand. (Chapter 7 explains this step.)

PMID Step 5: Explore your dream for possible **solutions** to problems, including changing (or affirming) your thoughts, attitudes, or behaviors. Consider your responses to each PMID model step, including Step 6, as you search for solutions and suggestions in this dream. Give primary attention to the power of your thoughts before your dream (PMID Step 2) to act as questions that your dream answers. (Chapter 8 explains this step.)

PMID Step 6: Explore your dream for **family and other relationship systems perspectives**, which are influences arising from reactions to family and other major relationships, both past and current. Use these perspectives to discover whether this dream reflects your reactions during experiences with family members or other important people in your life. Compare and comment on your dreaming and your waking-life reactions to the primary relationships in this dream. (If this dream is not about a relationship, type the words "Not Applicable" in this space.) (Chapter 9 explains this step.)

PURPOSE OF EACH PMID MODEL STEP

The purpose of Step 1 (connect your previous-day events to this dream) is to uncover the theme of the dream, which provides a foundation for the rest of the steps.

The purpose of Step 2 (connect your previous-day thoughts to this dream) is to determine whether the dream responds to any of the dreamer's pre-dream (often day-before-the-dream) thoughts. Our thoughts are powerful antecedents to our dreams and frequently act as questions that the dream answers.

The purpose of Step 3 (select and define major dream phrases and symbols from your write-up of this dream) is to find personal meanings for phrases (strings of words) taken directly from our recalled dream. Our ability to find personal meanings in our dream phrases frequently overlaps into Steps 4, 5, and 6. For instance, solutions (Step 5) found in our dreams can become apparent while we are interpreting dream phrases.

The purpose of Step 4 (compare your emotions in your dream with your pre-dream waking-life emotions about the issue in this dream) is to discover whether the emotions we feel in our dreams about the main issue accurately reflect our waking-life appraisal of how we feel about the main issue. When emotions in dreams and waking-life emotions are in disharmony, this is a clue that the dreamer's waking-life appraisal of his or her emotions is off target for that issue. But, be aware that dreams exaggerate. We all know that. *Disharmony* can refer to differences in intensity, direction, and types of emotions.

The purpose of Step 5 (explore your dream for possible solutions to problems, including changing [or affirming] thoughts, attitudes, or behaviors) is to assimilate all the responses from the other steps (including Step 6) to arrive at solutions to problems or issues the dreamer is facing. Solutions and suggestions are often connected to the waking-life events and thoughts that prompted this dream.

The purpose of Step 6 (explore your dream for family and other relationship systems perspectives) is for the dreamer to determine whether the dream contains information about his or her reactions (past or current) during relationship experiences and, if so, how those reactions affect his or her current functioning.

Note that Step 6 is only applicable to dreams about reactions to major relationships. The dreamer's responses to Step 6 should be considered when completing Step 5.

OVERALL STRENGTHS AND LIMITATIONS OF RESEARCH AND EXPLORATIONS OF THE PMID MODEL

The general goal of our PMID research and exploration projects was to increase the availability of professionally researched and explored dream interpretation models. The specific objective of projects beyond my thesis was to examine the efficacy of the PMID model in guiding participants to elicit problem-solving suggestions from their dreams and use those suggestions to alleviate stress. The focus of research was on relationship concerns.

A major strength of the PMID model projects is that they were all longitudinal, and lasting at least 3 months. The investigators in all the PMID model projects were either counselor education faculty members or degreed counselors, which lent credence to the conclusions.

Another strong point in the PMID projects was that both qualitative and quantitative measures were used, with the qualitative measures (the actual data, participants' dreams and interpretations) given the greater attention. Quantitative results are generally accepted in dream studies.

Qualitative studies are increasingly being given credence. For instance, one aim in Bulkeley's 2002 study of cultural differences in political ideologies was to "illustrate the fruitfulness of combining quantitative and qualitative modes of investigation. … Statistics … are important, but they do not by themselves tell the full story" (p. 65).

Advantages of qualitative assessments were presented by Goldman (1992). Qualitative studies, Goldman wrote, help participants become aware of and understand themselves, usually integrate several components of a situation, and tend to operate within a developmental framework and are conducive to intimate counselor–client relationships and flexible and adaptable to varied populations.

The PMID model projects used small sample sizes (ranging from 5 to 17 participants), which allowed me sufficient time to teach, facilitate, and explore individual uses of the model. Time spent on interactions with participants provides confidence in the outcome, although limiting sample sizes can lead to results that are unable to be generalized to other populations.

INSTRUMENTS DEVELOPED DURING THE PMID PROJECTS

Three key instruments were developed for the PMID model projects (see Appendix B for the format of these instruments). In 2000, Van Doren and I developed a screening application to evaluate applicants' emotional stability to work with their dreams. In 2002, I developed a periodic feedback instrument (PFI) and an emotional change instrument (ECI) to evaluate participants' self-rated success with the PMID model.

The PFI, which is a series of statements related to the PMID steps, was designed to increase participants' learning and self-awareness of the level of their success in using the model. Participants used this form to rate their abilities to do each step. Rating is on a 1-to-7 Likert-type scale, with 7 the highest rating.

The ECI is a series of questions designed to increase the dreamer's awareness of differences between his or her dreaming emotions and pre-dream, waking-life emotions regarding the people in the dreams. We used the ECI as one technique to evaluate each participant's progress in reducing stress while using the PMID model.

Our use of the screening application began with Van Doren and Duesbury's (2000) pilot study. Use of the PFI and ECI instruments began with Duesbury and colleagues' (2002) explorations. Thus, from 2002, participants submitted both qualitative and quantitative data.

QUALITATIVE DATA COLLECTED FOR THE PMID PROJECTS

The primary qualitative data were the participants' dream narratives and their corresponding interpretations. Participants also wrote paragraphs about the major people who appeared in their dreams. Collection was by means of a privately owned Internet Web site. Dreams and interpretations were examined for correct use of the PMID model.

Facilitative feedback was provided for each participant. Qualitative data were analyzed for all projects.

MULTICULTURAL USES OF THE PMID MODEL

Although the research and exploration projects of the PMID model covered mostly local, rural areas in the midwestern United States, six races, nationalities, and cultures were represented: White American, White European, Hispanic, Asian, African American, and Native American. The highest percentage was White American. Both genders were represented, with the higher percentage being female. Ages ranged from low 20s to the mid-70s, with the average age in the 40s. Representatives from all cultures showed that they were able to use the dream interpretation model. While the primary focus in all projects was on dreams about relationship concerns, participants also learned to use the PMID model for other types of dreams, such as those about work, education, health, and the spiritual realm.

Unsolicited endorsements from the participants' use of the PMID model include the following:

> "I think the PMID model could be used by people of multiple nationalities, not only by 'non-White' individuals, since it allows them to establish 'customized' meanings."
>
> "This project has changed my life!"
>
> "[This project] gives me a positive focus to interpreting my dreams! I think of dreams more in problem-solving terms than I ever have. All areas of interpretation help me to focus on the whole dream and the dream's relationship to real, waking life! I feel that my analysis skills of interpreting my dreams have been enhanced forever."
>
> "During these months I have been motivated to work on my dreams, despite the effort and amount of time it takes, as doing this research has been infinitely more fulfilling than any kind of therapy, holistic and not, and I feel that I have made great strides into coming closer to my subconscious."
>
> "I'm recognizing that dreams are our 'inner counselors.'"

I suggest that researchers in counseling fields offer opportunities to use the PMID model to races, nationalities, and cultures in addition to White Americans, Hispanic, Asian, African American, Native American, and White Europeans. Conclusions drawn from the proposed research will obviously be helpful in identifying additional cultures that could benefit from the model.

Use of the PMID model is explained and demonstrated throughout this section. Chapter 3 is an overview of the model. Chapters 4 through 9 give step-by-step examples of the use of the model plus literature and research support of each PMID step.

Chapter 10 explains and demonstrates the individual's series approach to interpreting dreams. Chapter 11 encourages reviewing earlier dreams and interpretations to refresh former meanings, discover new insights, and review the dreams for misinterpretation. Review is vital to our best use of our dreams. We can also review our past dreams and interpretations to look for indicators that concerns have been relieved, which means we can move on. Chapter 12 presents information on delivery modes (face to face and distance by way of the Internet) for communicating with clients and students. Included are discussions of how the number of sessions used for working with dreams can be diminished by using the PMID model.

Note that throughout this book pseudonyms are used to protect the confidentiality of dreamers and their dream interpretations. Dreams are italicized to distinguish them from the narrative text.

3

Overview of the Personalized Method for Interpreting Dreams

KIMBERLY TUESCHER, BRENDA O'BEIRNE, and EVELYN DUESBURY

Carlie sits down and we can see she has something all around her mouth. The counselor wipes it off. It is chocolate.

PURPOSES OF THIS CHAPTER

This chapter serves two purposes:

1. It is an overview of the Personalized Method for Interpreting Dreams (PMID) for practicing counselors who use this book for learning how to facilitate clients' interpretation of their dreams.
2. It is a one-class period, 3-hour presentation to introduce the PMID model to students in graduate-level counselor education courses that are other than dream interpretation courses.

Finding answers or solutions through use of dreams is the ultimate goal of the PMID model. The objective of this chapter is to introduce the PMID model to educators, counselors, students, and other readers. A dream about a childhood friend and the dreamer's interpretations demonstrate the model.

The initial incentive for this chapter was an invitation by counselor education professor Kimberly Tuescher (University of Wisconsin–Platteville) to Evelyn Duesbury to present information on the PMID model to Tuescher's advanced counseling techniques students. Later, counselor education professor Brenda O'Beirne (University of Wisconsin–Whitewater) invited Duesbury to make a similar presentation to her counseling practicum class. Each professor indicated a desire to help her students think intentionally about the use of dream interpretation in the overall context of their work.

The result is an introduction to the PMID model that is appropriate as both a one-time presentation and an introductory chapter in the whole book. As stated in the body of this chapter, it is important for university professors and other teachers to have some understanding of their own dreams before offering to coach others' use of dreams. The suggestions in this chapter apply to one-time presenters as well as to those who teach a semester-long dream interpretation course. Teaching dream interpretation is certainly much easier for those who have a passion for dreams, have worked with their own dreams, have experience with the PMID model, and are willing to work at the students' levels. (Students are often beginners at dream interpretation.)

We suggest that counselors, professors, and other teachers gain experience with the PMID model by studying the entire book from which this overview is taken. One option for purchase is as an e-book. Because e-books are low priced, this option is offered specifically to encourage purchase of the entire book. While this chapter is appropriate for a one-class period, 3-hour presentation to introduce the PMID model to students, those who teach the model need more academic learning and experience than this single chapter.

SUGGESTED PRESENTER GUIDELINES

Preclass Assignment

Invite students to recall and record:

1. One of their own dreams
2. One or more of the events from the day before their dream that could possibly connect in either symbolic or literal terms to this dream
3. One or more of their thoughts from the day before their dream that might possibly connect in either symbolic or literal terms to this dream

Let students know that you will not ask them to share their dreams during class, but that you will invite them to comment on their experiences of recording their dreams and pre-dream events and thoughts that might have prompted the dream. A major reason for avoiding dream sharing during class is that disclosure of specific dreams or meanings initiated by individuals might require the presenter's thoughtful responses, plus the dreamer's processing. Confidentiality and response time are important concerns for dream sharing.

Presenter's Preclass Preparations

1. A week before the in-class presentation, make copies of materials (a packet) to hand to each student. The packet should include the following items:

   a. Steps of the PMID model (Copy from the Section II Introduction of this book)
   b. The dream narrative, "Let Carlie Do the Talking—Now" (Copy from this chapter)
   c. *Dream recall* and *dream recording*: Copy the sections "Dream Recall" and "Dream Recording" from Chapter 2 of this book).
2. Make copies of the following for handing to each student during the presentation (narratives are included in this chapter):
   a. Handout for after completing the work with Steps 1 and 2: Rose's (the dreamer's) completed Steps 1 and 2.
   b. Handout for before beginning interactive work with PMID Step 3: List of all the dream words and phrases that Rose selected and defined. Leave all the definitions blank except these first two:
      i. **Carlie:** My childhood best friend, a girl.
      ii. **Room being dark:** There is something in the dream I do not understand. (This is a universal, or common, meaning.)
   c. Handout for after finishing interactive work with the rest of Rose's PMID Step 3 dream phrases: Rose's completed list of dream phrases and her definitions.
   d. Handout for after finishing interactive work with all the PMID steps: Rose's responses to PMID Steps 4, 5, and 6.
   e. Optional: Print each PMID model step (concise form) in large letters on 11 × 17 inch poster sheets. When presenting each step, place the related poster card on a bulletin or other type board at the front of the room.

SUGGESTED IN-CLASS NARRATIVES FOR PRESENTER

Welcome to Dreamland!

The counseling technique I present is the counselor's facilitation of clients' and students' interpretations of their dreams. The model we will use is the Personalized Method for Interpreting Dreams, PMID for short. Finding answers or solutions through use of dreams is the ultimate goal of the PMID.

As a warm-up, we'll go around the class. Tell me your first name [if the presenter is other than the regular teacher for this course] and what your emphasis is, if you have declared one.

For a further warm-up, let's see a show of hands in the affirmative for the following:

1. How many of you dream? (Research shows that all people dream.)
2. How many of you recall your dreams? (Not all people recall dreams. There is a page in your packet on dream recall.)
3. How many of you expect that at some time you will have students or clients bringing dreams to your sessions with them?
4. How many of you wonder whether people's reactions in past relationships affect how they react in current relationships?

5. How many of you did recall a dream and have brought one to class today along with your day-before-your-dream events and thoughts?

I won't ask you to share your dreams during class. Your sharing your dreams with the class could lead to disclosure of more than you care to reveal. While dreams often disclose more than we realize, *if* you did record a dream *and* did record events and thoughts from the day before your dream, this will help you understand the first steps in the model that I am going to present.

After we work through a dream and the dreamer's interpretations, we will return to day-before-your-dream events and thoughts and invite you to share your reflections, comments, or questions from your experiences of recording a dream and those two steps. These two steps (recording and connecting the previous day's events and thoughts) are the first two steps in the PMID model.

Note that there are several dream interpretation models, but few are researched models. The PMID model is a researched model. Participants in research and exploration projects of the PMID model included members of the American Counseling Association, the Wisconsin Counseling Association, students in counselor education courses, and the general public living in the southeast corner of Wisconsin. The emphasis on all projects was dreams about relationships. Sample sizes ranged from 1 (a case study) to 17. All projects lasted at least 3 months.

Key findings from those projects were that most participants did dream about relationships. A high percentage of active participants ("active" meaning contributing to the project's conclusion) reported that they were able to understand and use the PMID model within 8 weeks. A high percentage of active participants reported positive changes in emotions about one or more relationships in a period of between a few weeks to 2 months while using the PMID model. While researching a general population, investigators compared participants' self-reports of positive emotional change to content in their dreams and found almost 100% corroboration. Most active participants in all projects rated their use of the PMID steps before learning the PMID model to be very low, but after several weeks of using the PMID model, they rated their ability to do all six steps very high.

Facilitative comments from the coinvestigator on participants' use of the PMID model appeared to be an important factor in participants' increasing ability to use the model. For instance, investigators presented the following yes–no statement at the end of the general population study: "Comments from [the coinvestigator] were more helpful than I could have done on my own"; 100% answered yes.

In considering whether dreams have value, realize that some cultures from ancient times have connected dreams to daytime events and thoughts. The Chinese culture connects daytime events and thoughts to dreams. Synesius of Cyrene (1930), North African scholar and philosopher in the early fifth century AD, encouraged people to record their waking-life experiences at the time they recorded their dreams.

Techniques of connecting daytime events and thoughts to dreams and exploring personal meanings in dreams also have noteworthy effects in contemporary times. This is why you were invited to record your dreams and day-before-your-dream events and thoughts. Even if you were unable to connect those events and thoughts to your dream at the time of your dream, you still have valuable clues to use when dream interpretation becomes easier for you.

Notice that we are talking about you, the dreamer, as the interpreter. From ancient cultures to present times, the primary interpreters of dreams have been specialists of some kind. Today, some Western dream interpretation models have transitioned from using a specialist as the interpreter of dreams to letting the dreamer become the interpreter of his or her own dreams. Examples are Delaney's dream interview model (Delaney, 1988, 1996), Cartwright's RISC (recognize, investigate, stop, change) model (Cartwright & Lamberg, 1992/2000), Ullman's group dreaming model (Ullman, 1996), and Duesbury's PMID model (2000, 2001, 2007). When a counselor is involved, the counselor facilitates the process. That works well with members of the American Counseling Association because what we do in counseling is to help, or facilitate, the client find his or her own answers.

With the PMID model, you thus interpret your own dreams. If you are a counselor and your clients are bringing dreams to you, you will facilitate their interpretations of their own dreams. It is not as easy as it may seem to keep dreamers on track so that they pay close attention to each step in the PMID model. That is the facilitator's task.

It is significant that the PMID model is a stand-alone model. No other counseling approach is needed for a dreamer to reach this model's goals and purposes. The PMID model has the potential to provide information for other therapeutic approaches. For instance, a gem we can mine from the PMID model is the wealth of information dreamers reveal with each step, which is often appropriate to the particular counseling approach that you follow, whether it is cognitive behavior therapy or any of the other psychotherapy approaches. The PMID model can thus generally be incorporated within your theoretical orientation.

It is, of course, important for you to understand your own dreams before offering to coach others' use of their dreams. Coaching dream interpretation when you have little understanding of your own dreams is like coaching an athletic team when you have yet to play the game yourself. How well would you do? How long would top management keep you on staff?

Now, turn in your handouts to the PMID steps. [Note to presenter: As you discuss each step, you may want to place a card with that step written in concise form on a bulletin board or stand.]

I invite you to help the dreamer interpret this dream. In real life as a counselor, you facilitate the dreamer's interpretation instead of being an interpreter. Now, turn to the dream in your packet. Do we have a volunteer to read the dream out loud while the rest of us listen? [The dreamer's words are italicized.]

Presentation of Real Dream: Let Carlie Do the Talking—Now

[Permission to reprint given by Rose, the dreamer, a White American woman.] Dream: *The room is dark except for light where Carlie and I are sitting in seats, pew-like seats in a curve. Carlie is wearing a large red bow with what seems to be something else in it on the top of her head. There is a man counselor, tallish and slender, on stage in this room like an auditorium. … I suggest to Carlie to go up and have the counselor work with her. I think of myself as a knowing person who is superior to Carlie in knowledge about counseling. Carlie has never had counseling and I think she would find help with it. Carlie says, "But I don't know what to ask." I act as the dominant one here; Carlie is kind of innocent-like. I start to give her suggestions on what she might ask.*

All of a sudden, Mr. Roberts is here and reprimands me for telling Carlie what to say. He is quite disgruntled about my trying to tell Carlie what to say. I am surprised Mr. Roberts is here, did not see him sitting squeezed in sort of beside us on this same pew. …

There is a question of whether there is time for all the activities planned for the counselor. I feel a bit of concern that Carlie will not get to be on stage with the counselor, but it turns out there is time for her.

Later Carlie is on stage. The stage is quite dark on the right side of the counselor. Carlie sits down and we can see she has something all around her mouth. The counselor wipes it off. It is chocolate. As Carlie faces the audience, some chocolate comes out of her mouth and drips down her chin and neck, too. She seems innocent and embarrassed, too, as she wipes it off.

[To the reader] Thank you. Class, please picture yourselves as facilitators. What would you suggest to the dreamer to do first? [Expected response from the class: What happened the day before your dream that you believe connects in either literal or symbolic terms to this dream?] This is PMID Step 1. [Presenter reads PMID Step 1 and Rose's response to PMID Step 1]

> **PMID Step 1:** Connect your **previous-day** (often the day before) **events** to the dream to discover the theme of this dream. The events may appear in either symbolic or literal terms in your dream. Write down the appropriate events and record when they occurred.

Rose: **Yesterday** my husband put a big red bow with a little bell inside it on top of our Christmas tree in place of the star I had there.

We got quite a bit of chocolate candy for Christmas. **Last night** my husband took some Pepto-Bismol to calm his stomach from all the chocolate he ate.

Presenter: Is there anything in this dream that connects in either symbolic or literal terms to these events from yesterday? [Expected responses from the class are red bow on Carlie's head, chocolate candy coming out of Carlie's mouth.] The purpose of PMID Step 1 is to discover the dream's theme. What theme might Rose's event connections to this dream connote? [Possible response from the class: Reflections of Rose's husband and Carlie's actions.]

Now, and this is very important, let's see what thoughts Rose had that could have helped to prompt this dream. [Presenter reads the step and Rose's response to PMID Step 2.]

PMID Step 2: Connect your **previous-day** (often the day before) **thoughts** to your dream to detect which thoughts may have prompted this dream's responses. Like events, your thoughts may appear in your dream in either literal or symbolic terms. Write "I thought" statements and record when you thought them.

Rose: **Last night** I thought about two projects that I could do during my upcoming vacation. One project is to interpret my series of dreams about Carlie, but I decided there wasn't time to do both, and I thought I basically know what my dreams about Carlie mean.

I thought about the red bow my husband put on the Christmas tree, and though it just didn't look quite right to me, I decided it would do.

Presenter: What questions do these thoughts bring to mind that possibly this dream is responding to or answering? What does Rose mean by "series of dreams about Carlie?"

[Students may be unable to answer these questions. Here are some suggestions: Answer "Will I have to interpret my dreams about Carlie now?" with a subquestion, "Why can't I just plain tell my husband that, in my view, the red bow just doesn't fit on the tree?" Also, "A series of dreams is simply more than one dream about an issue or relationship."]

Presenter: What next would you, the facilitator, ask the dreamer to do? [Expected response: PMID Step 3] [Presenter reads PMID Step 3.]

PMID Step 3: Select and define **major dream phrases** and symbols from your write-up of this dream to discover the dream's personalized meanings. Consider effects of your events and thoughts of the day before your dream and earlier experiences on the meaning of each major dream phrase and symbol. The general definition for phrases as used in this step is "a string of words." The strings of words can be phrases, clauses, or whole sentences.

Presenter: This step of defining phrases (even clauses and whole sentences) from the dream instead of defining one-word symbols is unique with the PMID model. Instead of giving definitions for single words (as a dream dictionary does when it lists symbols), the dreamer and the facilitator will collaborate on selecting phrases from the dream for the dreamer to define in the context of the dream. The general definition for *phrases* as used in PMID Step 3 is "a string of words." A string of words can be a sentence, a clause, or a phrase.

"In the context of this dream—so what is the context of this dream? [Answer: PMID Step 1—day-before-the-dream events and PMID Step 2—day-before-the-dream thoughts, plus earlier experiences that connect to this dream.] Keep it tight to this dream.

[Note to presenter: For examples of other dreamers' definitions, see Chapter 6, "Dream Phrases: Products of the Amazing Creativity of the Dreaming Mind" and Table 6.2 regarding personal definitions for major dream phrases (PMID Step 3).]

For now, let's assume Rose's "Let Carlie Do the Talking—Now" dream is your dream (even if this is not even your gender), and you are interpreting it using the PMID model. Your packet contains a list of the dream phrases Rose decided on for her final interpretation of this dream. [Presenter waits while students locate this list.] Rose's definitions are provided for the first two dream phrases.

[For presenter convenience, here is the entire list of the dream words and phrases that Rose defined.]

1. **Carlie:** My childhood best friend, a girl.
2. **Room being dark:** There is something in the dream I do not understand. (This is a universal or common meaning.)
3. **Light where Carlie and I are sitting and where she sits on stage:** Suggests there is light being shed on my relationship with Carlie. (This is one universal meaning of light.)
4. **Large red bow on Carlie's head:** Symbol of my "Carlie-best-friend" relationship with my husband because he suggested putting the red bow on the tree yesterday.
5. **Give suggestions to Carlie:** Comes from my waking-life thoughts that I already know how my experiences with Carlie affect me.
6. **Man counselor:** I think of the rational reasoning faculty in all people (men and women) as masculine. For this dream, the male (man) in the dream connects to me and my prominent rational reasoning way to solve problems at the time of this dream.
7. **Counselor on stage:** Opportunity to analyze my reactions to Carlie is now on stage, a central issue for me.
8. **Carlie not knowing what to ask:** Actually, if I really look at this, I don't know where to begin to understand how my past reactions to Carlie affect me currently.
9. **Mr. Roberts's reprimands:** Professor who gave stern cautions about telling others what to do during a class project; here means to let my dreams about my reactions to Carlie do the talking. [Presenter: Obviously for this

one only Rose the dreamer would know the meaning. And always the dreamer gets to define that meaning.]

10. **Chocolate around Carlie's mouth:** Symbol of my "Carlie-best-friend" reactions to my husband who overdid eating chocolate yesterday.

Do you have any suggestions on meanings to any of the other dream phrases? Our emphasis here is on suggestions. Let's remember that this isn't your dream, so even if you believe you know the meanings, those meanings may not be the same that Rose would give. But, this will give you some practice. Are there any hints from Rose's Step 1, day-before-the-dream events, and Step 2, day-before-the-dream thoughts, that could be helpful in defining the dream phrases that Rose has selected.

To refresh your memory of Rose's responses to PMID Step 1 (day-before-the-dream events) and PMID Step 2 (day-before-the-dream thoughts), here is a handout with her responses. [Presenter, pass a copy of your handout of Rose's responses to PMID Step 1 and PMID Step 2.]

[Note to presenter: After concluding interactive discussion of Step 3, hand out copies of Rose's completed PMID Step 3 responses.]

Presenter: Rose's definitions of "large red bow on Carlie's head" and "chocolate around Carlie's mouth" are important connections between Rose's relationship with Carlie and her reactions to her husband.

Dreams and the dreamer's interpretations often unravel in mystery-like fashion as understanding grows. Moving onward with the detective work, what technique or step would you, as the counselor-facilitator, invite the dreamer to do next? [Expected response: PMID Step 4: Compare dreaming and waking-life emotions.] [Presenter reads PMID Step 4.]

PMID Step 4: Compare your **emotions in your dream** with your **pre-dream, waking-life emotions** to discover whether your waking-life emotions accurately reflect how you feel about the issue in this dream. Note that the issue may be a relationship issue. What differences, if any, do you find between your emotions in your dream and your waking-life emotions? It is useful to periodically review your emotions in your dreams regarding the main issue or relationship at hand.

Presenter: Hold to the issue and relationship in this dream. Avoid reaching out to possible other issues or other relationships. Did Rose record any of her emotions in her dream narrative for her "Let Carlie Do the Talking—Now" dream? [Expected responses from the class: Rose is surprised that Mr. Roberts is there and reprimanding her for telling Carlie what to say. At first, Rose is concerned whether Carlie will get to be on stage.]

Here is Rose's response to PMID Step 4:

Rose: In the dream, I am concerned whether there is time for Carlie to talk with the counselor. In waking life before this dream, I wasn't concerned enough to put that work ahead of the other project I had planned. In the dream, I am surprised that Mr. Roberts is there and reprimands me for telling Carlie what to say. In waking life before this dream, I felt content that I already knew what my dreams about Carlie mean.

Presenter: Emotions in dreams, though frequently exaggerated, are intrinsically honest sources of information (Jung, 1966; Ullman, 1996; Wolman & Ullman, 1986). Even when the individual feels confident of having identified the specific origins of stress, his or her ideas may be incorrect or incomplete. Which thoughts and which behaviors contribute to the dreamer's emotional stress can be difficult to pinpoint in waking-life cognitions. Dreams reach to the peripheries of the mind (Hartmann, 1995). Thus, dreams have potential to reveal earlier experiences that continue to influence the dreamer's current emotional responses, both positive and negative emotions.

Just as comparing "clients' self-reports of what they see, think, and feel with [the counselor's] observations of the client's behaviors" (Plesma, 2003, p. 91) is important, so is comparing clients' self-reports of what they think and feel in waking life with what they think and feel as reflected in their dreams. Making these comparisons gives us yet more clues to the mystery of Rose's dream about her childhood friend, Carlie.

What technique or step would you suggest to Rose now? [Expected response: Explore the dream for solutions, PMID Step 5.] [Presenter reads PMID Step 5.]

PMID Step 5: Explore your dream for possible **solutions** to problems, including changing (or affirming) your thoughts, attitudes, or behaviors. Consider your responses to each PMID model step, including Step 6, as you search for solutions and suggestions in this dream. Give primary attention to the power of your thoughts before your dream (PMID Step 2) to act as questions that your dream answers.

Presenter: The PMID steps are integrated from Step 1 through Step 6. For instance, PMID Step 2, day-before-the-dream thoughts, often helps the dreamer find the solutions explored in Step 5. Two thought questions developed from PMID Step 2 are "Will I have time to interpret my dreams about Carlie now?" and "Why can't I just plain tell my husband that in my view, the red bow just doesn't fit on the tree?" These seem like simple questions. In fact, they seem almost too minor for Rose's dreaming mind to bring up. But, clearly, Rose's dream addresses those concerns.

There are also some crossovers from step to step. For instance, in PMID Step 3, Rose's definition of the dream phrase, "Mr. Roberts's reprimands" is "Professor who gave stern cautions about telling others what to do during a class project; here means to let my dreams about my reactions to Carlie do the talking." This definition naturally crosses over to the solutions step, Step 5.

Another instance of possible crossover to PMID Step 5 is from emotions (PMID Step 4). Rose's responses [and the students' responses if they have correctly identified Rose's emotions in her dream] are "In the dream, I am concerned whether there is time for Carlie to talk with the counselor" and "In the dream I am surprised that Mr. Roberts is there and reprimands me for telling Carlie what to say."

Taking all the steps completed thus far into consideration, does anyone see solutions for Rose? [Probable responses from the class: The dream suggests, "Rose, put your study of your dreams about Carlie in top priority." And, "Rose, realize that there is more for you to learn about Carlie and your friendship than you currently understand in waking life."]

Solutions that Rose found in this dream are as follows:

Rose: The dream responds to my pre-dream decision that I wouldn't have time to work on my Carlie series of dreams and counters that decision by showing there is time to "counsel Carlie" now. My dream demonstrates that it is vitally important to my friendship with others, particularly with my husband at this time, to understand how my reactions to my childhood best friend affect my reactions to current friends.

Mr. Roberts's reprimand suggests I must let Carlie do the talking. That is, I must look to my dreams about Carlie for new insights about Carlie and my childhood friendship instead of depending on the waking-life appraisal of the circumstance as I have been doing.

Presenter: Notice that Rose, the dreamer, refers to "my Carlie series of dreams." She means more than one dream about Carlie. People often dream more than once about a specific topic or a specific relationship. More than one dream on a specific topic or relationship constitutes a dream series.

Rose has found solutions from her dream for what to do now. Isn't that enough? What else might Rose and her counselor-facilitator gain from this dream? [Possible response from the class: Maybe they need to know more about what happened during Rose and Carlie's friendship that carries on into Rose's waking life.]

[Presenter reads PMID Step 6.]

PMID Step 6: Explore your dream for **family and other relationship systems perspectives**, which are influences arising from reactions to family and other major relationships, both past and current. Use these perspectives to discover whether this dream reflects your reactions during experiences with family members or other important people in your life. Compare and comment on your dreaming and your waking-life reactions to the primary relationships in this dream. (If this dream is not about a relationship, type the words "Not Applicable" in this space.)

Presenter: The PMID model is useful for interpreting most types of dreams; for example, dreams about everyday activities such as work, education, health, and the spiritual. Only the first five steps are needed for those dreams. PMID Step 6 is for relationship dreams, those about major people in the dreamer's life.

PMID Step 6 is a family systems or relationships systems approach to an individual's interpretation of dreams. The systems approach to an individual's interpretation of dreams is the second unique technique in the PMID. Step 3, define dream phrases, is the first unique step. For Step 6, the dreamer compares his or her dreaming and waking-life reactions to each person in the dream.

Recall that for PMID Step 4 the dreamer addresses emotions: How did you feel in the dream? How have you felt about this issue or relationship in your waking life? In Step 6, the dreamer addresses reactions: What did you do in the dream and what do you do in waking life when reacting to the issues or relationships highlighted in this dream?

In the family systems approach to counseling, the counselor meets with the family or other major relationships. In contrast, in the systems approach of the PMID model to an individual's interpretation of dreams, the individual studies dreams about family or other major relationships. Neither the individual nor the counselor meets with the family or those in other major relationships. Consequently, intrarelational conflicts that might result from face-to-face meetings can be avoided. This approach respects the individual's personal meaning-making process, which can be related to others although not with others.

In the PMID model, the dreamer is encouraged (and assisted by working alone or with a counselor) to avoid blaming self or others. Assigning meaning and not blame is a major benefit in moving onward in overcoming stress instead of becoming stuck in blaming. "It is not a matter of who is at fault—it's a matter of changing who we can change most successfully … our own selves" (Duesbury, 2007, p. 58).

Further, each member of the system is so much a part of the system that if one member can change his or her reactions to other members, the system eventually changes to accommodate that one person's change (Allen, 1994). Thus, the potential result of positive change in the individual is positive change in the system.

Reactions in relationship experiences obviously extend from the individual's early life. Because dreams reach to the peripheries of the mind, the interpretation of dreams has potential for the individual to discover and alleviate stress that has bothered the individual since early life.

Regarding a question for the class, returning now to the dream, "Let Carlie Do the Talking—Now," who is Rose's primary relationship in this dream? [Probable responses from the class: Carlie or Rose's husband.] Rose's response to PMID Step 6 is as follows:

Rose: The primary relationship shown directly in this dream is with Carlie. In my dream, I react to her by suggesting she go on stage now. I also react to her by trying to be the dominant one. In waking life, I reacted to interpreting my dreams about Carlie by deciding that I already know how Carlie's leaving our friendship has affected me.

Instead of these dreams being about my current relationship with Carlie, I believe the dream is about my unresolved reactions to losing friendship with my one-time best friend, Carlie. I lost her friendship first when we were children and again when we were teenagers. That affects my reactions to other people who I currently call best friends. One current reaction is to my husband. I try very hard not to upset him. I guess I unconsciously think an angry best friend may leave me, as Carlie did.

Presenter: Notice that PMID Step 6 compels Rose to recall her childhood and adolescent reactions to a friend leaving her. Rose continues:

Rose: Carlie was my best friend from as early as I can remember, about six years old. She invited me to Sunday school with her. She chose me to travel with her family on an extended trip. She exchanged visits with me on Saturdays and during the summers. Then she left me for other best friends.

I think it was third grade when Selia moved into our school district and Carlie's devotion wavered between Selia and me as best friend. Sometime in junior high, Selia moved away, and Carlie and I were exclusive best friends again. Then Leah moved into the school district during high school and I lost Carlie as a best friend again, never to regain her. Honestly, I do not remember my reactions or my emotions when I lost Carlie as my best friend.

My husband is drawn into consideration for this dream because he is mirrored in Carlie's appearance in the dream. My recent reactions to my husband are: I began to call him my best friend and I recently gave a card to him that describes him as my best friend. I do react at times trying to figure out and do what pleases him, what will "keep his friendship." When he discovers what I am doing, he gets peeved at me and tells me to say what I really want to do. I admit to it being hard to stop reacting that way and even harder for me to figure out when I am being genuinely kind or just reacting to keep from upsetting a friend. I must feel threatened that an angry friend will leave me. My husband is not the only person I react to this way.

[Presenter: Hand out copies of Rose's responses to PMID Steps 4, 5, and 6.]

Rose's Other Dreams About Carlie

Rose understood from a later, very plain dream about Carlie that there was no reason for her to feel hurt from her experiences of losing Carlie as a best friend. That dream took Rose back to the youth building in her hometown where Carlie and the new friend left Rose and went on by themselves. In the dream, the girls are young women. The young women explain to Rose that what they were doing wasn't something that I should feel hurt about. It wasn't something that I would have been involved in anyway. Under Step 6 for that dream, Rose wrote:

Looking back I know that is true. Selia and Leah's interests were more akin to Carlie's than to mine at the time Carlie became friends with them. As adults their lives are very different from mine. So there is no reason for me to carry my reactions from childhood and adolescence into my current experiences with my current friends.

Presenter: In Rose's most recently volunteered dream, she is again back in the hometown youth building where Carlie and the new friend would leave her and go on by themselves. Prompters for that dream were Rose's thoughts that she might have offended a young man when he didn't return her telephone calls. Those thoughts took her into grief ("felt just awful").

Rose's New Dream: "Do I Really Want to Continue This Pain of Reminiscing?"

Excerpt from the dream: *The scene is in the youth building in my hometown. … I walk on out the front door and start to walk along the building toward the corner. I am in a grieving mode. I walk this way just to reminisce about the times I used to walk here. But I stop. Do I really want to continue around the corner and continue this pain of reminiscing what used to be, but no longer is?*

Presenter: The effects for Rose after interpreting this dream were as follows:

Rose: After I interpreted this dream, I felt tremendous relief. I realized without even trying that my earlier reactions had left me vulnerable to the current circumstance and that the awful feelings I had were unrealistic, very unrealistic. I realized anew that I had returned to the old "I lost Carlie's friendship" reaction instead of appraising the current circumstance for what it was, a casual meeting with a busy young man.

Presenter: Later, Rose wrote the following synopsis of what she learned from interpreting her dreams about Carlie:

Rose: I learned that my "Let Carlie Do the Talking—Now" dream was on target; I had not dealt with my childhood friend choosing other best friends over me and that affected my vulnerability in current friendships. I learned that my overanxious reactions with current friends were turnoffs for them. I learned I could deal with the past loss by looking to my current dreams instead of talking with Carlie or with my current friends about the stress I felt. I learned that it was my reactions instead of Carlie's behavior that initiated my stress. I learned to review and rereview my dreams to avoid misinterpreting them. I learned to be grateful for Carlie and my childhood friendship and grateful to realize that we indeed have far divergent adulthood interests. I learned that I continue to be at least a little vulnerable in relationship experiences. I learned to stop and ponder as well as look to my dreams before jumping to unrealistic conclusions.

Presenter: Now that we have worked with all six PMID steps, let's return to the first two. Please share your reflections, comments, or questions about your experiences of recording a dream of your own plus searching your day-before-your-dream events and thoughts for connections to your dream. [Presenter listens and responds to students' reflections.]

In conclusion, as Rose's dreams and interpretations reveal, work with our dreams gives us opportunities to discover solutions to current questions (for instance, To what activity do I need to give priority?) and solutions to long-term questions (for instance, What outdated reactions in relationship experiences do I continue?).

Thank you for your attention. Dream on!

BRENDA O'BEIRNE'S REFLECTIONS ON THE ONE-CLASS PERIOD, THREE-HOUR PRESENTATION

Within a counselor preparation program, the practicum course is designed to help counselor trainees enhance their skills while serving clients. Practicum students apply earlier learning, experiment with strategies and techniques, and receive ongoing feedback about their work. Practicum students also raise questions and continue their quest for new learning that will help them to build on the foundation of theory and practice already established.

It was within this context of learning that Duesbury shared her PMID model and helped students consider the possibilities in their lives and their work. Students were invited to read introductory materials before the class meeting and were asked to reflect on their own dreams; they were also encouraged to think about potential applications with clients they were working with at the time. Because the presentation was scheduled for midsemester, all practicum students had significant experience with clients and could speculate about the utility of the approach with selected clients.

The structure suggested in these guidelines was utilized by Duesbury to help students build an understanding of the model. The process was straightforward and clear; all members of the class were included (they reported feeling valued and included when asked later) in the exploration and discussion. Students' questions were encouraged and processed. While the content was new to most of the students, the approach helped them to feel open and confident. The working through of specific dreams was useful to all students in the group (based on feedback solicited later). Students were able to integrate earlier learning about theory and other counseling constructs with the dreamwork being presented. Students reported a desire to practice and learn more (several worked with dreams of clients later in the semester, and I am confident they would not have heard those openings had we not shared this time).

When we repeat a similar workshop, I will likely use a similar approach. What I might do differently has to do with the anticipation of the time and the prework that is assigned. With highly motivated and skilled students (and the practicum students are), it would be helpful for them to have some work done in advance so that even more time could be dedicated to discussion and exploration during the class period. Ideally, there could also be a follow-up session in which trainees use the new knowledge and then take time for feedback and additional learning. Each of those pieces was good learning for Duesbury and myself. Most important, all of the students who had the opportunity to participate in this training have another way to think about helping clients develop deeper understanding of themselves and another way of understanding self. Given that counselors' work is about making meaning, that is an invaluable outcome.

KIMBERLY TUESCHER'S REFLECTIONS ON THE ONE-CLASS PERIOD, THREE-HOUR PRESENTATION

In preparation for Duesbury's presentation, it was important for me to create a tone of active participation and openness to using a variety of techniques. The intent was to have my students consider these techniques for use in their future work as counselors. Prior to the presentation, students were asked to participate in a variety of technique-based exercises by taking roles of both counselor and client and then to reflect in writing about their experience from both perspectives. I believe this created a tone that was optimal for the preclass assignment and subsequent presentation of the PMID model and related exercises.

During the presentation, I became an active participant, much like the student role. My hope was to model active participation desired to gain the most benefit of the presentation exercises offered by Duesbury. I interjected responses on an intermittent basis in hopes to achieve this goal.

Follow-up consisted of having students reflect in writing as well as verbally processing in the subsequent lesson of the course. Students commented on the value of the exercise in their own life and expressed an interest in continuing to use this for personal growth. They highlighted that they did not want to minimize the impact this might have in the therapeutic process for future clients. The fact that they were able to feel the impact of the exercises was a valuable reinforcement of the potential for use in their future practice.

EVELYN DUESBURY'S REFLECTIONS ON HER PRESENTATIONS TO THESE TWO CLASSES

As a visiting presenter, I found that students in both classes were noticeably attentive and receptive to talking about dreams. I also found that the regular professors' participation encouraged their students' involvement. My approach to the two classes varied in one major aspect—I used "Let Carlie Do the Talking—Now" dream for one class and a more intense dream for the other. The dreamer's obvious waking-life connections (red bow and chocolate dripping from Carlie's mouth) and the relative straightforward solution in the "Let Carlie Do the Talking—Now" dream I believe worked best to inspire student comments and questions. Thus, whether presenters use the "Carlie" dream or another to give an overview of the PMID model, I suggest selecting a dream and related interpretations for which the dreamer's connections and solutions are straightforward. The professors' preclass preparations, plus their encouragement and inspiration to their students and to me, were significant in the resulting positive session outcomes, and I thank them for this.

SUMMARY

This chapter has dual goals: an introduction to the book for a full-semester course and a one-time, 3-hour introduction to dream interpretation for students in courses other than dream interpretation ones. An interactive format is used in presenting an actual dream ("Let Carlie Do the Talking—Now") that Rose, the dreamer, interprets by using the PMID model. In contrast to the dreamer's waking-life thought that I basically know what my dreams about Carlie mean, the dream convinces Rose to study her dreams about her childhood friend, Carlie. In the process, Rose realizes that loss of Carlie's friendship in childhood continues to affect how she reacts to others in adulthood. Professors O'Beirne and Tuescher reflect on their experiences of having a visiting presenter make the class presentation. Duesbury reflects on her experiences from a visiting presenter's perspective.

SELF-STUDY QUIZ: CHAPTER 3

1. This chapter serves two overall purposes. What are those two purposes?
2. List one key finding from research and explorations of the PMID model.
3. It is important for you to understand your own dreams before offering to coach others' use of their dreams. Why?
4. List one advantage of the dreamer working either alone or with a counselor instead of meeting with family and other major relationships to discuss family issues.
5. Which PMID step strikes you as the most practical to do and why?

4

Daytime Events *Reproduced in the Nighttime Theater of Dreams (PMID Step 1)*

It is hard work to play the part of myself.

INTRODUCTION

What happened yesterday or last night anywhere in the world is headlined in the morning newspapers. What happened yesterday or last evening to the individual is often headlined in morning dream recall, depending on its significance to the dreamer. A newspaper headline states the theme of the article below it. Themes can also be identified for dreams.

Why is it important to identify the theme of a dream? This is true for the same reason it is helpful to read newspaper headlines—to find out what the dream is about. Determining the theme is the purpose of the first step in the Personalized Method for Interpreting Dreams (PMID) model.

The counselor needs to learn how to use the PMID model with his or her own dreams before he or she is ready to facilitate clients' use of the model. Consider Appendix B to be teaching instruments for you and your clients.

To begin interpreting your dream, first decide whether any pre-dream (often day-before-your-dream) events appear either symbolically or literally in your dream. Record all events that possibly may tie into your dream. The most relevant ties often become intuitively apparent when you ponder events and dreams together. The action of writing these events on paper or typing them into a computer serves two functions: (1) It triggers your thoughts on possible event connections, and (2) you still have the events for later review. Later review is often necessary for full understanding of your dream.

PMID Step 1: Connect your **previous-day** (often the day before) **events** to the dream to discover the theme of this dream. The events may appear in either symbolic or literal terms in your dream. Write down the appropriate events and record when they occurred.

DREAM SPECIALISTS SUPPORT THAT PRE-DREAM EVENTS PROMPT DREAMS

Synesius of Cyrene (1930), a North African scholar and philosopher of the early fifth century, encouraged people to record their waking-life experiences at the same time as they recorded their dreams. "It should be a wise proceeding," he wrote, "even to [record] our waking and sleeping visions [dreams] and their attendant circumstances … to have records to remind us of the character of each of the two lives concerned" (par. 12).

Freud (1900/1955) likewise considered connecting the events of the previous day to the dream as one of the easiest ways of interpreting the dream.

One question that Gendlin (1986) suggested for finding a "felt sense" of associations to the dream is, "What did you do yesterday?" (p. 10).

Domhoff's dream content studies (1996, 2003) solidly support linking dream content and waking life. For his 1996 study, Domhoff explored the dream diaries of eight people, including Freud and Jung, for links between Domhoff's dream content categories and the dreamers' recorded waking-life thoughts and behaviors. The conclusion was that dreams give views of people's waking-life interests.

Strauch and Meier's (1996) research showed the dominant connections that preceding-day events have to dreams. Five participant dreamers recorded and rated 50 dreams for event connections: Of 80 leading characters, 67.6% were time dated to the previous day. Of 39 extra characters, 25.6% were time dated to the previous day. Of 74 settings, 47.3% were time dated to the previous day. Of 298 objects, 30.9% were time dated to the previous day.

Cartwright and Lamberg (1992/2000) suggest recording events daily in a journal to prime dream recall. Yet, in Cartwright's experience with sleep laboratory participants, dreams that connect to waking-life events may come a week or more later.

Schredl's (2006) research also shows significant incorporation of daytime events in dreams. Participants (46 psychology students, mean age 20.7 years; 40 women, 6 men) rated 105 of 254 dreams from a 2-week period as "having incorporated at least one recent daytime event" (p. 3). Sixty-four events were from participants' lists of chosen events prepared the day before their dreams. Forty-one of the 64 events were from the day before the dreams.

Hartmann (1968) traced "day residue" (events and thoughts) to 800 of his own dreams and found 94% incorporated in dreams of the same day, 70% "of the event's visual dream content; 15 per cent as thought elements" (p. 222). Hartmann recorded these items at the time of recording his dreams.

I also record my day-before-the-dream events (and thoughts) at the time I record my dreams, which is as soon as possible after I awaken from the dream. It is easy for me to verify the accuracy of Hartmann's high percentage of events and thoughts incorporated into dreams because my rates are consistently higher than 90% for both events and thoughts.

What often happens in the dreamer's waking life the day before the dream concerns relationship experiences. Hartmann (1995) wrote that dreams "often seem to be dealing with interpersonal problems, with the dreamer's current concerns about family, friends, lovers" (p. 215). Dreams "appear to make connections with other persons or experiences in the past" (p. 215). Hartmann (2001) frequently writes that "dreaming makes connections more widely than waking" (e.g., p. 11).

Two methods we can use to encourage a dream about a particular event are incubation and interpretation of our spontaneous responses to waking-life events. Delaney's (1988, 1996) dream interview model suggests that we ask for (incubate) dream answers to waking-life concerns. Obviously, one possible event represented in subsequent dreams is the dreamer's pre-dream incubation. Delaney's dream interview model also recognizes that dreams do respond spontaneously to waking-life events without incubation.

The PMID model looks first for spontaneous responses to waking-life events for connections to the dream. When we consider all our day-before-the-dream waking-life events, we have a selection of events that may have inspired our dream. If we choose to accept our incubation request instead of considering other day-before-the-dream events, this is akin to accepting only one possible event even before seeing the dream.

Table 4.1 presents a synopsis of our support of PMID Step 1.

As stated at the beginning of this chapter, events appear in either symbolic or literal terms in dreams. Table 4.2 contains both symbolic and literal dream parts that connect to waking-life events. (Associated dreams are not included here.)

Uses of the PMID model steps are demonstrated in six chapters, beginning with this chapter and continuing through Chapter 9. One dream by a woman, Gloria, and her counselor-facilitated interpretations demonstrate the use of the PMID model. With this model, as with some other contemporary dream interpretation models, such as Delaney's dream interview (1988-1996) and Ullman's group approach (1996), the dreamer is considered the ultimate authority on what his or her dreams mean. When a counselor is involved, the counselor facilitates the client's use of the PMID model.

APPLYING PMID STEP 1

We follow a dream, "When Did I Lose Control?" through six chapters as Gloria, the dreamer, facilitated by a counselor, finds a simple solution to a dilemma she faces. Whether the solution is easy to put into practice is, however, another scenario.

TABLE 4.1 Support for PMID Model Step 1 (Previous-Day Events)

Projects	Raters	Results (%)
A1: Duesbury (2000), 7 years, thesis RES, 1 PRT: 70 dreams No. of dreams per year: 18, 11, 3, 10, 16, 7, 5	PROF-R[a]	(No. met Step 1 criteria ÷ No. of dreams per year) 66.7, 55.5, 66.7, 50.0, 81.3, 42.9, 100.0
A2: Van Doren & Duesbury (2000), 3-month EXPL, 10 PRTs—24 pre-PMID, 9 post-PMID dreams	Duesbury	(No. met Step 1 criteria ÷ No. of pre-PMID or post-PMID dreams) Pre-PMID 28.6 Post-PMID 88.9
A3: Van Doren & Duesbury (2001), 4-month EXPL, 5 PRTs—13 pre-PMID, 33 post-PMID dreams	PFI[b]	(PFI median, Step 1 ÷ 7 [Likert scale]) After 2 PMID dreams 71.4 At 4 months 92.9
Rated 13 pre-PMID and 24 of 33 post-PMID dreams	PROF-R	(No. met Step 1 criteria ÷ 13 and 24) Pre-PMID 76.9, post-PMID 100.0
A4: Duesbury, Bynum, & Van Doren (2002), 3-month EXPL, 11 PRTs—81 dreams	PFI	(Wilcoxon signed rank tests) At 8 weeks: Significant change with $W- = 2$, $W+ = 64$, $N = 11$, $p \leq 0.00293$ At 14 weeks: Nonsignificant
A5: Duesbury, Bynum & Van Doren (2003), 3-month EXPL, 5 PRTs—36 dreams	PFI	(PFI median, Step 1 ÷ 7 [Likert scale]) Start 78.6 At 8 weeks 71.4 At 14 weeks 85.7
A6: Duesbury, Bynum, & Van Doren (2004), 3-month EXPL, 6 PRTs—29 dreams	PFI	(PFI median, Step 1 ÷ 7 [Likert scale]) Start 78.6 At 8 weeks 71.4 At 14 weeks 85.7
A7: Van Doren & Duesbury (2005–2006), RES ongoing, PMID use, 5 PRTs—4 gave PFIs, 46 dreams from earlier years, 10 current-year dreams	PFI	(PFI median, Step 1 ÷ 7 [Likert scale]) Earlier years PFI median ÷ 7: 92.9 Current year PFI median ÷ 7: 85.7
A8: Okocha & Duesbury (2005–2006), 6-month RES, 17 PRTs—222 dreams, 200 being from 8 PRTs who were active for full 6 months	PFI	(Wilcoxon signed rank tests–critical values of *W* for samples less than 10) At 2½ months: $W = 33$ $n_{s/r} = 8$, $p \leq = .05$ At 6 months: Nonsignificant

Note: See Appendix A for details. RES, research; EXPL, exploration; PRT, participant.

[a] PROF-R Van de Castle is an independent professional rater.

[b] PFI, periodic feedback instrument, formalized in 2002. See Appendix B for format. Likert-type rating scale 1 to 7, with 7 high.

Gloria's Dream: "When Did I Lose Control?"

Dream: *We, somebody else and I, are placed into the right-side seats in the Langley church. We simply and calmly observe a graduation ceremony. On the other side are graduates who are quite excited about their graduation.*

Punctuating this scene is a row of slender little girls. They all look very much alike. The little girls turn around and look toward us, the observers, instead of toward the graduates.

The director is standing at the front of the room, on the stage. He looks like Mr. Morgan, albeit his physique is smaller and his facial features are different

TABLE 4.2 Examples of Day-Before-Dream Event Connections to Dreams (PMID Step 1)

Example 1: Last evening, I prepared a short, hasty agenda for an upcoming meeting. During the night, I dreamed that a chairperson expects an organized agenda.

Literal Connection: Last evening's waking-life event is factually shown in the dream event: the agenda for an upcoming meeting. The theme of the dream is "agenda for upcoming meeting."

Example 2: Yesterday, I worked on some dreams about relationships in my life. During the night, I dreamed that my room in my parents' house was under construction.

Symbolic connection: Yesterday's waking-life event is symbolically shown in the dream as "my room in my parents' house under construction." Likely themes are "efforts to improve unhelpful early established patterns" and "efforts to change my reactions to my parents."

Example 3: Yesterday, I overcame several obstacles in my work. In the subsequent dream, I helped our team win a game in the 13th inning after being behind several times.

Symbolic connection: Popular superstition has it that the number 13 means bad luck. Winning in the 13th inning is thus picture language for overcoming bad luck, which the dreamer did when he overcame obstacles the day before. A possible dream theme could simply be "keeping a good attitude."

Note: Associated dreams for examples are not included here.

from Mr. Morgan's. [Director] *Mr. Morgan tries to calm the graduates, but he doesn't have much control. He is quite good-natured about it and just lets them cheer and carry on. He says to the rest of us, though, "You can go ahead and leave if you want to while we let these graduates carry on." But it doesn't seem that any of us leave.*

Step 1: Connect your **previous-day** (often the day-before) **events** to the dream to discover the theme of this dream.

Facilitator: Gloria, first look for clues in your dream that show how your dream possibly might connect to your waking life. This first clue is meant to help you discover what the dream is about; this is the theme of your dream. The theme provides a basis for completing the rest of the PMID steps.

Look first at your day-before-your-dream events, which are valuable clues toward understanding what initiated your dream and what issues the dream addresses. For that reason, it is important to record day-before-your-dream events at the same time as you record the dream. Otherwise, those clues will be lost from your immediate memory. Record all the events that seem to connect to the dream. You can later delete events that clearly have no ties to the dream.

So, Gloria, did you record any events from the day before your dream, and, if yes, do any seem to tie to your dream?

Gloria: The day before my dream, I wrote a bit of an interpretation of a snake dream from quite a while ago. I also reread a meditation piece I had written earlier. These could tie in.

Facilitator: Let's take these events one at a time. What makes you think that writing some interpretations about your snake dream the day before might have brought on your "When Did I Lose Control?" dream?

Gloria: Snake dreams dismay me. Sometimes they warn me. Sometimes they seem to be about spiritual growth. So maybe my snake dream links to my "When Did I Lose Control?" dream by the setting being in a church.

Facilitator: And what about the second event? What about the meditation piece that you had written earlier and reread the day before your dream?

Gloria: The part of the meditation that really caught my eye when I read it yesterday was, "It is hard work to play the part of myself and harder still to play the part of my Self."

Facilitator: I wonder which comes first for you—how to play the part of your self with the lowercase *s* or how to play the part of your Self with the uppercase *S*?

Gloria: They ought to come together, but to be honest I think the trouble I'm having with how to be me (the self with the lowercase *s*) is what I need to tackle first, before understanding how to go about the spiritual life (the self with the uppercase *S*).

Facilitator: Perhaps you will find that both of these day-before-your-dream events do connect to your "When Did I Lose Control?" dream. For now, though, which one do you believe most prompted your dream? Which one most helps you decide what your dream is about?

Gloria: After talking about each event just now, I think it's my reading the meditation piece again about how hard it is to play the part of myself. A tie in my dream that I see is the little girls who look very much alike. They clone each other and end up as identical copies. That is what I do. I copy others on how to act.

Facilitator: So the general theme of your dream seems to be?

Gloria: How about finding out how to be me?

Facilitator: That theme fits with the main event you tie to your dream. If that theme is on target, it will help you as you work with the rest of the PMID steps. If you find it doesn't fit, you can always come back to Step 1 and revise the theme you developed.

Keep in mind that although the counselor-facilitator discusses the dreamer's idea of a theme, the counselor-facilitator resists suggesting a theme he or she might see in the dream. The dreamer is the interpreter; the counselor simply facilitates the process.

SUMMARY

In this chapter, the first step in the PMID model is explained and demonstrated. Step 1 is to connect previous-day (often the day-before) events to the dream. These events appear in the dream in either straightforward or figurative terms. Record all events that possibly may tie to your dream and then ponder whether each does connect. Be encouraged that professional dream workers support pre-dream events as factors in bringing dreams.

To demonstrate Step 1, a counselor facilitates Gloria's ability to link day-before-her-dream events to her "When Did I Lose Control?" dream. Gloria decides that one event most connects to her dream: The day before her dream she had reread some words that she had written for a meditation piece, "It is hard work to play the part of myself and harder still to play the part of my Self." She decides the theme of her dream is "finding out how to be me."

SELF-STUDY QUIZ CHAPTER 4: APPLY PMID STEP 1 TO YOUR DREAMS

Before going on to the next chapter and the next step, spend some time studying and doing Step 1 with at least one of your own current dreams. Write the dream you have chosen and your response to PMID Step 1 for your dream. Explain how the events you list tie to the dream and state whether it or they are from the day before your dream.

LOOKING ONWARD TO THE NEXT PMID MODEL STEP

In the next chapter, Gloria searches for another clue to what brought on her "When Did I Lose Control?" dream. That clue takes her closer to understanding the purpose of her dream.

5

Daytime Thoughts *Questions That Nighttime Dreams Answer (PMID Step 2)*

I thought it truly is very difficult to feel comfortable with the way I act at times.

INTRODUCTION

Thoughts are powerful antecedents to our dreams. They frequently serve as questions that the dream answers in some way. In Chapter 4, we saw that our ability to connect pre-dream (often day-before-our-dream) events to the dream can reveal the theme of a dream. In this chapter, we can use Personalized Method for Interpreting Dreams (PMID) Step 2 to learn if a dream responds to any of our day-before-our-dream thoughts.

Caution. Be aware that events and thoughts are not the same thing. Address them separately when you begin to interpret your dream. When participants in our research and exploration projects recorded and considered events and thoughts separately, they often succeeded in finding the best personal meanings in their dreams.

Events are, however, few in comparison to the multitude of thoughts we think every day. Can you really determine which of your random thoughts connect to your current dream? Yes, you can, and your success will amaze you. But, be aware that this work takes dedication. A major reason it takes dedication is that dreams are more often symbolic or metaphoric than literal.

To help you make thought connections to the dream, write your recalled day-before-your-dream thoughts on paper or type them into your computer. As participants in our research and exploration projects attested, writing gets better results than just thinking about possible connections. Writing in a journal also prompts insights into meanings. Even if you are thinking, "Yes, I already know that," write the dream plus the events and thoughts down.

As an alternative to writing in a journal after waking up from the dream, before you go to sleep each night, write down your most prominent thoughts (and events) of the day. This alternative may be beneficial for beginners and for people who have difficulty making connections after the dream.

Keep in mind that it is *after* we have the dream that we explore which thoughts may have prompted the dream. It is like the board game and TV program *Jeopardy*, in which the contestant is given an answer and must supply the question. The contestant waits until after the answer is given before deciding what question requires that answer. As if you are playing *Jeopardy*, wait until after you have the dream before you decide what thoughts (questions) prompted your dream.

PMID Step 2: Connect your **previous-day** (often the day before) **thoughts** to your dream to detect which thoughts may have prompted this dream's responses. Like events, your thoughts may appear in your dream in either literal or symbolic terms. Write "I thought" statements and record when you thought them.

DREAM SPECIALISTS SUPPORT THAT PRE-DREAM THOUGHTS INITIATE DREAMS

Dream researchers have long recognized that thoughts passing through the waking mind are frequent and significant initiators of dreams (Kramer, Roth, Arand, & Bonnet, 1981).

Freud (1900/1955) wrote: "Dreams show a clear preference for the impressions of the immediately preceding days" (p. 163).

Schredl (2003, 2006) declared that measuring pre-dream waking-life thought connections to dreams is vital to assessing the continuity between waking life and dreams.

One of two time references that Strauch and Meier (1996) asked participants to report was "when these elements ['the very individuals, locations and objects that had made an appearance in their dreams'] last entered their minds" (p. 160).

Table 5.1 presents a synopsis of our support of PMID Step 2.

For assistance with connecting your day-before-the-dream thoughts to your dream, examine the examples in Table 5.2.

Returning to Gloria's "When Did I Lose Control?" dream, she addressed PMID Step 2 as the facilitator guided her.

APPLYING PMID STEP 2

Recall the predominant event that Gloria connected to her dream for Step 1—read the meditation piece again about "how hard it is to play the part of myself". The theme Gloria developed from that event was "finding out how to be me." Based on

TABLE 5.1 Support for PMID Model Step 2 (Previous-Day Thoughts)

Projects	Raters	Results (%)
A1: Duesbury (2000), 7 years, thesis RES, 1 PRT: 70 dreams No. of dreams per year: 18, 11, 3, 10, 16, 7, 5	PROF-R[a]	(No. met Step 2 criteria ÷ No. dreams per year) 61.1, 45.5, 66.7, 80.0, 87.5, 71.4, 100.0
A2: Van Doren & Duesbury (2000), 3-month EXPL, 10 PRTs—24 pre-PMID, 9 post-PMID dreams	Duesbury	(No. met Step 2 criteria ÷ No. pre-PMID or post PMID dreams) Pre-PMID 3.6 Post-PMID 66.7
A3: Van Doren & Duesbury (2001), 4-month EXPL, 5 PRTs—13 pre-PMID, 33 post-PMID dreams	PFI[b]	(PFI median, Step 2 ÷ 7 [Likert scale]) After 2 PMID dreams 71.4 At 4 months 92.9
Rated 13 pre-PMID and 24 of 33 post-PMID dreams	PROF-R	(No. met Step 2 criteria ÷ 13 and 24) Pre-PMID 7.7, post-PMID 100.0
A4: Duesbury, Bynum, & Van Doren (2002), 3-month EXPL, 11 PRTs—81 dreams	PFI	(Wilcoxon signed rank tests) At 8 weeks: Significant change with $W- = 0$, $W+ = 55$, $N = 10$, $p \leq 0.00195$ At 14 weeks: Nonsignificant
A5: Duesbury, Bynum & Van Doren (2003), 3-month EXPL, 5 PRTs—36 dreams	PFI	(PFI median, Step 2 ÷ 7 [Likert scale]) Start 28.6 At 8 weeks 71.4 At 14 weeks 85.7
A6: Duesbury, Bynum, & Van Doren (2004), 3-month EXPL, 6 PRTs—29 dreams	PFI	(PFI median, Step 2 ÷ 7 [Likert scale]) Start 78.6 At 8 weeks 71.4 At 14 weeks 85.7
A7: Van Doren & Duesbury (2005–2006), RES ongoing, PMID use, 5 PRTs—4 gave PFIs, 46 dreams from earlier years, 10 current-year dreams	PFI	(PFI median, Step 2 ÷ 7 [Likert scale]) Earlier years PFI median ÷ 7: 92.9 Current year PFI median ÷ 7: 85.7
A8: Okocha & Duesbury (2005–2006), 6-month RES, 17 PRTs—222 dreams, 200 being from 8 PRTs who were active for full 6 months	PFI	(Wilcoxon signed rank tests—critical values of *W* for samples less than 10) At 2½ months $W = 34$ $n_{r/r} = 8$, $p \leq = .02$ At 6 months $W = 21$ $n_{s/r} = 6$, $p \leq .05$

Note: See Appendix A for details. RES, research; EXPL, exploration; PRT, participant.

[a] PROF-R Van de Castle is an independent professional rater.

[b] PFI, periodic feedback instrument formalized in 2002. See Appendix B for format. Likert-type rating scale 1 to 7, with 7 high.

Gloria's Step 1 responses, her counselor-facilitator encouraged her to move on to Step 2.

Facilitator: Gloria, because you have been working with the PMID model on other dreams, I'm sure you recorded at least some of the thoughts you had the day before your "When Did I Lose Control?" dream.

Gloria: Yes, I did scribble a few thoughts in my dream diary. In looking back, it dismays me that I didn't record more at the time of my dream. Step 2 is complex, with all the thoughts that ramble though my mind daily.

TABLE 5.2 Examples of Day-Before-Dream Thought Connections to Dreams (PMID Step 2)

Example 1: Yesterday, I thought about some things to say to a person who had asked me to write to her. In the dream, when I hug her she stiffens and changes into an uptight person I know.

Connection: Day-before-the-dream thoughts about what to write to this person connect to the uptight person in the dream.

Example 2: Last night, I thought in remorseful terms about a past circumstance of being ignored by a friend. In the dream, I am standing at a wall and cry and moan.

Connection: My night-before-the-dream remorseful thoughts connect to the "wailing wall" in my dream.

Example 3: Yesterday, after first discovering a golden opportunity, in an afterthought I kicked myself because I thought I might have muffed it. In the dream, I turn in to the driveway of Mr. Swinerath, a negative person.

Connection: My turning a day-before-my-dream positive event into negative thoughts connects to turning in to the driveway of a negative person in my dream.

An experiment: Purposely think about some event that seems like a downer to you. Notice your emotions when you are thinking of the event in negative or discouraging terms. Next, think of some event that seems more upbeat. Notice that your emotions are different when you are thinking of that event in positive terms. Compare the effects of your thoughts on your emotions.

Note: Associated dreams for examples are not included here.

Facilitator: You are correct. Tracing day-before-your-dream thoughts to dreams can be hard work. As with all techniques, the more you practice, the more proficient you become.

Gloria: Well, yes. I know that linking the day-before-my-dream thoughts to my dreams is a chief clue to finding meanings. I believe I did okay for this dream. Here are the thoughts that I had the day before my dream that I think connect to it:

1. I'm doing better in intuitive "listening," although I admit to being too immersed in the world of objective thinking when I wrote the meditation piece.
2. It truly is very difficult to feel comfortable with the way I act at times. That thought came when I engrossed myself in rereading my words, "It is hard work to play the part of myself."

Facilitator: The best time, of course, to record your thoughts from the previous day is at the same time you record your dream. Besides developing "thought questions" for Step 2, as you do Step 3 (select and define major dream phrases and symbols from your write-up of this dream to discover the personalized meanings of the dream), insights will come on how your day-before-your-dream thoughts (and events) originated some of the dream phrases. Have you experienced that?

Gloria: Yes, I have.

Facilitator: Good. When we come to Step 3, we will see if and how your work in Steps 1 and 2 helps you interpret this dream. For now, let's discuss how you believe your recorded thoughts tie to your dream and thus could have had a part in prompting your "When Did I Lose Control?" dream.

First, how do your recorded thoughts about "doing better in intuitive 'listening,'" connect to your dream?

Gloria: Although that thought is true, by now it only seems like a loose link, if it links at all. Could more than one thought be tied to a dream?

Facilitator: Yes, of course. You can also use your day-before-your-dream thoughts to help find personal definitions when we come to Step 3.

Gloria: Actually, in pondering this now, the second thought I told you about (I thought it truly is very difficult to feel comfortable with the way I act at times) links the best to my "When Did I Lose Control?" dream. That's because the director, an unconventional person, loses control in the dream.

Facilitator: So, the director's losing control of the cheering graduates mirrors in some way you are losing control in waking life?

Gloria: Well, first, the director being like Mr. Morgan is a clue. Mr. Morgan just doesn't lose control in waking life. His natural way is being in control. I must not be acting naturally when I feel uncomfortable with the way I act at times.

Facilitator: Do I understand you correctly here that you consider yourself unconventional in some way, and that causes you to lose control at times?

Gloria: That's kind of how it is. I'm an unconventional person, not unconventional in the way that Mr. Morgan is, but unconventional because I feel most natural as an inward type of person, and that doesn't work very well at times. So, I try to join in with the more outgoing people, but I lose control at times.

Facilitator: You lose control in what types of settings? What do you mean by "lose control at times"?

Gloria: Well, it's in social-type settings. Chitchat stuff, you know. I start thinking I need to join in, to be part of the group, but then I have a tough time keeping from talking too much, becoming an actress really, and saying more than it feels natural for me to say.

Facilitator. It seems quite natural to me for people to cheer when they have accomplished such a feat as passing all the courses and meeting the other graduation requirements, as the graduates in your dream are doing.

Gloria: Yes, I realize that. But it doesn't work that way for me. You see, when I was growing up, I believed outgoing people were the normal people. I didn't think about being anything else, or even that I was anything else. I tried to be like them so I would fit in and be appreciated, I guess. The truth is that I'm not like that. I finally discovered, with testing, that my natural way is very inward, and that's one reason this trying to be one of the crowd is tough. This is a very serious matter for me. [Gloria is shedding tears now.]

Facilitator: [Gently inquires] Do you recall, Gloria, what tests you took that convinced you that your natural way is very inward?

Gloria: The Myers-Briggs Type Indicator and the Strong Interest Inventory.

Facilitator: Those are valid statistical tests. You should be aware that in addition to those quantitative measures, our nighttime dreams also have the potential to reveal evidence of personality type. Do you have any recall or records of dreams that might reflect whether your natural type is introversion or possibly bordering on extraversion?

Gloria: Not right now. I'll check my dream journal.

Facilitator: You could have dreams that reflect your personality type during our further work on the topic of finding out how to be you.

One reason it's important to tie pre-dream thoughts to the dream is that these thoughts often act as questions to the dreaming mind. With the question already in your mind, it is much easier to understand the answer. Do you want to put your predominant day-before-your-dream thought into one or more questions for your ongoing work with this dream?

Gloria: Sure. How about, "How can I stop overreacting in social settings?"

SUMMARY

In this chapter, the second step of the PMID model is explained and demonstrated. For Step 2, the dreamer connects pre-dream (often day-before-the-dream) thoughts to the dream. Thoughts frequently act as questions that the dream answers in some way.

Caution: Events (Step 1) and thoughts (Step 2) are not the same and should be addressed separately when interpreting dreams. It is amazing, but true, that although multitudes of thoughts cross the human mind every day, it is possible for the dreamer to become aware of which specific thoughts connect to the dream. One way to succeed is with dedicated practice in recording your thoughts. Another key is listening for intuitive thoughts or ideas that fall spontaneously into your mind regarding which thoughts connect to your dream. The best time to record thoughts from the previous day is when you record your dream. It is encouraging to know that professional dream workers support our concept that pre-dream thoughts, which are often emotion-packed thoughts, do bring dreams. In this chapter, Gloria, the dreamer, was facilitated by a counselor to tie her day-before-the-dream thought, "I thought it truly is very difficult to feel comfortable with the way I act at times" to her "When Did I Lose Control?" dream. From there, she develops a question, "How can I stop overreacting in social settings?"

SELF-STUDY QUIZ CHAPTER 5: APPLY PMID STEP 2 TO YOUR DREAMS

Before going on to the next chapter and the next step, spend some time studying and doing Step 2. Record and connect your day-before-your-dream thoughts to at least one of your own current dreams to detect which thoughts may have prompted responses to your dream. Write the dream and your responses to PMID Step 1 along with your responses to PMID Step 2. Explain how the thoughts that you list tie to the dream and state whether it or they are from the day before your dream.

You may use the same dream that you selected for your Chapter 4 self-study quiz, or you may choose one of your other dreams.

LOOKING ONWARD TO THE NEXT STEP

In the next chapter, Gloria, with the facilitator's guidance, unveils much of the mystery in her "When Did I Lose Control?" dream. Of all the PMID steps, Step 3 most assists the dreamer in becoming acquainted with his or her uniquely personal dreaming language.

6

Dream Phrases
Products of the Amazing Creativity of the Dreaming Mind (PMID Step 3)

All look very much alike: As I said when we were talking about Step 1, means copying others. They clone each other and end up as identical copies. That is what I do. I copy others on how to act.

DREAM PHRASES AND SYMBOLS

The ability to develop personalized meanings for dream phrases can enable people to find joy in dream guidance, perhaps for the first time in their lives. The Personalized Method for Interpreting Dreams (PMID) Step 3, which is defining a string of words, is unique to interpreting dreams. The technique is straightforward. Select major groups of words from your recorded dream narrative and define them in the context of the current dream. Selecting dream phrases is an evaluation made by the dreamer regarding which dream phrases are the most personally meaningful. The dreamer's spontaneous feelings are the best gauges for knowing the relative accuracy of meanings he or she has developed.

Although the technique is straightforward, our ability to become at ease with developing personal definitions takes dedication and time. Dreams often include images and use figurative language; further, there are no boundaries between the dreamer's past and current experiences. The incorporation of the dreamer's experiences in the dream confirms that each dreamer has a uniquely personal dreaming language. When the dreamer becomes acquainted with his or her own dreaming language, meanings will become accessible. Dedication to discovering one's individual dream language will result in rich rewards of discovering dream guidance.

PMID Step 3: Select and define **major dream phrases** and symbols from your write-up of this dream to discover the dream's personalized meanings. Consider effects of your events and thoughts of the day before your dream and earlier experiences on the meaning of each major dream phrase and symbol. The general definition for phrases as used in this step is "a string of words." The strings of words can be phrases, clauses, or whole sentences.

As the formal PMID Step 3 shows, the PMID way to find personal meanings in your dream is to select and define dream phrases, which are strings of words taken directly from your recorded dream narrative. Define those phrases in the context of your dream, the context being day-before-your-dream events, day-before-your-dream thoughts, earlier experiences, and intuitive insights.

It is common to find and accept the definitions for single words in the typical dream dictionaries. These definitions often give brief definitions of archetypal symbols. Dream dictionaries are useful but only as secondary sources. When you depend on dream dictionaries with their stereotypical definitions, you are limited in your ability to understand your personal dream messages. One example I use to demonstrate that point is the symbol *door*. As I wrote in my earlier book:

> Universal meanings of the word "door" are "challenge" and "opportunity." An example of a dream phrase is "locked the car doors," which one dreamer understood to mean, "I think I have to protect myself from danger on the road of life without my spouse." Another dreamer understood "closed the door" to mean he had overcome a difficult relationship issue that was represented in his dream. (Duesbury, 2007, p. 35)

When selecting your own dream phrases to define, it is often helpful to select exact phrases taken word for word from your description of your dream. What you write in your description of your dream is the closest report of the actual scenario that played like a movie in your dreaming mind. Using those exact words will thus help you uncover the intended messages of your dream. To trigger ideas about what those intended messages are, repeat the exact words from your dream by writing them down or typing them into your computer. In the process of writing or typing, ideas often come regarding the pre-dream events, pre-dream thoughts, and earlier experiences that inspired your dream. They clue you into literal and symbolic meanings for your dream.

When you become adept at selecting and defining dream phrases, you will have a vital technique for understanding your own unique, personal dream language. Dedication is important and will lead to an aptitude for both intuitive insight and rational reasoning. Intuition and rational reasoning are primary characteristics for achieving success with the PMID model, especially with Step 3. We have found that intuitive awareness not only is a helpful characteristic for working with dreams but also is often increased when using the PMID model.

DREAM SPECIALISTS SUPPORT THAT DREAM MEANINGS DERIVE FROM DREAMERS' EXPERIENCES

Synesius of Cyrene (early fifth century) wrote about the "obscurity" of dreams. That is, some of the most valuable meanings of dreams are difficult to understand. However, he said, this obscurity is best understood by the dreamer "for it [the dream] comes from us, is within us" (1930, par. 3).

Hildebrant (1895, cited in Van de Castle, 1994) claimed that it would be possible to explain every dream image if enough time were available to trace the image to the person's memory. Delaney (1988, 1996) also soundly supported the idea that dreams flow from the dreamer's experiences. Thus, the dreamer is the ultimate expert on meanings of his or her own dreams. LaBerge (2004) taught that dreams derive from "past experiences and motivations," which is "what we fear, hope for, and expect" (p. 14).

Table 6.1 presents a synopsis of our support of Step 3.

An added plus of doing well with Step 3 is that our interpretations frequently flow into information for other steps, as some of the examples in Table 6.2 show.

Let us return to Gloria and her work with her facilitator.

APPLYING PMID STEP 3

Gloria looks at her personal experiences to select and define major phrases from her "When Did I Lose Control?" dream. The dream (given in Chapter 4) is reprinted here for convenience. As you read Gloria's dream this time, however, be open to possible dream phrases that Gloria might have selected. After exploring the dream in this new way, see the phrases that Gloria, as guided by a facilitator, selected.

Gloria's Dream: "When Did I Lose Control?"

Dream: *We, somebody else and I, are placed into the right-side seats in the Langley church. We simply and calmly observe a graduation ceremony. On the other side are graduates who are quite excited about their graduation.*

Punctuating this scene is a row of slender little girls. They all look very much alike. The little girls turn around and look toward us, the observers, instead of toward the graduates.

The director is standing at the front of the room, on the stage. He looks like Mr. Morgan, albeit his physique is smaller and his facial features are different from Mr. Morgan's. [Director] *Mr. Morgan tries to calm the graduates, but he doesn't have much control. He is quite good-natured about it and just lets them cheer and carry on. He says to the rest of us, though, "You can go ahead and leave if you want to while we let these graduates carry on." But it doesn't seem that any of us leave.*

TABLE 6.1 Support for PMID Model Step 3 (Dream Phrases Defined)

Projects	Raters	Results (%)
A1: Duesbury (2000), 7 years, thesis RES, 1 PRT: 70 dreams No. of dreams per year: 18, 11, 3, 10, 16, 7, 5	PROF-R[a]	(No. met Step 3 criteria ÷ No. dreams per year) 100, 90.9, 66.7, 90.0, 81.3, 85.7, 100.0
A2: Van Doren & Duesbury (2000), 3-month EXPL, 10 PRTs—24 pre-PMID, 9 post-PMID dreams	Duesbury	(No. met Step 3 criteria ÷ No. of pre-PMID or post-PMID dreams) Pre-PMID 0.0 Post-PMID 33.3
A3: Van Doren & Duesbury (2001), 4-month EXPL, 5 PRTs—13 pre-PMID, 33 post-PMID dreams	PFI[b]	(PFI median, Step 3 ÷ 7 [Likert scale]) After 2 PMID dreams 71.4 At 4 months 71.4
Rated 13 pre-PMID and 24 of 33 post-PMID dreams	PROF-R	(No. met Step 1 criteria ÷ 13 and 24) Pre-PMID 0.0, post-PMID 66.7
A4: Duesbury, Bynum, & Van Doren (2002), 3-month EXPL, 11 PRTs—81 dreams	PFI	(Wilcoxon signed-rank tests) At 8 weeks: Significant change with $W- = 2, W+ = 53, N = 10, p <= 0.005859$ At 14 weeks: Nonsignificant
A5: Duesbury, Bynum & Van Doren (2003), 3-month EXPL, 5 PRTs—36 dreams	PFI	(PFI median, Step 3 ÷ 7 [Likert scale]) Start 28.6 At 8 weeks 71.4 At 14 weeks 71.4
A6: Duesbury, Bynum, & Van Doren (2004), 3-month EXPL, 6 PRTs—29 dreams	PFI	(PFI median, Step 3 ÷ 7 [Likert scale]) Start 35.7 At 8 weeks 64.3 At 14 weeks 78.6
A7: Van Doren & Duesbury (2005–2006), RES ongoing, PMID use, 5 PRTs—4 gave PFIs, 46 dreams from earlier years, 10 current-year dreams	PFI	(PFI median, Step 3 ÷ 7 [Likert scale]) Earlier years PFI median ÷ 7: 92.9 Current year PFI median ÷ 7: 85.7
A8: Okocha & Duesbury (2005–2006), 6-month RES, 17 PRTs—222 dreams, 200 being from 8 PRTs who were active for full 6 months	PFI	(Wilcoxon signed rank tests—critical values of W for samples less than 10) At 2½ months, $W = 30$ $n_{s/r} = 8, p \leq .05$ At 6 months, $W = 28$ $n_{s/r} = 7, p \leq .02$

Note: See Appendix A for details. RES, research; EXPL, exploration; PRT, participant.

[a] PROF-R Van de Castle is an independent professional rater.

[b] PFI, periodic feedback instrument; formalized in 2002. See Appendix B for format. Likert-type rating scale 1 to 7, with 7 high.

Step 3: Select and define major dream phrases and symbols from your write-up of the dream. Define them in the context of this dream.

Facilitator: Gloria, let's start by reviewing your responses to the first two PMID steps. The primary day-before-your-dream event that you connected to your dream for Step 1 was "Read words about it being 'hard to play the part of myself.'" (Note: Step 1 is explained and demonstrated in Chapter 4.) Your primary day-before-your-dream thought that you connected to your dream for Step 2

TABLE 6.2 Examples of Personal Definitions for Major Dream Phrases (PMID Step 3)

Example 1: From a dream titled "Jogging Will Heal My Knees"

Dream phrase: *Cane made especially for me.*

Dreamer's definition: Points the finger directly at me and asks me to stop acting as if I have a weakness.

Example 2: From a dream titled "I Understand the Substitute Teacher Better Than I Understand the Regular Teacher"

Dream phrase: *Book from which my regular teacher teaches.*

Dreamer's definition: Symbolizes my usual logical thought process. Logical reasoning is the way most lessons are taught in my waking-life environment.

Dream phrase: *Female substitute teacher*:

Dreamer's definition: Represents my feminine intuitive nature that I listen to temporarily. (I subscribe to the symbolic description of the feeling intuitive nature of both men and women as feminine.) Here, my dream advises me to consistently listen for intuitive thoughts.

Example 3: From a dream titled "Passing Grade Is Seventy-Six"

Dream phrase: *Seventy-five is the figure in my mind for a passing grade.*

Dreamer's definition: Instilled in my mind is that 75 is a passing grade. It is the passing grade for the certified public accountant (CPA) examinations, examinations that I passed.

Dream phrase: *Teacher saying the percentage we need to pass this class is 76.*

Dreamer's definition: Suggests that I need to learn through my "sixth" sense, my intuitive sense.

Note: Associated dreams for examples are not included here.

was "It truly is very difficult to feel comfortable with the way I act at times." From there, you developed the thought question, "How can I stop overreacting in social settings?" (Note: Step 2 is explained and demonstrated in Chapter 5.) Gloria, do I have these correct?

Gloria: Yes. Fine.

Facilitator: Good. Now let's talk about Step 3. I assume you have already done some work with Step 3 for your "When Did I Lose Control?" dream.

Gloria: Well, when I had this dream, I didn't tumble to where the scene came from. After working with it later, it struck me that that's a real scene from my waking life!

Facilitator: Good. Can you select a phrase from the dream and define it by telling me where the scene comes from? Your personal definition is as simple as that. Do you understand what I am asking you?

Gloria: I understand the following as what you mean by putting personal definitions to dream phrases:

Graduation ceremony: Is like the real ceremonies when I graduated from continuing education classes at a school of religion last summer. The ceremony was in a church sanctuary.

Facilitator: Great! I suspect you have produced definitions for several more phrases.

Gloria: Yes. This fascinates me because it's like fitting puzzle pieces together. The more dream phrases I define, the closer my dream is to a picture that makes sense. Here are two more dream phrases that I defined:

Somebody else and I: In the situation of this dream, the "somebody else" is my quiet cousin who came for my graduation.

Placed into the right-side seats: During the graduation ceremony last summer, my cousin and I did not sit with the graduates. Instead, we sat over at the side (just like we are doing in this dream).

Facilitator: I'm curious about this. I imagine that most times you choose to sit away from the main activity.

Gloria: Well, no. My cousin never puts on façades, so she easily sits away from the crowd. That gave me a chance to sit away from the crowd, too, despite the fact I was one of the graduates.

Facilitator: Okay. Go on with other dream phrases and your ideas of definitions based on your personal experiences.

Gloria: Here are two more:

Langley church: I grew up in the Langley church. I was very active in that church. Sure never sat on the side.

Graduates who are quite excited about their graduation: During the actual ceremony last summer, the other graduates were so exuberant that they started to sing the songs before the ceremony began. When the master of ceremonies came to the stage, his first words were, "When did I lose control of this ceremony?"

Facilitator: It's good that you have selected whole phrases to define. People often need several tries to learn the secret of selecting dream phrases (strings of words) instead of picking out single words to define from their dreams.

Another notable aspect of your definitions is that each ties to your life. That is, they all come distinctly from your experiences. Now, are any of your definitions leading you closer to answering the dilemma you believe this dream responds to on how to overcome, to use your words, "the way I act at times" and "how can I stop overreacting in social settings"?

Gloria: That's a piece of the puzzle I'm still deliberating.

Facilitator: The dreamer is the only person who can ultimately know with certainty because the dreamer is the one whose events and thoughts bring the dreams. I can help you by suggesting phrases from your dream for you to define. Define those by contemplating (that is, using rational reasoning together with listening for intuitive ideas) on what each means in the background of this dream.

Gloria: Step 3 says to select and define all major phrases. I've done that, haven't I? The scene, who I'm sitting with, where we are sitting, the Langley church, the cheering graduates. Those are all major phrases, aren't they?

Facilitator: True. They're all major phrases. But every phrase in your dream could be major for contributing to your full understanding of this dream. Are you game for seeing how many more you can define?

Gloria: Of course.

Facilitator: I'll suggest some for you to contemplate, and you can let me know later if any helped. Here they are, taken directly from your "When Did I Lose Control?" dream.

> Little girls
> All look very much alike
> Smaller stature and different facial features from Mr. Morgan's
> Tries a bit to calm the graduates
> But doesn't have much control

At a later counseling session, Gloria shared the following definitions she had developed for these suggested phrases:

Little girls: Maybe bringing up when I was a little girl. Maybe that is when I "lost control," so to speak, of being my natural self at times.

All look very much alike: As I said when we were talking about Step 1, means copying others. They clone each other and end up as identical copies. That is what I do. I copy others on how to act.

Smaller stature and different facial features from Mr. Morgan's: Not being himself in the dream. Like I'm not always myself in social settings.

Tries a bit to calm the graduates: This makes me stand in awe because this totally happened at the graduation ceremonies last summer. The master of ceremonies stood on the stage and tried to calm the graduates from their carrying on and cheering.

But doesn't have much control: It did work last summer for the cheering graduates. The graduates calmed down when the ceremonies began. Here, this points to my losing control at times.

Gloria: I picked out even more phrases from my "When Did I Lose Control?" dream than those in your list. I became so taken with the unfolding mystery that I kept choosing and defining groups of words from my dream. Shall I tell those to you?

Facilitator: Of course. That's the idea. We collaborate. That is, I suggest dream phrases only if the dreamer selects just a few. You are doing very well to select more on your own.

Gloria: How about these?

Look toward us, toward the observers, instead of toward the graduates: This puzzled me at first. The little girls, for sure, should have been looking toward the director on stage. That's pretty plain. A funny thing is when I first wrote this phrase down to interpret it, I miswrote it. I wrote, "Girls, the clones, all look back at the cheering graduates." Then, when I looked at my dream again, I noticed the right words were, "Girls turn around and look toward us, toward the observers, instead of toward the graduates." That's like saying to myself, "Pay attention to us, Gloria."

Just lets them cheer and carry on: Mr. Morgan, like, does that in my dream. That's strange because the master of ceremonies at the graduation brought the cheering graduates back to attention. Must be a clue here to my carrying on during social activities.

Can go ahead and leave if you want to while we let these graduates carry on: If the dream is talking about me, then it must be declaring, "Gloria, there are times when you could choose to leave from carrying on when you are in supposedly casual social settings."

Doesn't seem any of us leave: There are opportunities when I could leave, so to speak, from acting unnaturally. But, obviously, I don't cue into that all the time.

Notice three critical techniques that Gloria used to develop her Step 3 definitions:

1. She retained her dream as originally recorded.
2. She reviewed her first definitions to look for new insights.
3. She used words from her recorded dream narrative (as modeled by the facilitator) and defined those instead of creating new phrases. Gloria also caught her earlier mistake when she saw that in her dream narrative the little girls were looking toward Gloria and her cousin, the observers, not toward the cheering graduates.

Also notice in Gloria's work with Step 3 that she had already discovered something about her emotions, something about possible solutions in connection with her desire to overcome feeling uncomfortable "with the way I act at times," and something about relationship systems effects. In addition, notice that Gloria's work with Step 3 revealed information that would fit well with conventional therapies.

When working with Step 3, I find it most expedient and productive to copy and paste my write-up of the whole dream under Step 3. Next, I examine each sentence for whether there are phrases, or even whole sentences, that I can define in the context of my pre-dream events, pre-dream thoughts, earlier experiences, and intuitive insights.

For Gloria's dream, you probably have ideas regarding a solution in Gloria's dream just from reading Gloria's personal definitions. Thus, you may be tempted to give less attention to the last three PMID steps. But, would you stop reading midway through a fascinating mystery novel? Each new step contributes to the full meaning and usefulness of the dream.

SUMMARY

In this chapter, Step 3 is explained and demonstrated. For Step 3, the dreamer selects, defines, and interprets dream phrases he or she used to describe the dream. Definitions are foremost made in the context of the current dream, the context being the dreamer's day-before-the-dream events, day-before-the-dream thoughts, and earlier experiences. Prominent dream workers agree that dreams come from the dreamer's personal repertoire of experiences and thus must be interpreted in terms that are specific to the dreamer. The selection of phrases to define is often done in collaboration between the counselor-facilitator and the dreamer, especially if the dreamer selects only a few at first. Two key phrases from her dream that Gloria defines are

Placed into the right-side seats: During the graduation ceremony last summer my cousin and I did not sit with the graduates. Instead, we sat over at the side (just as we are doing in this dream).
Row of little girls: May be bringing up when I was a little girl.

In the unfolding mystery of interpreting her dream, Gloria has already discovered something about her emotions, something about possible solutions in connection with her desire to overcome feeling uncomfortable with "the way I act at times," and something about relationship systems effects.

SELF-STUDY QUIZ CHAPTER 6: APPLY PMID STEP 3 TO YOUR DREAMS

Before going on to the next chapter and the next step, spend some time studying and doing Step 3 for at least one of your own current dreams. You may use the same dream that you selected for your Chapter 4 or Chapter 5 self-study quizzes, or you may choose one of your other dreams.

1. Write the dream and your responses to PMID Steps 1 and 2.
2. Select at least three major phrases from your dream. (Remember, dream phrases are words taken directly from your recorded dream. The general definition for *phrases* as used in this step is "a string of words." The strings of words can be phrases, clauses, or whole sentences.)
3. Write definitions for each major phrase that you have selected from your dream.
4. Review the definitions you wrote for each phrase. Are your definitions personalized to the context of this dream? Do they tie to any of the following: your previous (often day-before) events (PMID Step 1), your previous (often day-before) thoughts (PMID Step 2), or any other experiences in your life? Do intuitive insights come to you after you have concentrated on the phrases in this way?

5. Review the definitions you wrote for each phrase. Do any lead to or indicate a solution? If so, which ones?

LOOKING ONWARD TO THE NEXT STEP

Emotions, an area explored in conventional therapies, are addressed in Step 4. In the next chapter, Gloria compares the emotions she felt in her dream with her waking-life emotions about the main issue addressed by her dream "When Did I Lose Control?"

7

Emotions in Dreams
Intrinsically Honest (PMID Step 4)

In the dream I am calm. In waking life,
I often become hyper after seemingly easily joining with the group.

INTRODUCTION

The dreaming mind exaggerates. A major area of dreaming exaggeration is emotions. Emotions in dreams are, however, intrinsically honest, even while being exaggerated. This honesty is noteworthy because it means that dreams can tell us when our waking-life appraisals of emotions are inaccurate. Consider how helpful the emotional content in a client's dreams can be in the counseling process. Besides assessing accuracy, comparisons over time about a particular issue or relationship help trace a client's progress in alleviating stress.

Because emotions are essential elements of the dreaming process, record the emotions in each dream narrative at the time you record your dream. Also, record your associated waking-life emotions about the main issue represented in your dream.

PMID (Personalized Method for Interpreting Dreams) Step 4: Compare your **emotions in your dream** with your **pre-dream, waking-life emotions** to discover whether your waking-life emotions accurately reflect how you feel about the issue in this dream. Note that the issue may be a relationship issue. What differences, if any, do you find between your emotions in your dream and your waking-life emotions? It is useful to periodically review your emotions in your dreams regarding the main issue or relationship at hand.

DREAM SPECIALISTS SUPPORT THAT STUDYING EMOTIONS IN DREAMS LEADS TO STRESS REDUCTION

Jung (1966) claimed that the intrinsic honesty of emotional content in dreams helps dreamers set their dreams within recent emotional experiences and, consequently, helps people apply their dreams to their waking lives.

Cartwright and Lamberg (1992/2000) wrote the following:

> Working with people while they were awake was frequently slow going. They often didn't want to face the feelings that were undermining them. With tremulous voices, they would say, "I'm not scared. Who says I'm scared?" However, they could recognize a dream that demonstrated their fears and uncertainties in a way that was clear and undeniable. (p. x)

Siegel (2002) says that the "wisdom of dreams can guide us to … resolve the challenges of life transitions" by "allowing us to identify and reclaim powerful hidden feelings that undermine our ability to move forward" (p. 18).

Kramer (1993, 2007) finds that emotions are dominant dream themes.

Hartmann (2001) writes that the "connecting process is not random. It is guided by the emotions and emotional concerns of the dreamer" (p. 3). Again, according to Hartmann, "dreams make connections more widely, more broadly, than waking and … the connections are guided by emotion" (p. 11).

Wolman and Ullman (1986) contend that the dreaming mind is often a more accurate reflection of the person's emotions than the person outwardly expresses or knows.

Gendlin's (1986) model asks the dreamer questions in an attempt to elicit a "felt sense" in the body. One question in the Gendlin model is "What did you feel in the dream?" (p. 9).

Table 7.1 presents a synopsis of our support of Step 4.

It is important to compare your emotions in your dreams with your appraisal of how you felt about the associated issue before your dream. Study the examples in Table 7.2 for assistance with making such comparisons.

Let us return to the PMID model and Gloria's work with her dream "When Did I Lose Control?" and see how Gloria, facilitated by a counselor, applies Step 4.

APPLYING PMID STEP 4

For Step 4, Gloria compares her emotions in her dream with her waking-life emotions about the main issue in this dream. First, a summary of the Gloria's responses to PMID Steps 1, 2, and 3 are as follows:

Step 1: Based on the day-before-her-dream event that Gloria connected to her dream, she decided a possible theme of her dream is "finding out how to be me."

Step 2: Based on the main day-before-her-dream thought that Gloria connected to her dream, "It truly is very difficult to feel comfortable with the

TABLE 7.1 Support for PMID Model Step 4 (Emotions)

Projects	Raters	Results (%)
A1: Duesbury (2000), 7 years, thesis RES, 1 PRT: 70 dreams No. of dreams per year: 18, 11, 3, 10, 16, 7, 5	PROF-R	(No. met Step 4 criteria ÷ No. dreams per year) 88.9, 100.0, 100.0, 70.0, 100.0, 100.0 100.0
A2: Van Doren & Duesbury (2000), 3-month EXPL, 10 PRTs—24 pre-PMID, 9 post-PMID dreams	Duesbury	(No. met Step 4 criteria ÷ No. of pre-PMID or post-PMID dreams) Pre-PMID 32.1 Post-PMID 44.4
A3: Van Doren & Duesbury (2001), 4-month EXPL, 5 PRTs—13 pre-PMID, 33 post-PMID dreams	PFI	(PFI median, Step 4 ÷ 7 [Likert scale]) After 2 PMID dreams 71.4 At 4 months 92.9
Rated 13 pre-PMID and 24 of 33 post-PMID dreams	PROF-R	(No. met Step 4 criteria ÷ 13 and 24) Pre-PMID 92.3, post-PMID 95.8
A4: Duesbury, Bynum, & Van Doren (2002), 3-month EXPL, 11 PRTs—81 dreams	PFI	(Wilcoxon signed rank tests) At 8 weeks: Significant change with $W- = 2$, $W+ = 43$, $N = 9$, $p \le 0.01172$ At 14 weeks: Nonsignificant
A5: Duesbury, Bynum & Van Doren (2003), 3-month EXPL, 5 PRTs—36 dreams	PFI	(PFI median, Step 4 ÷ 7 [Likert scale]) Start 42.9 At 8 weeks 71.4 At 14 weeks 85.7
A6: Duesbury, Bynum, & Van Doren (2004), 3-month EXPL, 6 PRTs—29 dreams	PFI	(PFI median, Step 4 ÷ 7 [Likert scale]) Start 35.7 At 8 weeks 71.4 At 14 weeks 72.9
A7: Van Doren & Duesbury (2005–2006), RES ongoing, PMID use, 5 PRTs—4 gave PFIs, 46 dreams from earlier years, 10 current-year dreams	PFI	(PFI median, Step 4 ÷ 7 [Likert scale]) Earlier years PFI median ÷ 7: 92.9 Current year PFI median ÷ 7: 78.6
A8: Okocha & Duesbury (2005–2006), 6-month RES, 17 PRTs—222 dreams, 200 being from 8 PRTs who were active for full 6 months	PFI	(Wilcoxon signed rank tests—critical values of W for samples less than 10) At 2½ months: $W = 28\ n_{s/r} - 7, p \le .02$ At 6 months: Nonsignificant

Note: See Appendix A for details. RES, research; EXPL, exploration; PRT, participant.

[a] PROF-R Van de Castle is an independent professional rater.

[b] PFI, periodic feedback instrument, formalized in 2002. See Appendix B for format. Likert-type rating scale 1 to 7, with 7 high.

way I act at times," she developed a possible thought question: "How can I stop overreacting in social settings?"

Step 3: Gloria selected phrases from her dream and developed personal definitions based on the context of her dream. For instance,

1. **All look very much alike:** Means copying others. They clone each other and end up as identical copies. That is what I do. I copy others on how to act.

TABLE 7.2 Examples of Emotions in Dreams Compared With Waking-Life Emotions (PMID Step 4)

Example 1: From a dream titled "Mom's Name Is Eunice Now"

Dreamer's comparison: In my dream I feel calm around my mother-in-law (whose name in my dream is Eunice). In waking life at the time of this dream, I also feel calm about her, although I have felt stressful around her from time to time. Eunice is not my mother-in-law's given name in waking life, but it is appropriate in this dream because it means "gloriously victorious." My calm emotions in this dream show that I am "gloriously victorious" in overcoming stressful emotions about my mother-in-law.

Example 2: From a dream titled "Help!"

Dreamer's comparison: I wake up from my dream with a labored, alarmed, desperate shout of "Help!" Before the dream, I felt agonized as a result of trying to play a role in another person's life that the person did not want, although I certainly did not feel alarmed then.

Example 3: From a dream titled "The Silver Platter"

Dreamer's comparison: In the dream, I feel very mad at a man who cusses at a herd of donkeys. This dream points to my feeling mad at his stubbornness. Before going to sleep and having this dream, I was feeling intensely guilty for giving this man some materials I looked on as silver platter quality, materials that upset him a lot when he read them.

Note: Associated dreams for examples not included here.

2. **Placed into the right-side seats:** During the graduation ceremony last summer, my cousin and I did not sit with the graduates. Instead, we sat over at the side, just as we are doing in this dream.

Facilitator: Gloria, adding to your interpretations for the first three PMID steps, let's turn to Step 4 and compare your emotions in your dream with your waking-life emotions during times when you believe you are not being your natural self. What emotions did you feel during your "When Did I Lose Control?" dream?

Gloria: In the dream, I am calm. I "simply calmly watch a graduation ceremony," although I'm one of the graduates.

Facilitator: Gloria, recall when we explored PMID Step 2, day-before-your-dream thoughts, I asked you a couple of questions: "You lose control in what types of settings? What do you mean by 'lose control at times'?"

Your response was, "Chitchat stuff, you know. I start thinking I need to join in, to be part of the group, but then I have a tough time keeping from talking too much, becoming an actress really, and saying more than it feels natural for me to say."

Gloria: Yes, I recall. That's how I lose control at times.

Facilitator: What emotions do you feel after you say more than it feels natural for you to say?

Gloria: Hyper, very hyper. Then, it's tough for me to calm down from how keyed up I become.

Facilitator: So, I'm wondering why your dream shows a time when you were calm when you are looking for how you can stop overreacting and becoming hyper afterward.

Gloria: I see that. It leads right to the solution I believe this dream puts forth on what I can do to act more natural in group-type occasions.

SUMMARY

The fourth of six steps in the PMID model is explained and demonstrated in this chapter. While many counseling approaches explore the client's waking-life emotions, we have found that dreams are fruitful resources for going one step onward to affirm or disaffirm the accuracy of a client's reports on how he or she feels about a particular issue or relationship. Here, Gloria realizes that her dream points to a time when she was successful in calming her waking-life emotions. She immediately sees that as leading to a solution for her quandary on what she does that makes her feel uncomfortable.

SELF-STUDY QUIZ CHAPTER 7: APPLY PMID STEP 4 TO YOUR DREAMS

Before going on to the next chapter and the next step, spend some time studying and working with Step 4 with at least one of your own current dreams. You may use the same dream that you selected for your Chapter 4, 5, or 6 self-study quizzes, or you may choose one of your other dreams. Write the dream and your responses to PMID Steps 1, 2, and 3. Now, focus on completing PMID Step 4 for this dream. Compare your emotions that you reported in your dream with your pre-dream, waking-life appraisal of your emotions about the main issue or relationship in this dream.

LOOKING ONWARD TO THE NEXT STEP

The dilemma Gloria faces in her waking life is how to overcome feeling uncomfortable with how she acts at times in social settings. The solution she finds in her "When Did I Lose Control Dream?" is revealed in the next chapter.

8

Solutions and Suggestions in Dreams

Answers to the Dreamer's Waking-Life Issues (PMID Step 5)

My dreaming mind simply pops in an event from the past when I handled myself well.

INTRODUCTION

A major outcome assessment in family counseling and cognitive behavior therapies is problem solving. A major outcome from the use of the Personalized Method for Interpreting Dreams (PMID) model is the dreamer's ability to discover problem-solving suggestions.

"This method [the PMID model] is especially helpful in identifying, clarifying, and resolving relationship problems. During our waking hours, we often feel frustrated that our rational attempts to solve life challenges are unsuccessful. It is then that our dreams often provide innovative and unexpected answers" (S. Krippner, personal communication, March 2, 2001).

Unexpected answers found in dreams are often couched in symbolic language. The dreamer needs to interpret this symbolic language to understand the answers. The counselor-facilitator encourages the dreamer to put together all the responses from the other PMID steps (including Step 6) and study the results before deciding which answers, solutions, and suggestions are embedded in the dream.

Note that Steps 1 through 5 are useful for interpreting most kinds of dreams, including dreams about work, education, health, and the spiritual realm. Step 6, which deals with the dreamer's reactions in relationship experiences, is used only for dreams about reactions to family or other major people in the dreamer's life. Step 6 can be considered simultaneously with Step 5, explore for solutions.

PMID Step 5: Explore your dream for possible **solutions** to problems, including changing (or affirming) your thoughts, attitudes, or behaviors. Consider your responses to each PMID model step, including Step 6, as you search for solutions and suggestions in this dream. Give primary attention to the power of your thoughts before your dream (PMID Step 2) to act as questions that your dream answers.

DREAM SPECIALISTS SUPPORT THE PROBLEM-SOLVING FUNCTION OF DREAMS

The discussion that follows concerns books that present the authors' findings on the discovery of problem-solving suggestions in dreams.

In Krippner and Dillard's (1988) *Dreamworking: How to Use Your Dreams for Creative Problem-Solving*, the authors asked:

> Are you aware of your full creative capacity? If you had a tool allowing you to tap hidden reservoirs of creativity for practical purposes, how would you use it? … We believe your night-time adventures can teach you methods of creative problem-solving that may dramatically improve your personal and professional life. (p. 1)

According to Cartwright and Lamberg's (1992/2000) *Crisis Dreaming: Using Your Dreams to Solve Your Problems*, "We can learn from our dreams when things are not right in our bodies, our minds, or our relationships with other people before we are likely to recognize these facts when we are awake" (p. 269).

Siegel (2002), in *Dream Wisdom, Uncovering Life's Answers in Your Dreams*, wrote the following: "Dreams give us access to hidden feelings and unexpressed needs. They highlight issues we need to work on and point to creative solutions to emotional roadblocks we are facing" (p. 15).

Delaney reported in several books, including *New Directions in Dream Interpretation* (1993), that the dream provides answers to the thought questions put to it.

Synesius of Cyrene (1930), in his *Dreams* (early fifth century AD), wrote: "Many of the things which present difficulties to us awake, some of these it makes completely clear while we are asleep, and others it helps us explain" (par. 9).

Table 8.1 presents a synopsis of our support of PMID Step 5.

For assistance in understanding Step 5, see the examples that follow. First are solutions found in "everyday" dreams (Table 8.2). For the purposes of the PMID model, an *everyday dream* is any dream that focuses on common activities, such as work, recreation, career, education, health, and the spiritual realm. Following the everyday dream examples are examples of solutions found in relationship dreams (Table 8.3). While dreams that focus on everyday activities are often easiest to interpret, it is frequently most productive to work concurrently with both everyday dreams and dreams about relationships. In addition, it is vitally important to take

TABLE 8.1 Support for PMID Model Step 5 (Find Solutions)

Projects	Raters	Results (%)
A1: Duesbury (2000), 7 years, thesis RES, 1 PRT: 70 dreams No. of dreams per year: 18, 11, 3, 10, 16, 7, 5	PROF-R[a]	(No. met Step 5 criteria ÷ No. dreams per year) 94.4, 81.8, 100.0, 100.0, 100.0, 100.0, 100.0.
A2: Van Doren & Duesbury (2000), 3-month EXPL, 10 PRTs—24 pre-PMID, 9 post-PMID dreams	Duesbury	(No. met Step 5 criteria ÷ No. of pre-PMID or post-PMID dreams) Pre-PMID 21.4 Post-PMID 100.0
A3: Van Doren & Duesbury (2001), 4-month EXPL, 5 PRTs—13 pre-PMID, 33 post-PMID dreams	PFI[b]	(PFI median, Step 5 ÷ 7 [Likert scale]) After 2 PMID dreams 71.4 At 4 months 85.7
Rated 13 pre-PMID and 24 of 33 post-PMID dreams	PROF-R	(No. met Step 5 criteria ÷ 13 and 24) Pre-PMID 15.4, post-PMID 100.0
A4: Duesbury, Bynum, & Van Doren (2002), 3-month EXPL, 11 PRTs—81 dreams	PFI	(Wilcoxon signed rank tests) At 8 weeks: Significant change with $W- = 1$, $W+ = 54$, $N = 10$, $p \le 0.00391$ At 14 weeks: Nonsignificant
A5: Duesbury, Bynum & Van Doren (2003), 3-month EXPL, 5 PRTs—36 dreams	PFI	(PFI median, Step 5 ÷ 7 [Likert scale]) Start 28.6 At 8 weeks 71.4 At 14 weeks 71.4
A6: Duesbury, Bynum, & Van Doren (2004), 3-month EXPL, 6 PRTs—29 dreams	PFI	(PFI median, Step 5 ÷ 7 [Likert scale]) Start 28.6 At 8 weeks 50.0 At 14 weeks 85.7
A7: Van Doren & Duesbury (2005–2006), RES ongoing, PMID use, 5 PRTs—4 gave PFIs, 46 dreams from earlier years, 10 current-year dreams	PFI	(PFI median, Step 5 ÷ 7 [Likert scale]) Earlier years PFI median ÷ 7: 85.7 Current year PFI median ÷ 7: 85.7
A8: Okocha & Duesbury (2005–2006), 6-month RES, 17 PRTs—222 dreams, 200 being from 8 PRTs who were active for full 6 months	PFI	(Wilcoxon signed rank tests—critical values of *W* for samples less than 10) At 2½ months: $W = 26$ $n_{s/r} = 7$, $p \le .05$ At 6 months: Nonsignificant

Note: See Appendix A for details. RES, research; EXPL, exploration; PRT, participant.

[a] PROF-R Van de Castle is an independent professional rater.

[b] PFI, periodic feedback instrument, formalized in 2002. See Appendix B for format. Likert-type rating scale 1 to 7, with 7 high.

refreshing and inspirational breaks from intensive work with relationship dreams. (See Appendix D for encouragement.)

For dream solutions to make a difference, those solutions must be used in waking life. Bulkeley (2000) reminded us that a dream "cannot in and of itself solve a waking-life problem; what is always necessary is the willingness of the dreamer to pay conscious attention to the dream, to test its workability, and finally to act on its guidance" (p. 190). Drawing on three of the dream solutions presented in Tables 8.2 and 8.3, we can illustrate the wisdom of Bulkeley's words:

TABLE 8.2 Examples of Solutions Found in "Everyday" Dreams" (PMID Step 5)

Example 1: Dream solution about distress over negative nightly TV news program

After watching the national news in which the emphasis was on negative events, Grace, the dreamer, dreams she is bantering back and forth with a friend she hasn't seen in a while and whose *very sophisticated humor makes the dream real-like and makes me feel good.* Grace's interpretation of this dream is that the solution to the distress that she feels from watching the negative nightly news is to *increase my humor in this day and age, as is appropriate. May not want to watch the nightly news so much. May need to do some more constructive work during news broadcasts.*

Example 2: Dream solutions for health

The nurse *asks: "How would you do with giving up food?" This comes from my request last night for a dream about a health condition I've had for several months. My dream says, "Stop eating solid foods." By inference: "Drink only liquids." Several weeks later, my boyfriend finally won out on his insistence that I ask my doctor about my mostly liquid diet. The doctor said, "Irritable bowel syndrome is what you have." I'd never heard the term before. He said parents think doctors are crazy to prescribe liquid diets for kids that have diarrhea, but the liquid diet works, and it worked for me, as long as I kept to it.*

Example 3: Dream solution about classroom teaching

A dream about a coach and a gymnastics team persuaded a professor to cut back on assignments for a class in auditing. In the dream, a superior student-athlete becomes so stressed he quits the team.

My dream, the teacher says, *shows that I am assigning excessive paperwork for students in my auditing class. For the young athlete-scholar, intense practice is his style. But the "gymnastics" (unnecessary paper work) required by students in my class, coupled with the demands placed on him as a superior athlete are de-energizing him.* [After this dream] *I immediately cut back on the work assignments for* [my] *class.* (Duesbury, 1994)

Note: Associated dreams for examples are not included here.

1. Grace's dream about negative nightly news can provide emotional release from the preponderance of negative thoughts that the TV news presses on her. She worries about the "daily events in and of our country." She accepts the solution of her dream to "increase my humor in this day and age, as is appropriate. May not want to watch the nightly news so much. May need to do some more constructive work during news broadcasts."
2. The woman who dreamed about a solution for her irritable bowel syndrome learned that she needed to follow the dream nurse's advice. The solution helped her. "It worked for me, as long as I kept to it."
3. Janet, who interpreted her "Passing a Heart Around" dream to mean "that I need to express my grief to others instead of keeping it inside in tremendous fear that I believe others will think I am weak and worthless if I emote in front of them," receives help from the dream suggestion when she acts on this guidance.

We need to pay attention to the solutions our dreams give us. Sometimes, we need to engage in new, ongoing activity suggested by our dreams. The woman who dreamed the solution for her irritable bowel syndrome only needed to stay on liquids for a while. The other dreamers' solutions, however, required dedication until the changes in thoughts, attitudes, emotions, and behaviors became

TABLE 8.3 Examples of Solutions Found in Relationship Dreams (PMID Step 5)

Example 1: Dream solution to alleviating the stress arising from a dispute

In Ruthanne's dream, she and a town official end up at Ruthanne's aunt's cabin, her favorite childhood vacation place. In waking life, the town official's decisions regarding Ruthanne's neighborhood have upset her. Although she does not know this before her dream, the town official's passion for traveling in search of family heritage is similar to Ruthanne's own devotion to family, past and present. This is revealed by the symbol of her aunt's cabin in the dream. The dream responds to Ruthanne's conscious change to having more positive thoughts about the town official and rewards her with the revelation of a common interest that she and the town official can share.

Example 2: Dream solutions for handling failure

The evening before he had this dream, Grant did poorly in a baseball game. He is usually an excellent player, but he became very angry at the umpire and was kicked out of the game. In his dream, Grant is back in childhood. He loses a board game to his brother. It is a game Grant usually excels in playing. In his dream, Grant becomes angry at his brother, but he is even angrier at himself. *It's interesting*, he reports, *that in the dream I projected my anger at myself onto my brother, since during childhood I routinely projected my anger on Carl after losing to him in competitive games.* Grant understands the solution given in his dream as *I need to work on dealing with anger I direct at myself rather than projecting it onto others. I also need to address why it is so important to do well all the time and why failure isn't okay in activities where I am generally successful.*

Example 3. Dream solution of prayer as the first option when dealing with a friend's problem

In her dream, Joyce receives an e-mail from God. *I am looking at a list of my e-mails*, she reports, *and I realize there is one from God at the top of the list. But I look at the others first and open and read those first!* Joyce identifies the source of her dream: *I've been trying to figure out a game plan. I've taken a stand on a problem with one of my closest friends, and now I am thinking, and I realize it's ridiculous, that other people might be more help to me in this sticky situation than God.* The solution Joyce finds in her dream is this: *I think in my unconsciousness, and in my waking heart of hearts, I know I must go on my knees to him for guidance and affirmation.*

Example 4: Dream solutions and suggestions for dealing with losing a family member

Janet is dealing with her emotions after the death of a young family member: She titles her first dream, "Passing a Heart Around." Her solution: *That I need to express my grief to others instead of keeping it inside in tremendous fear that I believe others will think I am weak and worthless if I express my emotions in front of them.* Janet's second dream is "Providing Sympathy." Her solution: *That I can cry with someone and that's okay. Instead of watching events unfold at a distance, I can try to keep myself present and in the moment and not lose sight of how exquisite the pain of a loss is for anyone at any level.*

Note: Associated dreams for examples are not included here.

natural to them. Look at your own dreams to determine whether you have followed Bulkeley's (2000) reminders on how to use your dream solutions.

Let us return to Gloria's "When Did I Lose Control?" dream. Using Step 5, Gloria, facilitated by a counselor, shows how to find a dream solution.

APPLYING PMID STEP 5

For Step 5, Gloria explores her dream for possible solutions or suggestions on changing (or affirming) thoughts, attitudes, or behaviors.

First, however, let us summarize Gloria's responses to Step 4, her emotions. In the dream, Gloria is calm, although the other graduates (her classmates) are "cheering." Regarding her waking-life emotions in social-type circumstances, at times Gloria feels compelled to say more than it feels comfortable for her to say. Afterward, she feels extremely hyper.

Facilitator: Gloria, by the time you completed the first four PMID steps, you believed you already knew what your "When Did I Lose Control?" dream suggests for what you can do to, in your words, "feel comfortable with the way I act at times." Step 6 sheds light on reactions in relationship concerns, so we could go on to Step 6 before you decide on a solution.

Gloria: I'm more certain than ever that the solution I see is the one my dream has moved into. My dreaming mind simply pops in an event from the past when I handled myself well. I handled myself well during the graduation exercises last summer. Reminiscences of the graduation are in my dream. Hence, the solution in my dream is, "Gloria, do what you did to keep calm during the graduation exercises. Do not let your cheering emotions continue into hyper feelings and blot out your natural inward self."

Facilitator: Okay, share with me how you accomplished remaining calm during the graduation exercises last summer. Your dreaming mind seems to have picked up on a valuable capability that you already possess. You have recognized it as an achievable technique.

Gloria: Well, prior to and during the graduation exercises, I consecrated myself to feeling content within myself. I did this intentionally because I wanted very deeply to savor my accomplishment of graduating. Hence—aha!—that is the solution for remaining calm in future casual situation gatherings. Before and during social events, persistently keep my thoughts on feeling content. Consciously do that. Do not let my cheering emotions continue into hyper feelings and blot out my natural, reserved self.

I am in a bit of awe of the simple solution so clearly pictured in my dream: "Look you can do this Gloria. You can stay calm. You were a part of the group because you were a graduate, but you sensibly sat on the side instead of acting out of character and becoming hyper afterward."

Facilitator: That's great, Gloria. I assume you have yet to try this.

Gloria: Acting on this solution is more difficult for me than it sounds, I assure you of that.

Facilitator: So, you've tried it?

Gloria: Well, I missed an opportunity to remain calm in a social setting even after I'd talked with you about my "When Did I Lose Control?" dream and finding out how to remain calm!

Facilitator: Share your experiences with me.

Gloria: The setting was a meeting with old friends I had worked with on a long-term project. I had no idea I'd be struggling to be my natural self there because I was very at ease when I worked with these people. Hence, I didn't coach myself before the event to keep my thoughts to myself. I jumped into the conversation full force. Afterward, I talked to myself, scolded myself you know, until I became hyper. That night I had a dream about messing up again.*

Facilitator: Keep up your confidence, Gloria. You did receive an excellent and simple, but not necessarily easy, suggestion from your "When Did I Lose Control?" dream. That's excellent progress. I assure you that it's a common phenomenon that people who come to counseling discover simple solutions for relieving stress but afterward find that those "simple" solutions are difficult to carry out. This is the dilemma you face.

Step 6 is an opportunity for you to compare your dreaming reactions (what you do in your dream) with your current waking-life reactions when you are with other people during social settings with how you have reacted to others in the past. When we dig up the roots of our unnatural reactions to others, it often helps to make sense of and change our current unnatural reactions.

Gloria: Oh, I don't want to blame others.

Facilitator: We will walk gently, Gloria, as we explore your dreams for help in using the simple solution you've found in your dreams. Even if others are involved, we'll still only work with your dreams. With the PMID model, there is no blaming. We don't blame the dreamer; we don't blame other people. That is one beauty of working only with dreams instead of confronting other people.

SUMMARY

In this chapter, Step 5 is explained and demonstrated. The PMID process is an integrated process. Thus, during the procedure of working on Step 5, we can also review the dreamer's responses to the other steps, including Step 6 (relationship systems perspectives). The discussion between Gloria and the facilitator regarding this point in Gloria's "When Did I Lose Control?" dream led Gloria to a simple solution for how to be more comfortable in social circumstances: "Before and during social events, persistently keep my thoughts on feeling content. Consciously do that. Do not let my cheering emotions continue into hyper feelings and blot out my natural, reserved self."

Counseling implications drawn from the use of Step 5 are suggested. Changing (or confirming) thoughts, attitudes, emotions, and behaviors is commensurate with the objectives of psychotherapy. A common phenomenon in counseling is that

* The facilitator and Gloria discuss that dream, titled "Missed a Test," in Chapter 10.

clients may find simple solutions difficult to carry out. Gloria, our dreamer, has discovered this.

SELF-STUDY QUIZ CHAPTER 8: APPLY PMID STEP 5 TO YOUR DREAMS

Before going on to the next chapter and the next step, spend some time studying and working with Step 5 with at least one of your own current dreams. You may use the same dream that you selected for your Chapter 4 to 7 self-study quizzes, or you may choose one of your other dreams. Write the dream and your responses to PMID Steps 1 throughout 4. Now, focus on completing PMID Step 5 for this dream. Explore your dream for possible solutions to problems, including changing (or affirming) thoughts, attitudes, or behaviors. Look for answers to your day-before-your-dream thoughts.

LOOKING ONWARD TO THE NEXT STEP

Gloria has discovered a solution to her dilemma, "How can I stop overreacting in social settings?" What else is left to uncover in this dream? Relationship systems perspectives (reactions in relationship experiences) are shown in Gloria's "When Did I Lose Control?" dream. In the next chapter, she explores for relationship systems effects in efforts to understand and change her current stressful reactions.

9

Interpretation of Dreams From Family and Other Relationship Systems Perspectives

Further Clues to Relieving Stress (PMID Step 6)

It seems so easy for me to change those patterns.
I am finding it very difficult to change.

INTRODUCTION

The Personalized Method for Interpreting Dreams (PMID) model uses family and other relationship systems perspectives to interpret dreams. The family systems perspective as it relates to counseling is defined as influences arising from reactions to family and other major relationships, past and current. As used in PMID Step 6, the term *family and other relationship systems perspectives* means dreamers study their dreams about influences arising from reactions to family and other major relationships, both past and current, to discover whether their reactions in the dream connect to past circumstances or whether their reactions originate from present circumstances only.

Allen (1994) developed the family systems approach to individual psychotherapy (currently renamed unified therapy), which is based on Bowen theory (1978). As the original name implies, Allen's approach is the integration of individual counseling techniques with family counseling techniques to resolve family problems. With Allen's approach, the therapist usually meets with only one family member. Changes in one person's reactions compel other family members to act differently because the system has changed.

With the PMID model, the dreamer, counselor facilitated or alone, studies his or her dreams about family and other major relationships instead of meeting with others in the system of relationships to discuss concerns. This feature avoids blaming. It is not a matter of who is at fault; it is a matter of changing the person the dreamer can most easily change—the dreamer. Dreams guide the process of change. When the individual can change his or her thoughts, attitudes (emotions), or behaviors, the system of relationships must adjust to accommodate that one person's change (Bowen, 1978; Kerr & Bowen, 1988).

In the 1960s and 1970s, psychodynamic, behavioral, and humanistic approaches (called the first, second, and third forces, respectively) dominated counseling and psychotherapy. "Today, the various approaches to family systems represent a paradigm shift that we might call the 'fourth force'" (Corey, 2008, p. 411). In this respect, the PMID model might be called a fourth-force counseling approach because it addresses family and other relationship systems perspectives.

People may say that they can endure their own stress. However, those same people may, and it seems very likely, be impelled to change their thoughts, attitudes, emotions, and behaviors when they realize their children and other close relationships might be affected.

At the same time, patterns can be so engrained in us that it becomes difficult for us to realize when our behaviors are unnatural to our own individualities. Studying our dreams is one pathway to finding and unraveling dysfunctional patterns and finding solutions that will change those patterns.

Note that Step 6 is applicable only to dreams about relationships, and for this reason is the last step in the list. However, the dreamer's responses to Step 6 should be considered when completing Step 5.

PMID Step 6: Explore your dream for **family and other relationship systems perspectives**, which are influences arising from reactions to family and other major relationships, both past and current. Use these perspectives to discover whether this dream reflects your reactions during experiences with family members or other important people in your life. Compare and comment on your dreaming and your waking-life reactions to the primary relationships in this dream. (If this dream is not about a relationship, type the words "Not Applicable" in this space.)

DREAM SPECIALISTS SUPPORT THE PRESENCE OF FAMILY AND OTHER RELATIONSHIP SYSTEMS PERSPECTIVES IN DREAMS

Krippner and Dillard (1988) wrote:

> The dreamer pulls upon his or her memory bank, which is programmed with the initial images of the dream and the feelings associated with them. A flock of

> images from the past swiftly emerges. These images sometimes go all the way back to childhood, and are in some way related to the current issue. (p. 52)

Cartwright and Lamberg (1992/2000) wrote:

> Dreams may be at the core of our ability to assimilate major changes in our lives, good and bad, successes and failures. At such time, dreams review the experiences that give rise to strong feelings and match them to related images from the past. (p. 269)

As recounted in other parts of this book, Hartmann (1995) found that dreams "often seem to be dealing with interpersonal problems, with the dreamer's current concerns about family, friends, [and] lovers." Dreams also "appear to make connections with other persons or experiences in the past" (p. 215).

Dreamers' reactions based on their childhood and adolescent experiences can last into adulthood dreaming. For instance, 81% of the 122 dreams about relationships in Okocha and Duesbury's 2005–2006 (see Appendix A) general population research contained influences from the past. (Of the 122 dreams, 103 were from the eight continuing active participants.)

Table 9.1 presents a synopsis of our support of Step 6.

For assistance in understanding PMID Step 6, see the examples in Table 9.2.

APPLYING PMID STEP 6

Let us revisit Gloria again. For Step 6, she and her counselor explore her dream for systems effects that may have originated from her reactions to family or other major relationships. Gloria will decide who the primary relationships are in her dream and will compare her dreaming and waking-life reactions to them.

Facilitator: Gloria, just to remind you, this step deals with your reactions, which are what you do in this dream and what you do or have done in the past during your waking life in response to the people either directly shown in your dream or implicated in it. What you do—your behavior—is closely linked to your emotions, but in the PMID model, as you remember, emotions are addressed separately in Step 4. Recall that for Step 4 you compared how you feel in the dream with how you sometimes feel in waking life in supposedly casual settings.

To begin Step 6, then, who is the primary relationship in your "When Did I Lose Control?' dream?

Gloria: I believe it is me, although I am sitting on the side just watching.

Facilitator: I agree that you are the primary person shown by your dream. Many do consider themselves as the primary person in their dreams. In fact, with the PMID model the dreamer is assumed to be the primary person. However, what we are looking for in PMID Step 6 are other people who the dreamer is reacting to or has reacted to in some way.

TABLE 9.1 Support for PMID Model Step 6 (Systems Perspectives)

Projects	Raters	Results (%)
A1: Duesbury (2000), 7 years, thesis RES, 1 PRT: 70 dreams No. of dreams per year: 18, 11, 3, 10, 16, 7, 5	PROF-R[a]	(No. met Step 6 criteria ÷ No. dreams per year) 66.7, 72.7, 33.3, 90.0, 56.3, 14.3, 60.0
A2: Van Doren & Duesbury (2000), 3-month EXPL, 10 PRTs—24 pre-PMID, 9 post-PMID dreams	Duesbury	(No. met Step 6 criteria ÷ No. of pre-PMID or post-PMID dreams) Pre-PMID 17.9 Post-PMID 11.1
A3: Van Doren & Duesbury (2001), 4-month EXPL, 5 PRTs—13 pre-PMID, 33 post-PMID dreams	PFI[b]	(PFI median, Step 6 ÷ 7 [Likert scale]) After 2 PMID dreams 71.4 At 4 months 92.9
Rated 13 pre-PMID and 24 of 33 post-PMID dreams	PROF-R	(No. met Step 6 criteria ÷ 13 and 24) Pre-PMID 69.2, post-PMID 87.5
A4: Duesbury, Bynum, & Van Doren (2002), 3-month EXPL, 11 PRTs—81 dreams	PFI	(Wilcoxon signed rank tests) At 8 weeks: Significant change with $W- = 5.50$, $W+ = 60.50$, $N = 11$, $p \leq 0.00977$ At 14 weeks: Nonsignificant
A5: Duesbury, Bynum & Van Doren (2003), 3-month EXPL, 5 PRTs—36 dreams	PFI	(PFI median, Step 6 ÷ 7 [Likert scale]) Start 51.7 At 8 weeks 71.4 At 14 weeks 85.7
A6: Duesbury, Bynum, & Van Doren (2004), 3-month EXPL, 6 PRTs—29 dreams	PFI	(PFI median, Step 6 ÷ 7 [Likert scale]) Start 85.7 At 8 weeks 71.4 At 14 weeks 71.4
A7: Van Doren & Duesbury (2005–2006), RES ongoing, PMID use, 5 PRTs—4 gave PFIs, 46 dreams from earlier years, 10 current-year dreams	PFI	(PFI median, Step 6 ÷ 7 [Likert scale]) Earlier years PFI median ÷ 7: 78.6 Current year PFI median ÷ 7: 64.3
A8: Okocha & Duesbury (2005–2006), 6-month RES, 17 PRTs—222 dreams, 200 being from 8 PRTs who were active for full 6 months	PFI	(Wilcoxon signed rank tests—critical values of W for samples less than 10) At 2½ months, $W = 28$ $n_{s/r} = 7$, $p \leq .02$ At 6 months, $W = 21$ $n_{s/r} = 6$, $p \leq .05$

Note: See Appendix A for details. RES, research; EXPL, exploration; PRT, participant.

[a] PROF-R Van de Castle is an independent professional rater.

[b] PFI, periodic feedback instrument, formalized in 2002. See Appendix B for format. Likert-type rating scale 1 to 7, with 7 high.

Gloria: Oh, I get it. Well, Mr. Morgan, who doesn't look like himself, is one relationship in my dream, although I believe he is only there because he is so individualistic and isn't bothered by being different. I just don't know then who the main relationship would be.

Facilitator: Let's make that plural. Who are the main relationships in this dream?

Gloria: That makes huge sense! The cheering graduates, you bet. They are the social group here. I should have put that in PMID Step 3. Cheering graduates: A social group like those in which I sometimes overdo talking.

TABLE 9.2 Excerpts From Dreams About "Influences Arising From Reactions to Family and Other Major Relationships, Past and Current" (One Technique in PMID Step 6)

Example 1: In a dream Saundra, the dreamer, is hiding in the closet she hid in as a child when her parents were fighting. In the dream, she is hiding because there is a battle going on, much like the waking-life battles in Iraq highlighted in the news the day before her dream.

Example 2: In a dream, the car that Conway is driving *swings around of its own accord* and stops at the *simple little nursery school where I went.* Conway is envious of the creative activities of the children. He tells them, *"I came to this school, too, when I was small." I* [have] *a strong desire to find someone who could have been my teacher to tell me how I behaved as a kid. Was I as relaxed as these kids and how did I relate to other kids?* Conway decides: *Looks like I need to go back to explore things in my childhood.*

Example 3: In a dream, Nicole arrives at her grandparents' house (her second childhood home), where a relative who is *waiting on the porch makes negative comments to me.* Although Nicole is *tempted to say something about that, [she chooses] not to say anything.* Her definition of "chooses not to say anything" is that *this has meaning to me from my Native American grandfather, as he taught me the importance of observation and to take time in using words."*

Note: Associated dreams for examples are not included here.

Facilitator: Dreams do make sense, don't they? Okay, what were your reactions to the cheering graduates in your dream? What did you do in reaction to the cheering graduates while you were dreaming this dream?

Gloria: Like I said before, my cousin and I just sat off to the side. I was a graduate, but I didn't join with the cheering and carrying on.

Facilitator: Now, compare those reactions with what you do, how you react to others when the result is that you become hyper afterward.

Gloria: A real contrast. I transfer into being an actress and overtalk. Then afterward, I think about what I said, about whether I left anyone out, those type rehearsals, you know. I talk to myself and think to myself until by the time I go to bed I am sky-high hyper. That's very different from what I did in my dream.

Facilitator: I wonder how others usually react when you, as you term it, transfer into being an actress and overtalk.

Gloria: Well, they generally pay attention. One thing that bothers me a lot afterward is that what I think to say often changes the topic of the conversation.

Facilitator: What you think of to say is your attempt to be casual?

Gloria: No way what I say is what I consider casual. Well, if I throw in something I think is just kidding chitchat, it usually falls like a lead ball. No, what I usually say is like I'm compelled to say it. Something that seems to me is important for the others to know. Plus, as I said, I want others to know they are attended to. That they are paid attention to, given credence, you know.

Facilitator: Gloria, you talk about being compelled to say something important for others to know when you are in casual-type conversations. I'm wondering how you react in work circumstances.

Gloria: Oh, I'm fine there. I don't recall becoming upset with myself from what I say or do at work.

Facilitator: I assume your work position is one in which you work by yourself.

Gloria: Well, no. I'm in customer service. It's needful for me to talk and be in charge there. I'm there to help others and give customers important information to help them.

Facilitator: Do you enjoy your job?

Gloria: I love my job. I love helping people.

Facilitator: Do you maintain calmness during and after a workday in which you have had many interchanges with customers?

Gloria: Yes, I'm fine with talking there. I do keep from overrunning them with conversation, but I do enough talking to be what I consider a very good customer relations person.

Facilitator: Yet, you cannot tolerate your behavior when you act in similar fashion when you are in social circumstances?

Gloria: No, I cannot. That is out of place there. Other people can relax and enjoy their conversations. I just am very uncomfortable joining in supposedly casual-type conversations. I'm just ignorant on social talk, you know. I suppose I just don't know how to do it. So, its far better that I do what I did at the graduation ceremonies last summer. That is the very best for me. It was so easy then to be my quiet self. Why is it so tough when I am at home and with people I know?

Facilitator: Actually, as I understand it, you have spent many years repeating unnatural reactions to others. That pattern isn't working for you now. Perhaps never did really work. It is something you can change now.

Gloria: You know, and this is changing the train, but as I mull this over I'm thinking I don't treat these others very fair when I put on an acting personality. They don't even get to know me. Baffling that I never even thought of that until we worked with my "When Did I Lose Control?" dream.

Facilitator: Summing your interpretations to date, you have answered the question in the title you chose for this dream "When Did I Lose Control?" You interpret that the little girls who look alike may represent that you were a young girl when you began to copy others. In addition, you have an excellent solution for how to change that pattern and prevent overreacting in social settings in the future. Perhaps this is the extent of what you can glean from your "When Did I Lose Control?" dream. Does it seem that way to you?

Gloria: I admit, yes, it does. I still have questions in my mind, though.

Facilitator: Such as?

Gloria: Well, albeit this started when I was a little girl, I don't know the root of it. I guess I shouldn't have to know the why. I do know the when and that helps me understand somewhat of why it is so tough to change. The pattern started a long time ago.

Facilitator: If you can find the root of who you may have copied, if you did copy someone or some people, it could be very helpful to you in changing the pattern. For instance, were people's reactions that you may have copied extraverts? Or could she or he or they have been experiencing the same type of stress that you experience at times in social circumstances?

Gloria: Well, I did look for whether Mom and Father were in my "When Did I Lose Control?" dream. They just are not there.

Facilitator: It is very understandable to look first to our parents. But, as you say, it doesn't seem your parents are even implicated in your dream. Further, with the PMID model, we make no assumptions unless others are either directly pictured or at least implicated in a dream.

However, you may have new dreams as you work with using the solution you found in your "When Did I Lose Control?" dream that will indicate one or more persons whom you may have copied when you were a little girl.

In addition, Gloria, and this is very important, each of us is an individual, unrelated to family history. Recall the theme you decided on for this dream was "finding out how to be me."

Gloria: I'm feeling really fine that my dreams are so tuned into my natural self. Just need to control being myself all the time.

Facilitator: Keep confidence, Gloria. You do have an excellent simple, granted not easy, suggestion from your "When Did I Lose Control?" dream.

Gloria: I am ever so glad for your patience in helping me with the PMID model and with this dream. Maybe I'll be back to let you know when I don't have any more "Missed a Test" dreams!

Facilitator: Speaking of your "Missed a Test" dream, I am wondering if I could help you look closer at that dream. Concentrating on more than one dream on a particular theme offers opportunities for expanded insights.

Gloria: Oh, I don't think I need any more counseling. You've been a huge help for me with the PMID model. With what we talked about just now, I pretty well think I'll do better. Just need to do what I know to do. Gee whiz, I should have chucked this stuff into the wastebasket a long time ago.

Facilitator: It is natural to struggle in changing long-embedded patterns, Gloria. Sometimes it helps to have a person who is uninvolved to touch bases with and to give support. Also, referring to PMID Step 6, I am wondering if your "Missed a Test" dream contains other relationships from when you were a young girl.

Gloria: Mom and Father are in that dream.

Facilitator: Those connections could, of course, expand your use of PMID Step 6. If you discover that you need a little help, just let me know.

Gloria: A bit of humbleness here. I had a dream a couple weeks ago where a man wants me to go for more counseling help. I resisted in the dream, and I didn't tell you about it at the time. But when you talk about a little more help, maybe I do need a little more.

Facilitator: We'll continue to look to your dreams as we follow your progress in using the solution that you found in your "When Did I Lose Control?" dream. In addition, perhaps you will find a past dream or have a new dream that pictures or otherwise addresses your personality type.

Note that facilitation of dreamwork, as with most counseling approaches, includes monitoring the client's emotions. New insights, although ultimately uplifting, frequently result in distress for the client-dreamer. That is what happened to Gloria. Her counselor's invitation to meet for a few more sessions not only provided opportunities for facilitating Gloria's continuing work with her dreams, but also gave the counselor occasion to observe changes in Gloria's emotions. (Appendix C contains a caveat on bad or worrisome dreams.)

KEY FACTOR: INNATE INDIVIDUALITY

A key factor when exploring for relationship systems effects is the person's individuality. Separate from any consideration of effects that might have originated from other people's actions is the fact that each person is an individual unlike any other human being. Thus, an individual's stressful reactions could be influenced in part by the person's inability to discover his or her innate individuality, unrelated to family history.

Being able to differentiate what is natural and what is repeating unnatural distressing patterns is frequently difficult when involved in relationship systems (as we all are). Gloria discovered that she was repeating a stressful behavior that she began as a young girl. There is no way that she can return to the past to change her reactions from her earlier experiences. If she blames others and consequently becomes engulfed in negative emotions about the others, she could become stuck in those disabling scenarios. Further, in the process of focusing on others' actions, Gloria might become deterred from recognizing her own individuality.

MORE ON SYSTEMS EFFECTS

This section contains excerpts from Duesbury, 2007 (pp. 57–58).

> Reactions to others based on earlier experiences—systems effects—can be very difficult to recognize in our waking lives, especially since most of us have established our patterns over years, often since early childhood. The good news is that once we begin to recognize negative patterns, we can immediately begin to change the dynamic.
>
> One person's reactions do affect how others react. That means you don't have to change everyone around you (nor can you). But you can change your own thoughts, emotions and actions, and these will absolutely change your relationships with others.

> Initially … people [might] hesitate at making changes in themselves to address relationship issues. This is especially true if the other person seems obviously to be the cause of the problem. The common reaction is, "Why should I change when I haven't done anything wrong, and the other person is creating all the problems?"
>
> It's not unusual to feel that you're letting the other person off the hook, or that you are somehow admitting to being the "bad" person because you're taking responsibility for your role in the relationship. Certainly, "others" have issues to work through. But the PMID dream interpretation model is based on … practice that repeatedly demonstrates it is not a matter of who is at fault—it's a matter of changing who we can change most successfully … our own selves.
>
> Dreams also reflect repeated emotional patterns within relationship systems from generation to generation (Bynum, 2003), again reflecting what is happening in people's waking lives. "In the case of a healthy family system, [explorations into dreams] can increase true empathy and acceptance of differences, thus avoiding irresolvable conflicts" (Bynum, 1984, p. 31). In the case of conflicting relationships, an individual's explorations into dreams can yield suggestions for changing [or affirming] thoughts, attitudes and behavior currently, and reduce the possibility of conflicting patterns getting repeated in the next generation.

Notice that although Gloria is having difficulty very soon after discovering solutions in a dream on how to act naturally in casual group-type settings, she is continuing her efforts to use the solutions (prior to and during the occasion simply dedicate myself to feeling content within myself instead of becoming hyper, plus be content to sit on the sidelines of social type conversations and actions). For more on Gloria's continuing efforts to use her solution to her "When Did I Lose Control?" dream and other dreams that connect to the theme "finding out how to be me," consult Chapter 10, "Dreams Build on Each Other: The Individual's Series Approach to Interpreting Dreams."

You may wonder how many dreams Gloria might have had over the years in response to her stressful reactions and been unaware of those dreams and of the guidance they contained. A case is made here that use of dreams early in life could be resourceful in preventing stressful reactions from becoming embedded in the person's reflexes.

SUMMARY

This chapter demonstrates family and other relationship systems perspectives, which is a major feature of the PMID model. The systems perspective as used in the PMID model means the dreamer explores his or her dreaming reactions to others. The objective is to discover whether the dreamer is reacting to others based on a pattern established in the past. Knowing the source of reactions helps to identify how to change long-established stressful patterns and consequently react more naturally in current relationship experiences. During Gloria's work with her "When Did I Lose Control?" dream, she had another dream about her reactions in social circumstances. Gloria and her counselor agree to look closer at that dream ("Missed a Test") when next they meet.

SELF-STUDY QUIZ CHAPTER 9: APPLY PMID STEP 6 TO YOUR DREAMS

Before going on to the next chapter and the next step, spend some time studying and working with Step 6 with at least one of your own current dreams. You may use the same dream that you selected for your self-study quizzes in Chapters 4–8, or you may choose one of your other dreams. Write the dream and your responses to PMID Steps 1–5. Now, focus on completing PMID Step 6 for your dream. Explore your dream for relationship systems perspectives (influences arising from reactions to family and other major relationships, both past and current). Compare and comment on your dreaming and your waking-life reactions to the primary relationships in your dream.

LOOKING ONWARD TO THE INDIVIDUAL'S SERIES APPROACH TO INTERPRETING DREAMS

Dreaming more than once about an issue, as Gloria has done, is demonstrated fully in the next chapter, "Dreams Build on Each Other: The Individual's Series Approach to Interpreting Dreams." The series of dreams could be about one relationship or about one issue.

10

Dreams Build on Each Other

The Individual's Series Approach to Interpreting Dreams

She listens and doesn't say anything. I finally say to her, "I apologize." She says, "That is all you needed to say."

INTRODUCTION

Using the "individual's series approach to interpreting dreams," the dreamer learns about hivs or her reactions to one or more relationships or issues by studying a series of dreams about each relationship or issue.

GLORIA'S SERIES OF DREAMS AND INTERPRETATIONS, CONTINUED

In this chapter, Gloria and her counselor will more deeply examine the concept of studying a series of dreams. In the process, they will look for answers to two questions that came up during the Personalized Method for Interpreting Dreams (PMID) work with Gloria's "When Did I Lose Control?" dream: (1) Do Gloria's other dreams contain suggestions for how Gloria can more easily achieve the solution she found in her "When Did I Lose Control?" dream, and (2) does Gloria have dreams that support the results of her quantitative personality tests?

Recall that even after Gloria discovered a simple solution for remaining calm during social events ("before and during social events, persistently keep my thoughts on feeling content. Consciously do that. Do not let my cheering emotions continue into hyper feelings and blot out my natural, reserved self"), she overreacted during and after a meeting with old friends. Afterward, she talked to herself, scolded herself, until she became hyper. That night she had a dream, "Missed a Test," that she connected to the circumstances.

Gloria's Dream: Missed a Test

Dream: *I need to get to a class I'm taking. I think there will be a test, but am unsure of it. First I struggle with finding the right clothes to wear. Then, I struggle with driving to class.*

Mom is here. I ask her for permission to drive Father's new car, and she says to ask Father. Father tells me I can drive his new car. Although I can use his new car, I ask him if my old car will still work. He says, yes, it will work, so I start down the drive in my old car. But when I push the brakes, they just don't take hold. Father says push very hard. I do so, and the brakes work.

Alas, I arrive at the class just at the end of the period. A student coming out the door tells me the teacher did give a test. I try to talk my teacher into letting me take the test I missed. I give her the reasons why I was late for the test. She listens and doesn't say anything. I finally say to her, "I apologize." She says, "That is all you needed to say."

Facilitator: Such a lot of content in that dream. And did you find a solution in this dream?

Gloria: You know, I did. Another simple solution. Apologize to myself for making excuses when talking too much if indeed I fail to stay calm during future gatherings. That way, I will avoid talking myself into feeling hyper afterward.

Facilitator: Another reasonable solution. Congratulations. I see it connects to the event (Step 1) you had the evening before your dream. To refresh your memory, here's what I have in my notes as the event you connected to your "Missed a Test" dream:

"Met with old friends had worked with on a long-term project. No idea would struggle to be relaxed there because had felt at ease with them before. So didn't coach herself before the event to keep her thoughts on feeling content. Resulted in feeling very hyper afterward."

Are my notes still accurate on what happened the night before your "Missed a Test" dream?

Gloria: Yes, that's what happened.

Facilitator: Moving to Step 2, what thoughts did you record from before you went to sleep and dreamed this dream?

Gloria: Well, I sure was thinking about messing up and talking too much again! I thought that maybe there's no way to avoid it when in those circumstances. Maybe I'll never get over this. I did think on whether I would have any dreams on how to do the "simple, but … not easy, solution" from my "When Did I Lose Control?" dream.

Facilitator: So, those thoughts, together with feeling upset about missing an opportunity to remain calm, brought a dream with some further help.

Gloria: Yes. What to do if I mess up again. Just do what I did at the end of my dream. I apologized. In my dream, after arriving late for a test, I talked to the teacher. At first I did what I do when I end up becoming hyper. I just kept making excuses for messing up and being late. After I finally apologized for being late, the teacher said, "That's all you needed to say."

Facilitator: I'm impressed with your dream and with your work in finding another straightforward solution to acting your natural self and staying calm.

Gloria: These solutions might seem obvious, but as you know, I didn't catch on to them quickly. I worked long and hard for them.

Facilitator: Gloria, it's common for people to struggle to find solutions in their dreams, especially when it's a long-time pattern. As you discovered from your "When Did I Lose Control?" dream, social settings have apparently been a bit tough for you from the time you were a little girl. Sure, the solutions you found are obvious to me now, but I wouldn't have been able to understand your dreams at all without all the work you did in pulling from your experiences to find the meanings of the dreams.

Dreams that deal only with current times or are on other topics than relationships often take much less effort to understand. Of course, the more the dreamer becomes accustomed to using the PMID model, the easier it is. Have you experienced that?

Gloria: Oh, yes. That's a delight. Sometime, I'll share some of my dreams with you that are on other topics! For now, are we done with my "Missed a Test" dream?

Facilitator: I wonder if there's more help in your "Missed a Test" dream.

Gloria: You mean about Mom and Father?

Facilitator: Yes. I'm curious about your father's new blue car and why you decided to drive your old vehicle instead.

Gloria: That is curious.

Facilitator: But, first tell me how you defined your dream phrase "struggle with finding the right clothes to wear."

Gloria: Oh, that's easy. That's the theme of my dream. Clothes regularly mean personality to me. I am struggling to be my natural self, my natural personality.

Facilitator: And that is a universal meaning of clothes: personality, what individuals use to cover themselves. Here's another phrase from your dream that I'm wondering about: "can drive his [Father's] new car."

Gloria: Where shall I start? A new car is just that, something new and something to drive.

Facilitator: I'm wondering what driving means to you. Is your father driven by any behavior? Would that be helpful to you to use?

Gloria: Oh, he's driven all right!

Facilitator: How so?

Gloria: He's a real talker, a driven talker. That's a great word, *driven*.

Facilitator: In your dream, your father drives a new car. Help me with what that could mean for you.

Gloria [thinks for a minute]: New! Another great word! Long story, trust me. Father isn't always comfortable with overtalking and being outgoing. I didn't think about that until recently. In my youth and far into adulthood, I always believed Father was an outgoing person.

Facilitator: Okay. Go on.

Gloria: I have a family of my own now, so I don't live with Mom and Father anymore. When I pondered this, a picture just fell into my mind of Father after he'd been on one of his chatting sessions. He talks to himself. He'll even swipe a hand across his face like he's said something he wished he hadn't. I talk to myself when I overdo in social settings.

Facilitator: So, this is your new awareness? That your father's being so driven to talk wasn't always comfortable for him?

Gloria: Yes. He seems quiet at home most of the time. It's only in social settings that he gets carried away.

Facilitator: Are you quiet at home?

Gloria: You bet. Most of the time.

Facilitator: Let's continue with the phrases in your "Missed a Test" dream. Here are a couple more I'm wondering about: "Start down the drive with my old vehicle" and "Brakes don't take hold."

Gloria: Okay, here goes.

Start down the drive with my old vehicle: That's easy now that I understand the driving pitch. I don't always overtalk and drive myself into feeling hyper. Sometimes I do. That is when I go back to old ways of driving myself.

Brakes don't take hold: Tying this in with Father telling me to push very hard just shows how hard it is for me to put on the brakes, so to speak, to keep from running away with overreacting and overtalking. Push very hard in coaching myself to stay calm even before I get to social events.

Facilitator: Good. So, now that you understand more about your father's behavior, your dream brings him in a helping role.

Gloria: It truly explains why it's so hard for me to keep under control in social groups. As Father says, I need to push very hard. In my dream I get the brakes to work, but not in time to get to the test on time. That translates into not in time the day before my dream to keep me from overtalking.

Facilitator: Notice, too, that you have also found a solution (Step 5) in your definition of "Brakes don't take hold."

Gloria: Yes, you are right. "Push very hard in coaching myself to stay calm even before I get to social events."

Facilitator: Now, let's move to Step 6. Do you see the systems perspective? Who are the primary relationships in this dream?

Gloria: Father has to be the main relationship. In my dream I react to him by not doing what he would allow me to do. Symbolically speaking, I could have realized, okay, Father, isn't acting natural, either, when he takes control of conversations, so to speak.

Facilitator: Linking your dreaming reactions to your father with your waking-life reactions when you "act like your father" …

Gloria: It's like I'm the little girl copying Father. Oh, but I don't like blaming Father. He can't help it, I guess. Look, he is helping me in my dream.

Facilitator: A helper in your dream, very touching.

Gloria, another person in your "Missed a Test" dream is your mom. I'm curious why she says to ask your father whether you can drive his car.

Gloria: I'm a bit like Mom. She isn't relaxed in social groups, either. Most times, she doesn't go with Father when he goes out socializing. When she does go, or did when I lived at home, she'd come home and say, "Loafing just wears me out!"

Facilitator: And by "loafing," she means?

Gloria: Social activity. Like it does to me. Mom is very thoughtful and courteous of others. I guess that's the reason she takes part as much as she does at social events.

Facilitator: Gloria, with both your parents apparently lacking in social skills, do you suppose some coaching in social skills might help you to feel more at ease in social settings?

Gloria: Sure. That stands to reason. Just the same, I'm not very enthused to be a chitchatter. Granted, visiting helps lots of people to feel relaxed, but still, I've proved over and over it doesn't work that way for me.

Facilitator: I tend to agree with you. We are not about transforming you into being even farther away from reacting naturally.

You now have two dreams in a series of dreams on the theme "finding out how to be me." Have you had any more dreams that you believe are on that theme?

Gloria: Yes! I did have another dream. Good news is that dream echoes my success in remaining calm during a social-type gathering. Also, it just might contain a bit of a forecast for the beginning of a new trail for me. Remember the words that caught my attention the day before my "When Did I Lose Control?" dream, "It is hard work to play the part of myself, and harder still to play the part of my Self"?

Facilitator: Yes, I do remember those words.

Gloria: Just maybe my new dream says a bit about playing the part of my Self, with the capital S.

Facilitator: Fascinating. Tell me about your dream and your interpretations of it.

Gloria: I titled my new dream "Shutter Stairs Success." I dreamed it the night after I did just fine in using the solution I found in my "When Did I Lose Control?" dream. First, I'll tell you the events that led up to my dream.

Facilitator: Good. Day-before-your-dream events, PMID Step 1, will help me understand your interpretations.

Gloria: Here are the events: During the afternoon before my dream, I attended a social event that I knew would put me in a susceptible position of overtalking, overacting, and becoming hyper afterward. Hence, I coached myself before and during the event to keep my thoughts on feeling content within myself.

Then, during the actual event, apart from the socializing, a woman I'd never met before struck up a conversation with me about a topic that I've come across during my customer relations work. I admit I was cautious. Didn't want to miss another test, you know. Our exchanges were exciting, yes, but they weren't hyperexciting. They were natural expressions on activities that we each love to do. Neither of us dominated the conversation. I learned a lot, and I think the other woman did, too.

Then, we were all invited to go down to the main part of the room and form small groups where we could do what I call chit-chatting with each other. As the guests were seated, I was given a chance to sit among the conversationalist group, so to speak, or to sit on the sidelines. I chose to sit on the sidelines. Amazing how easy it was to choose the sidelines. I remained on track with being my natural inward self. That means I enjoyed being part of the group without joining the lively talk. I stayed calm the rest of the day and evening, slept deeply during the night, and woke in the morning with a wonder-filled dream.

Facilitator: Good job of setting the scene. Now, how did your dream respond?

Gloria: As I said, I titled the dream "Shutter Stairs Success."

Gloria's Dream: "Shutter Stairs Success"

My dream symbolizes some of the events from the gathering the previous day, even to the exchange that led to my choice to sit on the sidelines during the main chitchatting socializing. Then, still in my dream, a woman and I are standing at the head of a stairway that has shutter-like steps. That is, the steps are only partly open, like shutters on a window can be. The woman and I talk about the main topic that the businesswoman and I discussed the day before this dream.

Facilitator: Fine connections to the events that prompted your dream (Step 1). It is obvious that your before-your-dream thoughts (Step 2) on feeling content within yourself helped to prompt your dream. Now, to

Step 3, are you willing to share your personal definitions for some of the phrases from your dream?

Gloria: I am sure that the dream woman was a replica of the businesswoman I met at the social gathering. So, I'll start there and then define the shutter-type steps that are partly open:

Woman and I standing at the top of the stairs: Ties to the businesswoman and my conversation the day before this dream. We stood at the head or top of the room when we visited before the social part of the meeting began. Our standing at the top of the stairs in my dream likely points to the type conversations that bring forth my peak or top natural self.

Shutter-type steps partly open: Ties to my day-before-my-dream success in remaining calm during the social part of the gathering the day before this dream. I believe the shutter-type steps symbolize my natural social disposition—not completely shut off but also not completely opened to chitchatting. That is how I reacted during the social time.

Do those definitions sound naïve?

Facilitator: Of course not. Do those meanings bring an intuitive sense to you that they are on target?

Gloria: Well, yes, they do. I did some mulling over before I came to having a "Yes, they are on target" sense.

There is some more in this dream. I also take the woman and I standing at the head of the steps to tie to something else.

Facilitator: And that is?

Gloria: Well, just maybe, it connects to the main topic we discussed (conversation about a subject that I've come across during my customer relations work). That topic, while I'm not prepared to share any details just yet, ties to my possible opening up a little bit to playing the part of my Self, with a capital S.

Facilitator: And the suggestions (Step 5) that you found in your dream?

Gloria: First, be confident that I can easily remain calm during social circumstances. Second, be alert for a possible new trail in my customer relations work.

Facilitator: Congratulations on your waking-life success with easily remaining calm during the social event that prompted this dream, Gloria. Although dreams more often present solutions to problems than successful use of dream solutions, I am glad that your dream does reflect your success.

As to a possible new trail in your customer relations work, your future experiences will help you understand whether that interpretation is on target. Be certain to pay close attention to your dreams before assuming your work is taking a different direction.

Now, Gloria, let's talk again about the theme you decided for this series, the one you selected when you interpreted your "When Did I Lose Control?" dream.

Gloria: Yes, "Finding out how to be me." I still think the real me is inward.

Facilitator: Last time we visited, I asked you if you had discovered any dreams that supported your belief that your natural personality is inward as your personality tests show. We are interested in dream support because we certainly want to avoid misreading your personality type for your future interactions with others.

Your interpretations of your "Missed a Test" dream reveal that your parents both show signs of being naturally reserved, especially your mom. Now, I see that your "Shutter Step Success" dream gives you some assurance that your personality tests were on target. Did you find any other dreams than your "Shutter Steps Success" that you interpret as pointing to your nature as introversion?

Gloria: You know, I did stumble onto a dream I had a few years ago that I believe points to my true nature as inward. Wish I'd understood it back when I dreamed it. This dream came the night after I learned that my Aunt Jayne had died, and I was grieving for her. I brought a copy of the dream and my work on each PMID step for you to look at.

Gloria's Dream: "Grieving for Aunt Jayne"

Dream: *I know a child is being cared for at a place that is like Willow Lodge. I know of someone named Oscar. I have an intuition that the child is this Oscar. I go to the house and ask to visit the apartment where this child is. The lady of the house takes me to the apartment. It is in a corner of the basement.*

When I go in, I see a little red-haired boy. He is probably 15 months to 2 years old. He is sitting on the floor. I ask the young woman taking care of him if that is Oscar. She says, "Yes." She also says he is having an unhappy day. Things are not going well it seems, for either of them.

PMID Step 1: Connect your **previous-day** (often the day before) **events** to the dream to discover the theme of this dream. The events may appear in either symbolic or literal terms in your dream. Write down the appropriate events and record when they ovccurred.

What I did the day before this dream that most ties to this dream is I had just learned that my Aunt Jayne had died, and I immediately fell into a deep, surprised grief. I say surprised because it had been several years since my growing up time when Aunt Jayne and her family and my father and his family had gatherings together. I had not been with her in some time. Hence, I honestly did not expect that her passing would affect me so much.

PMID Step 2: Connect your **previous-day** (often the day before) **thoughts** to your dream to detect which thoughts may have prompted this dream's responses. Like events, your thoughts may appear in your dream in either literal or symbolic terms. Write "I thought" statements and record when you thought them.

> I thought about and wondered why I felt the grief so deeply. The dream comes back with a reason that Aunt Jayne's death affected me so deeply.

PMID Step 3: Select and define **major dream phrases** and symbols from your write-up of this dream to discover the dream's personalized meanings. Consider effects of your events and thoughts of the day before your dream and earlier experiences on the meaning of each major dream phrase and symbol. The general definition for phrases as used in this step is "a string of words." The strings of words can be phrases, clauses, or whole sentences.

1. **Willow Lodge:** A women's rooming house where I stayed for a few years. It was a time to be alone.
2. **Oscar:** Acting is one of Oscar's professions.
3. **Red hair on Oscar:** That's very strange because in real life Oscar doesn't have red hair. I think Oscar's hair being red is a clue that there is something about Aunt Jayne that is like Oscar. Aunt Jayne had flaming red hair.
4. **In a corner of the basement:** Could be my very low feelings and wanting to hide myself from facing anyone because my grief was so deep.
5. **Not been a very good day:** Comes from my feeling loss brought on by my aunt's death.
6. **Oscar is a child:** Could be my immature, childlike innocence in understanding Aunt Jayne.

PMID Step 4: Compare your **emotions in your dream** with your **pre-dream, waking-life emotions** to discover whether your waking-life emotions accurately reflect how you feel about the issue in this dream. Note that the issue may be a relationship issue. What differences, if any, do you find between your emotions in your dream and your waking-life emotions? It is useful to periodically review your emotions in your dreams regarding the main issue or relationship at hand.

In my dream, as revealed by the child, I "was not having a good day" emotionally. Before I went to sleep, I was grieving for my Aunt Jayne.

PMID Step 5: Explore your dream for possible **solutions** to problems, including changing (or affirming) your thoughts, attitudes, or behaviors. Consider your responses to each PMID model step, including Step 6, as you search for solutions and suggestions in this dream. Give primary attention to the power of your thoughts before your dream (PMID Step 2) to act as questions that your dream answers.

It strikes me that Aunt Jayne was such a great actress. I bet she was like me, acting unnaturally. I bet that wasn't how she really was. That's an answer to my questioning thoughts on why I was grieving so very deeply about Aunt Jayne. I was grieving for my lost self. Look at what I say about Oscar for Step 6. My most natural personality is an inward type.

PMID Step 6: Explore your dream for **family and other relationship systems perspectives,** which are influences arising from reactions to family and other major relationships, both past and current. Use these perspectives to discover whether this dream reflects your reactions during experiences with family members or other important people in your life. Compare and comment on your dreaming and your waking-life reactions to the primary relationships in this dream. (If this dream is not about a relationship, type the words "Not Applicable" in this space.)

Aunt Jayne has to be my main relationship in this dream. I was so down when I heard she had died. What I did in the dream was I went to a place where I could be alone. Yesterday, when I heard about Aunt Jayne's death, I went back to bed. I wanted to be alone. When I was growing up, most times I laughed at Aunt Jayne. She was usually the center of attention. She generally put on a great performance that kept people laughing. I never tumbled to the idea that wouldn't have been her true personality.

As I wrote under Step 3, Oscar is an actor. He does other things, too, but I surmise that this dream is about him as an actor. I say that because I think this dream is pointing to Aunt Jayne as an actress and comparing her to Oscar the actor. Now for the kicker: One time when I was sitting by Oscar's girlfriend when Oscar was on stage acting up a storm, his girlfriend said to me, "That isn't how Oscar really is. He's very different from that."

I grieved for Aunt Jayne because she, like me, was surely an inward type. Somehow, she got on track of acting the part of an extravert. Just like I did. Sure, I grieved for her, but I sense this dream is saying, "Gloria, you are really grieving for your natural self."

Albeit I haven't pulled together other dreams about Aunt Jayne, I have dreamed about her from time to time. One dream I can think of is where her slip is showing. It strikes me as strange I haven't noticed her slipups in my dreams before and realized they pointed to some slipups I had made before those dreams.

Facilitator: [At this point in the session, Gloria is sobbing. The facilitator waits for her to recover, then comforts her.] Fine work, Gloria. I'm pleased for your thorough and productive work with your dreams.

Notice that your conscious efforts to understand how your reactions to two major relationships, your father and your mom, resulted in expanding your explorations into other major relationships, here your Aunt Jayne. It often takes several weeks into months before our dreams extend from one major relationship to others. Perhaps you will decide to study a series of your dreams about your Aunt Jayne in the future.

Gloria: I'm eager to do just that, get to know Aunt Jayne as I become well acquainted with myself.

Facilitator: Gloria, in closing our sessions together, let's review the main solutions you will continue to use as you change the pattern that comes up now and then when you play a part that isn't natural for you.

1. From your "When Did I Lose Control?" dream: "Before and during social events, persistently keep my thoughts on feeling content. Consciously do that. Do not let my cheering emotions continue into hyper feelings and blot out my natural, reserved self."
2. From your "Missed a Test" dream: "Apologize to myself for making excuses when talking too much if indeed I fail to stay calm during future gatherings. That way I will avoid talking myself into feeling hyper afterward." Also, "Push very hard in coaching myself to stay calm even before I get to social events."
3. From your "Shutter Stairs Success" dream: "First, be confident that I can easily remain calm during social circumstances. Second, be alert for a possible new trail in my customer relations work."
4. From your "Grieving for Aunt Jayne" dream: Be assured "my most natural personality is an inward type."

Readers, recall that Gloria at first debated whether the beginning dream in her series of dreams was about relationship concerns or about spiritual matters. It is somewhat common that relationship concerns and spiritual quests are linked. Let us briefly address the possibility of such a link.

LINK BETWEEN RELATIONSHIP CONCERNS AND SPIRITUAL QUESTS

On the topics of relationships and spiritual values, Delaney (1988/1996) wrote:

> I can think of nothing more profound than learning to see, cope with, and enjoy reality as it presents itself in our daily experience of affiliation, love, productive work, and creativity. In my opinion, the proof of our connection to transpersonal and spiritual values is in the sometimes sticky pudding of daily living. (pp. 44/pp. 59–60)

Of the people who were accepted for our projects (excepting the 10 participants in our 3-month research in 2000), 31% volunteered comments to the effect that spiritual understanding was an important factor, either as a sign of success (11 participants) or as a frustrating lack of connection (3 participants) in their lives. Those same applicants rated their agreement with the statement, "I wonder if my past relationships affect how I function in my current relationships," at a median of 6 on a scale of 1 to 7, with 7 being the highest agreement. After being accepted in a project, those same applicants presented dreams and their interpretations that showed stressful reactions they were experiencing in their relationships.

These findings and Gloria's dream series give support to Delaney's (1988/1996) view that proof of connection to spiritual values is in the "sometimes sticky pudding of daily living."

SUMMARY

This chapter explains and demonstrates an innovative concept implemented by the PMID model: "An individual's series approach to interpreting dreams." With this approach, the dreamer learns how to reduce stress from his or her reactions to others by studying a series of dreams that connect to the stress that he or she is experiencing.

In this chapter, Gloria works with dreams that connect to her "When Did I Lose Control?" dream, which is the focus of previous chapters. By working with more than one dream, a series of dreams, she gains a fuller picture and, consequently, a more comprehensive understanding of the issue she is dealing with and the solutions she is working to achieve.

SELF-STUDY QUIZ CHAPTER 10: APPLY THE INDIVIDUAL'S SERIES APPROACH TO INTERPRETING A SERIES OF YOUR DREAMS

1. Select two or more of your recorded PMID interpreted dreams that seem to be about one similar theme or topic. List the titles here.
2. Write the theme and the dates of each dream after your dream titles.
3. Review the contents of each dream again. Do you still believe that the dreams that you selected are about one similar topic or one similar theme? If not, look for other dreams in your dream file.

4. Review your responses to each PMID model step for each dream in your series. Did you gain any new insights, confirmations, missing pieces, or other knowledge from exploring more than one dream about an issue or theme? If yes, list those.
5. Do you still have unanswered questions about the theme or issue in this series? If yes, list those. (Expect future dream responses to your questioning thoughts about this theme or issue. Wait patiently.)

11

Review Dreams for New Insights
It May Be Time to Move Onward

When people neglect to revisit their dreams and interpretations, at least the major ones, it seems analogous to counselors keeping running records of their work with clients and then never referring to those records again.

REVIEW AND REVISE DREAM INTERPRETATIONS FOR NEW INSIGHTS

Serious dream workers repeatedly review their significant dreams and associated interpretations until the specific messages of the dreams are clear—or until they reach an impasse on one dream and go on to the next. Revisiting dreams and reviewing earlier interpretations to refresh former meanings, discover new insights, and review for misinterpretations are critical to our best use of our dreams. All dreamers who contributed their dreams and interpretations to this book had reviewed their interpretations at least once before offering them to me.

When people neglect to revisit their dreams and interpretations, at least the major ones, it seems analogous to counselors keeping running records of their work with clients and then never referring to those records again. Reviewing past dreams and interpretations for new insights reduces the need for the dreaming mind to repeat a message in future dreams. Repetitions of messages are marvelous, though, when the dreamer needs them. One instance of need for a repeated message is when the dreamer misinterprets the original message. Dreams provide light on other dreams. Be alert for later dreams that reveal your misinterpretations.

When you review your earlier dreams and interpretations, keep in mind that we all change and vary over time in attitudes, moods, emotions, behaviors, perceptions, preferences, and the like, depending on our individual differences and experiences. Consider those variations and changes when you review your dreams and interpretations from previous weeks, months, or years.

Continuing with benefits from reviewing dreams, the more you work with your dreams, the more opportunities you have to become familiar with your personal dreaming language. Another benefit is that reviewing significant dreams brings new dreams and more help, as we have demonstrated in this text.

There comes a time, though, that we look forward to reaching. This is a time when an issue we have been working on is finished. It is time to move on. Will dreams let us know when that time comes? The next section examines some indicators for when that could be happening.

FIND INDICATORS FOR WHEN TO SHUT THE DOOR ON SPECIFIC RELATIONSHIP CONCERNS

One challenge for the counselor-facilitator is to help the client recognize when it is time to close the door on specific relationship concerns and move on. It is done. The client has his or her answers.

Another challenge is how to keep that door closed. Clinicians see many people having troublesome relationship experiences. Yet, how do clients know when the learning is complete? People's dreams can reveal when a specific concern has been settled, and it is time to move forward. Dreams can also alert the dreamer when he or she has reopened an issue that is already settled in the dreamer's emotional consciousness. The discussion next provides indicators that tell us when it is time to walk away from pursuing more dreams about a particular theme.

First, verify that the dreamer is able to tie the dream to the specific issue or relationship. Then test for the following three indicators:

1. Both the dream and the dreamer's interpretations contain at least one clear message that the issue may be finished.
2. Neither the dream nor the dreamer's interpretations contain new or unused past solutions to the current issue.
3. Neither the dream nor the dreamer's interpretations give hints that the specific concern still bothers the dreamer.

Look for all three of these signs. The following dreams and interpretations demonstrate (a) when it is clearly time to close the door, (b) when there are only subtle indications that an issue is finished, and (c) when it is ambiguous whether a long-standing concern has been overcome.

WHEN IT IS CLEARLY TIME TO CLOSE THE DOOR

Dream Series Issue: Possible childhood molestation. During times of feeling intense stress, a woman had dreams that she understood indicated she had been molested during infancy. Later, the woman overcame the stress without discovering specifics about the possible molestation. Curiosity and need for material for an article led her to ask for another dream. That night, she had a nightmare.

Dream Title: "Why Is It Taking the Man So Long to Die?"*

Dream excerpt: *I am in a room with other people sitting at tables at a meeting or a class. I prefer to sit at the side of the table, but there doesn't seem to be room there. Oh, well, it's okay to sit at the head of the table, so that's where I sit. When the meeting class is over, the rest of the group decides to go someplace else for some relaxation. I say I cannot go. …*

The scene changes, and I am out in front of this place. … Oh, my goodness! [A man] has a long-barreled gun. … He quickly lifts the barrel to his mouth and unloads a barrage of pellets, fires them into his tongue. I am beginning to feel terror. Now he points the gun at his head and shoots and shoots and shoots. His head is bleeding. Parts of his head are blown away. I'm sure he will die soon. I feel relief when he turns the gun on himself, and he will die. I won't need to be afraid of him anymore. But why is it taking so long for him to die? How much damage to his head can he sustain without dying?

I awake and think, "Oh, this is the worst nightmare I have ever had!"

PMID Step 1: Connect your **previous-day** (often the day before) **events** to the dream to discover the theme of this dream. The events may appear in either symbolic or literal terms in your dream. Write down the appropriate events and record when they ovccurred.

I am writing an article about abusive behaviors and need a topic for the article. Last night, I asked for another dream about possible childhood molestation.

PMID Step 2: Connect your **previous-day** (often the day before) **thoughts** to your dream to detect which thoughts may have prompted this dream's responses. Like events, your thoughts may appear in your dream in either literal or symbolic terms. Write "I thought" statements and record when you thought them.

Last evening, although I felt concern about asking for another dream on a matter that is settled, I thought I needed more details for the article. Also, I became curious about what might have happened.

* Adapted from Duesbury (2007, pp. 122–125).

PMID Step 3: Select and define **major dream phrases** and symbols from your write-up of this dream to discover the dream's personalized meanings. Consider effects of your events and thoughts of the day before your dream and earlier experiences on the meaning of each major dream phrase and symbol. The general definition for phrases as used in this step is "a string of words." The strings of words can be phrases, clauses, or whole sentences.

1. **Man firing pellets into his tongue:** Caution, silence your words. Hold your tongue. You should not have asked for another dream about this issue.
2. **Points the gun at his head and shoots and shoots and shoots:** Why do I keep shooting myself in the head over this issue?

PMID Step 4: Compare your **emotions in your dream** with your **pre-dream, waking-life emotions** to discover whether your waking-life emotions accurately reflect how you feel about the issue in this dream. Note that the issue may be a relationship issue. What differences, if any, do you find between your emotions in your dream and your waking-life emotions? It is useful to periodically review your emotions in your dreams regarding the main issue or relationship at hand.

The terror I feel when the man shoots himself shows that I have terrorized myself. Relief that he turns the gun on himself shows that I am the only one being hurt by continuing to bombard myself with thoughts about this issue. My dream shows that I am needlessly concerned about possible childhood incest still being an issue for me.

PMID Step 5: Explore your dream for possible **solutions** to problems, including changing (or affirming) your thoughts, attitudes, or behaviors. Consider your responses to each PMID model step, including Step 6, as you search for solutions and suggestions in this dream. Give primary attention to the power of your thoughts before your dream (PMID Step 2) to act as questions that your dream answers.

Solution: Stop shooting myself in the head over this issue.

Verification that the dream is tied to the specific issue: Verified. The specific issue is possible sexual molestation. This dreamer clearly ties the dream to that issue.

Test for the three indicators:

1. Both the dream and the dreamer's interpretations contain at least one clear message that the issue may be finished.
   Indicator met: Three events in the dream remind the dreamer that her concern about possible molestation is finished: "the meeting or class is over," the "rest of the group decides to go someplace else for some relaxation," and when the dreamer does not go someplace for relaxation, she is presented with the "shooting in the head" message.
2. Neither the dream nor the dreamer's interpretations contain new or unused past solutions to the current issue.
   Indicator met: The only solution that the dreamer found in this dream relates to having asked for a dream on an issue that she had already overcome.
3. Neither the dream nor the dreamer's interpretations give hints that the specific concern still bothers the dreamer.
   Indicator met: The nightmare's trauma relates only to the dreamer having asked for another dream on an issue that was already settled.

The dreamer immediately dropped the idea of writing an article on sexual molestation and vowed that she would let the matter be closed. The next night she dreamed "A door is closed, very intentionally, closed with impact." Several years have passed since that nightmare. The dreamer reports no further dreams on the subject of possible childhood molestation.

WHEN THERE ARE ONLY SUBTLE INDICATIONS THAT AN ISSUE IS FINISHED

Dream Series Issue: A female dreamer's reactions to experiences with her mother-in-law and subsequent effects on her relationship with her husband, her mother-in-law's son. The dreamer had earlier dreams about how her unresolved reactions to her mother-in-law affected her relationship with her husband. Finally, she dreamed of flowers popping up beside her mother-in-law's house when she pulled weeds. It looks like the issue is settled—or is it?

Dream Title: "Weed Pulling and Flowers Popping Up"

Dream: *My very young son and I are here in a place that looks at first like our house, but then later it is Paul's mom's house. At first I see only a little dirt on the floor. When the dirt increases, I start to use the sweeper, but a sock-like thing on the end has come unstitched. I decide to let my little boy do the sweeping. I'll go stitch this sock-like thing up right away.*

My little boy pulls the sweeper canister by the cord. I was afraid of that! I scold him, "Do not pull the sweeper by the cord!"

Paul's mom is taking up Paul's time. That peeves me. Paul's hair is very curly. I bet his mom put a permanent in his hair. But, gee whiz, why would he let her? He even has pigtails. Somehow, I know for sure that the curls and the pigtails are only temporary.

I go out in back of the house to pull some weeds near a pretty little creek along the house. Paul's mom is standing in the doorway. I pull up a couple of plants I think are weeds. My goodness! I see they really are flowers. I am surprised! I gingerly pull on a couple more plants. More flowers come up. But I'm worried with Paul's mom standing here. I don't want to damage anything. Thus, I don't pull up the plants anymore.

This is really quite a lovely place. Yet in spite of that, Paul's Mom's presence irritates me. I know she wants things just a certain way. It surprises me, though, that I'm irritated.

PMID Step 1: Connect your **previous-day** (often the day before) **events** to the dream to discover the theme of this dream. The events may appear in either symbolic or literal terms in your dream. Write down the appropriate events and record when they ovccurred.

I was surprised to feel irritated at Paul when he came to bed last night. No reason. Yesterday I told Paul I had never been upset at my child in a dream. Then, last night in this dream, I became upset at my child.

PMID Step 2: Connect your **previous-day** (often the day before) **thoughts** to your dream to detect which thoughts may have prompted this dream's responses. Like events, your thoughts may appear in your dream in either literal or symbolic terms. Write "I thought" statements and record when you thought them.

Last night, I wondered where in the heck my irritation at Paul came from.

PMID Step 3: Select and define **major dream phrases** and symbols from your write-up of this dream to discover the dream's personalized meanings. Consider effects of your events and thoughts of the day before your dream and earlier experiences on the meaning of each major dream phrase and symbol. The general definition for phrases as used in this step is "a string of words." The strings of words can be phrases, clauses, or whole sentences.

1. **My mother-in-law's house:** Could be unwitting feelings about something Paul did yesterday that unconsciously reminded me of the way his mother did things.
2. **Increasingly seeing more dirt:** In the background of this dream, the more I think negatively about something, the more negative it seems. Could be talking about (gee, I don't like admitting this) how I got to thinking about Paul's mother at times.
3. **Stitch the sock-like end up right away:** Here, I act a lot like my mother-in-law. I used to marvel that she'd mend things on the spot. She never let it stack up the way I do. As they say, "A stitch in time … ."
4. **Scold my little boy for pulling the sweeper by the cord:** A fussy concern for me. Reminds me of my mother-in-law's fussing ways. Yet that is about the way I act when I scold my little boy for pulling the sweeper by the cord in my dream.
5. **My child:** Maybe the child is here to show me if my child can irritate me for something seemingly minor, when that has never happened in a dream before, my mom-in-law could be more irritated at me for something that seemed minor but was actually high priority for her.
6. **Paul's mom has been away**: Paul's mom died a couple of years ago.
7. **Paul's mom occupies his time:** That comes from my jealousy that she took so much of Paul's attention at times.
8. **Hair:** Hair is the usual symbol for thoughts coming out of the head.
9. **Paul's mom having put curls in Paul's hair:** The way she influenced Paul's thoughts. At least this is how I saw it.
10. **Curls are not permanent:** The hair work, this "thought influence," isn't a permanent influence on Paul. He is his own self.
11. **Pull out a couple plants I think are weeds:** In the background of this dream, weeds mean something I need to get rid of, unflowerlike thoughts about my mother-in-law. I imitate her here again. She was so fastidious that when we walked around our garden, she pulled any weeds she saw. I took it as an insult.
12. **Really are flowers:** This is going over into problem solving, Step 5, but it's good here in Step 3, too. When I pull weedlike thoughts, flowering thoughts appear.
13. **Concerns with Paul's mom being near while I work in the flower beds:** Really brings a strong memory. I never wanted to make any mistakes in front of her.
14. **Know she wants things just a certain way:** My mother-in-law's exacting disposition.
15. **Is really quite a lovely place:** Reminds me that Paul's mom's place in my life was really quite a lovely place. Deep down, I know that is right!

PMID Step 4: Compare your **emotions in your dream** with your **pre-dream, waking-life emotions** to discover whether your waking-life emotions accurately reflect how you feel about the issue in this dream. Note that the issue may be a relationship issue. What differences, if any, do you find between your emotions in your dream and your waking-life emotions? It is useful to periodically review your emotions in your dreams regarding the main issue or relationship at hand.

In the dream, I feel angry with my little boy for pulling the sweeper by the cord, flowers popping up surprise me, I'm worried I'll damage the plants in front of Paul's mom, I feel irritated from her standing here, and I'm surprised that I'm irritated. In waking life, last night I was surprised to feel irritated at Paul when he came to bed.

PMID Step 5: Explore your dream for possible **solutions** to problems, including changing (or affirming) your thoughts, attitudes, or behaviors. Consider your responses to each PMID model step, including Step 6, as you search for solutions and suggestions in this dream. Give primary attention to the power of your thoughts before your dream (PMID Step 2) to act as questions that your dream answers.

Pull the negative thoughts about Paul's mother out of my mind right now, just like Paul's mom did with her mending. She did it right away.

PMID Step 6: Explore your dream for **family and other relationship systems perspectives,** which are influences arising from reactions to family and other major relationships, both past and current. Use these perspectives to discover whether this dream reflects your reactions during experiences with family members or other important people in your life. Compare and comment on your dreaming and your waking-life reactions to the primary relationships in this dream. (If this dream is not about a relationship, type the words "Not Applicable" in this space.)

The primary relationship, I guess, is my mother-in-law. In the dream, I stop pulling weeds when she watches me. In waking life, when I was afraid of what she would say, I usually tried to keep from letting her know what I was doing. On how I treated Paul when I felt irritated at him the night before this dream, I didn't write that down, and I don't remember now what I did. But when I react to Paul as a result of something that happened between his mom

> and me (as I believe my dream shows), that is way, way off base and very unfair to Paul! When I am able to pull negative thoughts from my mind (weeds from the flower bed) about Paul's mother, then I'll be far more apt to react to Paul based on our relationship instead of partially based on my unresolved reactions to my mother-in-law.

Verification that the dream ties to the specific issue: Verified. The dreamer clearly ties the dream to her unresolved reactions to her mother-in-law and the effects on her reactions to her husband, Paul.

Test for the three indicators:

1. Both the dream and the dreamer's interpretations contain at least one clear message that the issue may be finished.
   Indicator met: Flowers pop up when the dreamer pulls the weeds (negative thoughts) beside her mother-in-law's house.
2. Neither the dream nor the dreamer's interpretations contain new or unused past solutions to the current issue.
   Indicator not met: One solution the dreamer finds is to "Pull the negative thoughts out of my mind right now, just like Paul's mom did with her mending. She did it right away." Yet in the dream, the dreamer stops pulling the weeds—figuratively she stops pulling negative thoughts about her mother-in-law's influence from her mind.
3. Neither the dream nor the dreamer's interpretations give hints that the specific concern still bothers the dreamer.
   Indicator not met: In the dream, the dreamer is "worried with Paul's mom standing here. I don't want to damage anything. Thus, I don't pull on the plants anymore." The dreamer continues to hold on to her old fear of being imperfect in the eyes of her mother-in-law. Until she can drop that fear, she has not yet used this dream's solution, and the potential remains for these unsettled fears to affect her reactions to her husband.

Incidentally, later the dreamer reported that she had additional dreams about her mother-in-law. In the last dream she shared for this book, her mother-in-law's name was changed from her given name to Eunice. The dreamer reported:

> Eunice means "gloriously victorious." My dream shows that I have become "gloriously victorious" in overcoming negative thoughts and emotions about Paul's mom. Paul is in that dream, also. The night before the dream, while sitting beside Paul I looked at him and thought, "I wonder how he looks and seems to others." I wondered if they see him differently from the very solid, intelligent, and wise upper-level person that I see.

A capsule of that dream is presented in Chapter 7, Table 7.2, "Examples of Emotions in Dreams Compared With Waking-Life Emotions (Step 4)."

WHEN IT IS AMBIGUOUS WHETHER A LONG-STANDING ISSUE HAS BEEN OVERCOME

Dream Series Issue: Sensitivity to feeling inferior. Ted, a White American man, had experienced fear of rejection and consequent sensitivity to feeling inferior throughout his work career. One evening after receiving news that his recent article manuscript had been rejected and that the reviewers' comments would be postal mailed to him, Ted staunchly vowed that he would not become upset from the comments. That night, he had a dream with hints of his partial success.

Dream Title: "Dr. Charles's Criticism Changes to Softness"

Dream: *It is darkish in here. I am standing in my work office. Dr. Charles is the boss. My place is right beside him in a line. … Dr. Charles complains that something is very messy. He announces this in scolding to us employees.*

Dr. Charles is now standing up at the counter. As he talks with someone he is almost in front of my place. I peek through to see whether there is room for me. He is asking a person, a woman, about needing articles on the innovative work we do here at this company. He needs articles this afternoon for something. I timidly say that I have many articles that I have written on the work that we do. They are up in my office. I think of my office up on a higher floor. "However," I say, "they are all my own writings." As I say this to him (and by now I am standing in my place), my eyes are watering. There is a bright light shining into my eyes, but it doesn't seem that the light is so bright that it is the cause of my tears. I do have difficulty looking into the light. As I talk, though, tears roll down my face, and some of the tears do come from my compassion, it seems on recall. I feel embarrassed about the tears. I tell Dr. Charles though that I will look for other people's writings on the type work we do here. I think how I could find some in the library, and I picture going to the library as I talk about this.

Then, I feel Dr. Charles's hand on my right shoulder. My eyes are so blinded with the light that I don't open them to see whether he truly does have his hand on my shoulder. I wonder if I have just imagined it, or if he really does have his hand on my shoulder in compassion. He talks softly to me now. I ask him what time he needs these writings. I know it is for a presentation he has this afternoon. He says, "2:00."

After Dr. Charles moves away I see Abel, but he doesn't look quite like himself. He is sort of lying over the upper part of my workstation. The predominant color I see is blue. Abel is dressed in blue, even seems to have a blue complexion. He shows a coat to me that he bought. He says that he bought, and he names a number, seems like six, coats. Seems faintly that he won some money, somehow has some money, came into some money. This is exquisite. I feel it. I am very pleased for him. I say, something like, "You must have come into a million dollars." (Though I don't recall exactly what I said about million in the dream, I do clearly recall that I said the word "million.")

PMID Step 1: Connect your **previous-day** (often the day before) **events** to the dream to discover the theme of this dream. The events may appear in either symbolic or literal terms in your dream. Write down the appropriate events and record when they ovccurred.

Yesterday, I expected reviewers' critiques from a recent rejection of my article manuscript to be in my postal mail. In preparation for receiving the critiques, I repeatedly vowed, "I will not let the reviewers' comments overwhelm me as has happened in the past." However, the critiques were not in my mail yesterday.

PMID Step 2: Connect your **previous-day** (often the day before) **thoughts** to your dream to detect which thoughts may have prompted this dream's responses. Like events, your thoughts may appear in your dream in either literal or symbolic terms. Write "I thought" statements and record when you thought them.

Although the critiques were not in my mail yesterday, I continued to think about how I will control my reactions when they do come. In the process, I thought about a dream I had after my article manuscript was rejected the first time. The dream had encouraged me so extensively that I rewrote the manuscript and submitted it to the journal the second time. Now, my article manuscript has been rejected a second time.

Yesterday, I first thought about writing to the reviewers in rebuttal. Yet, that was too unprofessional for me. Then, I thought of sending proposals to other publishers. Finally, I decided to change my strategy and write about how other professionals produce similar products to the one we create at our company. Then, I thought about going to the local libraries to research that prospect.

Last night, I thought about Abel, about the lingering effects of my reactions to him from when we were teenagers.

Yesterday, I thought a bit about my need for more casual clothes. I do have some from an uncle that I could wear, but I feel more comfortable in clothes that I choose for myself.

PMID Step 3: Select and define **major dream phrases** and symbols from your write-up of this dream to discover the dream's personalized meanings. Consider effects of your events and thoughts of the day before your dream and earlier experiences on the meaning of each major dream phrase and symbol. The general definition for phrases as used in this step is "a string of words." The strings of words can be phrases, clauses, or whole sentences.

1. **Dr. Charles, the boss:** The managing partner at the first company I worked for after I graduated from college.
2. **Complains that something is very messy:** Complaints that I anticipate will be in the reviewers' comments. My personal association here is that Dr. Charles was very critical of me at the start of my employment. I thought I was doing okay until at one of the first coffee breaks Dr. Charles asked me, "Do you think you are doing okay?" His tone of voice made me realize that he thought my work was inferior.
3. **Announces this in scolding to us employees:** This is fair-minded. I am not the only one reviewers scold.
4. **Almost in front of my place:** Coming closer to the specific topic that I write about.
5. **Peek through to see whether there is room for me:** Room for, a place for, me to be heard by those in authority regarding the topic of my article.
6. **Needs articles this afternoon:** Very soon. Write a new article immediately.
7. **My own writings:** My articles that appear to be lacking in quality.
8. **Bright light shining in my eyes that I have difficulty looking at:** I don't know. Maybe this promulgates my need to picture the rejections in a brighter light. Maybe the dream replicates the considerable strain it takes for me to maintain confidence when presented with rejections.
9. **Think how I could find some in the library, and I picture going to the library as I talk about this:** Last night, I thought about researching for published articles about similar products to the one we create here at our company.
10. **Feel Dr. Charles's hand on my right shoulder:** The only time an advisor put a hand on my shoulder in this manner was at a writers' conference. It happened when an editor was excited about my work.
11. **Talks softly to me:** After being in Dr. Charles employment for several years, I resigned for a new opportunity. Dr. Charles expressed deep sadness at my leaving. He told me that I had advanced so well with his guidance that he felt like he was losing a family member from the fold.
12. **Two o'clock:** Makes me think a bit of the intuitive ability I had for a long while when I woke during the night and knew the time was 2:00 a.m. exactly. Conceivably, 2:00 ties to my intuitive sense that helps me write.
13. **Abel … doesn't look quite like himself:** Conventional definition of people who appear in other than their actual features is that the dreamer is ascribing inaccurate attributes to the person pictured.

PMID Step 4: Compare your **emotions in your dream** with your **pre-dream, waking-life emotions** to discover whether your waking-life emotions accurately reflect how you feel about the issue in this dream. Note that the issue may be a relationship issue. What differences, if any, do you find between your emotions in your dream and your waking-life emotions? It is useful to periodically review your emotions in your dreams regarding the main issue or relationship at hand.

In the dream, I am timorous, shy when talking about my own articles. I acknowledge that there are times, and this is one, when my waking-life lack of confidence in my writing appears in my dreams. My spontaneous tears counteract my tough waking-life vow that I will refuse to let the reviewers' comments overwhelm me.

PMID Step 5: Explore your dream for possible **solutions** to problems, including changing (or affirming) your thoughts, attitudes, or behaviors. Consider your responses to each PMID model step, including Step 6, as you search for solutions and suggestions in this dream. Give primary attention to the power of your thoughts before your dream (PMID Step 2) to act as questions that your dream answers.

A suggestion: Look closer at my confidence level. I am failing a bit to keep my vow of last night: "I will not let the reviewers' comments overwhelm me as has happened in the past."

A solution: Do what I did for Dr. Charles after his criticism. I did everything in my power to learn the job and do quality work. He changed dramatically in how he accepted my work. I must learn to write better before reviewers will accept my articles.

Another solution: My decision last night to search the library for others' writings is an alternative I offer to Dr. Charles in my dream. My own writings have been rejected twice. I will search the library for others' writings and prepare an article from there.

PMID Step 6: Explore your dream for **family and other relationship systems perspectives,** which are influences arising from reactions to family and other major relationships, both past and current. Use these perspectives to discover whether this dream reflects your reactions during experiences with family members or other important people in your life. Compare and comment on your dreaming and your waking-life reactions to the primary relationships in this dream. (If this dream is not about a relationship, type the words "Not Applicable" in this space.)

Dr. Charles appears to be the main person I react to in the dream. I react to him in the dream by attempting to please him, even giving up my own articles. In waking life (I reported this under Step 5, too), I reacted to Dr. Charles's lofty expectations of me (beginning with criticism) by working very hard to reach his high standards. In comparison, my waking-life reactions to what the reviewers' critiques might be was defiance.

Abel is in my dream in an image that is somewhat unlike his waking-life appearance, which prompts me to deduce that I still respond to criticism based on my teenage reactions to him. Abel's superior status in comparison to mine weighed so intensely on me that I finally reacted to him by leaving the friendship.

Verification that the dream ties to the specific issue: Verified: Ted connects the dream with his sensitivity to feeling inferior.

Test for the three indicators:

1. Both the dream and the dreamer's interpretations contain at least one clear message that the issue may be finished.
   Indicator met: Ted finds a solution in his dream that is a positive acceptance of his need to improve his writing. Do "everything in my power to learn the job and do quality work."
2. Neither the dream nor the dreamer's interpretations contain new or unused past solutions to the current issue.
   Indicator not met: The solution that Ted finds in his dream "I must learn to write better before reviewers will accept my articles" appears to be a solution that he had not considered necessary for his article. At least, he must have thought his writing was good enough to be accepted without further finessing.
3. Neither the dream nor the dreamer's interpretations give hints that the specific concern still bothers the dreamer.
   Indicator not met: In the dream, Ted turns away from offering his own writings. He obviously feels inferior when he says, "However … these are my own writings." He also interprets that his teenage reactions to Abel continue to influence his current reactions when in situations that have potential to make him feel inferior.

REVIEW AND REVISE DREAM INTERPRETATIONS FOR NEW INSIGHTS—REVISITED

Let's follow Ted's work with this dream further. Ted reported that he returned to this dream after having at least two later dreams that contradicted his interpretation to use other specialists' writings. Those later dreams confused Ted on how he could have misunderstood his "Dr. Charles's Criticism Changes to Softness" dream.

I refer you to the first paragraph in this current chapter, repeated here for emphasis:

> Serious dream workers repeatedly review their significant dreams and associated interpretations until the specific messages of the dreams are clear—or until they reach an impasse on one dream and go on to the next. Revisiting dreams and reviewing earlier interpretations to refresh former meanings, discover new insights, and review for misinterpretations are critical to our best use of our dreams. All dreamers who contributed their dreams and interpretations to this book had reviewed their interpretations at least once before offering them to me.

You will be amazed at what Ted found when he reviewed his "Dr. Charles's Criticism Changes to Softness" dream and his original interpretations. According to Ted, it was "about the fifth time" he had looked at them. His revised interpretations are much expanded; he finally took my advice from chapter 6 of this book:

> When working with Step 3, I find it most expedient and productive to copy and paste my write-up of the whole dream under Step 3. Next, I examine each sentence for whether there are phrases, or even whole sentences, that I can define in the context of my pre-dream events, pre-dream thoughts, earlier experiences, and intuitive insights.

Examining every sentence is fundamental for significant dreams. Read Ted's revised and expanded PMID Steps 3–6 for his "Dr. Charles's Criticism Changes to Softness" dream. (The background information, Steps 1 and 2, and some of Ted's earlier definitions for Step 3 remain the same.)

PMID Step 3: Select and define **major dream phrases** and symbols from your write-up of this dream to discover the dream's personalized meanings. Consider effects of your events and thoughts of the day before your dream and earlier experiences on the meaning of each major dream phrase and symbol. The general definition for phrases as used in this step is "a string of words." The strings of words can be phrases, clauses, or whole sentences.

The following is a continuation of the list of dream phrases that Ted selected and defined. (Ted's original selections and definitions that he retained are repeated following his new selections and definitions.)

9. **Darkish in here:** Conventional definition, something I fail to see connected with the context of this dream. Specific to this dream, I fail to recognize all that my dream reveals regarding the theme of this dream, which is my preliminary reactions to receipt of the reviewers' critiques.
10. **Asking … about needing articles on the innovative work we do here at this company:** Specifically associating my dream with the

topic of the writing that I do. Let me ponder this a while. As I review this part (this is about the fifth inspection I have made of this dream and my interpretations), I notice that I wrote the word "articles" when I recorded my dream. "Articles," plural, means more than one article. More than one article could connote a book.

11. **Needs articles this afternoon:** There is an immediate need for a book of articles about the product that we produce at our company.
12. **Timidly say that I have many articles that I have written on the work that we do:** Continuing with the idea of many articles pointing to a whole book instead of the article that was rejected, concurrent with offering this one article for publication, I have been writing a book about our company's product.
13. **Think of my office up on a higher floor:** This is my dream, and I need a boost. I will boast here. Higher floor, a higher knowledge level than mainstream about the product that our company creates.
14. **Standing in my place, my eyes are watering:** My belief in the value of the uncommon version of the product that we create at our company is intense. Regardless that my article about it has been rejected, I remain fervent in my devotion to the product.
15. **Bright light shining into my eyes, but it doesn't seem that the light is so bright that it is the cause my tears:** Could this possibly imply that there is brightness or enlightening about my writings?
16. **Do have difficulty looking into the light:** I admit that, although I am greatly devoted to the product that our company creates and my writings about that work, in the face of rejections it is difficult for me to conceive of my writings as superior.
17. **"However," I say, "they are all my own writings":** Apologetic for my writings.
18. **Tell Dr. Charles though that I will look for other people's writings on the type work we do here:** Association to my last night's change in strategy (PMID Step 2) when I decided to search for published writings about similar products instead of resubmitting my writings about our company's specific product.
19. **Feel Dr. Charles's hand on my right shoulder:** Publishers will welcome my book. This is a precognitive part of my dream. The date of my dream is 3 days *before* I met with an editor at a writers' conference. The only time an advisor put a hand on my shoulder in this manner was at that writers' conference. It happened when an editor was excited about my work. At first the editor was nonplussed as he listened to me describe the product that our company creates. His mood changed dramatically when he read my synopsis of a book that I have in progress about that product. He put his hand on my right shoulder and told me publishers will welcome my book. It wasn't until I reviewed this dream after a few earlier readings, retrieved my notes from the writers' conference, and compared dates that I realized the precognitive part of my dream.

20. **Eyes are so blinded with the light that I don't open them to see whether he truly does have his hand on my shoulder:** My lack of confidence, reticence for fear of rejection to exploring whether my writing is as good as the editor ascribed to it.
21. **Don't open them to see whether he truly does have his hand on my shoulder:** Could this mean that my sensitivity to feeling inferior deludes me from being open to the reviewers' comments?
22. **Wonder if I have just imagined it, or if he really does have his hand on my shoulder in compassion:** Even when there is good news, I think it is my imagination instead of bona fide accolades.
23. **Talks softly to me now:** Could this be that reviewers will, in the future, talk softly to me in appreciation and honor of my writings just as Dr. Charles "talked softly to me" after he came to respecting my work?
24. **Time he needs these writings:** The time that Dr. Charles needs my writings, according to my dream, is "this afternoon." That means there is a current need for books about the uncommon product that our company creates. I already have a book in progress.
25. **Abel lying over the upper part of my workstation:** Associates to my thoughts last night about Abel and my vow to keep from becoming overwhelmed by the reviewers' critiques of my article.
26. **Predominant color I see is blue:** My foremost personal association for the color blue is men, strong men. I am a man. I have difficultly in the face of criticism to picture myself as a strong man.
27. **Shows a coat to me:** My inclination is that Abel's new coat is associated with my yesterday's thoughts about my casual clothing. Picturing Abel in new clothing might connote my improvement to now seeing him as a rich part of my life. Guessing, though. Read what I write under "Million."
28. **Million part of it is right:** Evidence that my feeling inextricably inferior to Abel is valuable beyond my expectations (symbolically "worth a million"). To explain, in the process of striving (unconsciously and consciously) to move beyond feeling inferior, I increasingly uncover my individuality, my own talents. My own talents are vastly different from Abel's.

Ted retained the following dream phrase definitions from his original interpretations:

1. **Dr. Charles the boss:** The managing partner at the first company I worked for after I graduated from college.
2. **Complains that something is very messy:** Complaints that I anticipate will be in the reviewers' comments. My personal association here is that Dr. Charles was very critical of me at the start of my employment. I thought I was doing okay until during one of the first

coffee breaks Dr. Charles asked me, "Do you think you are doing okay?" His tone of voice made me realize that he thought my work was inferior.

3. **Announces this in scolding to us employees:** This is fair-minded. I am not the only one reviewers scold.
4. **Peek through to see whether there is room for me:** Room for, a place for, me to be heard by those in authority regarding the topic of my article.
5. **Almost in front of my place:** Coming closer to the specific topic that I write about.
6. **Think how I could find some in the library, and I picture going to the library as I talk about this:** Last night, I thought about researching for published articles about similar products to the one we create here at our company.
7. **Two o'clock:** Makes me think a bit of the intuitive ability I had for a long while when I woke during the night and knew the time was 2:00 a.m. exactly. Conceivably, 2:00 ties to my intuitive sense that helps me write.
8. **Abel ... doesn't look quite like himself:** Conventional definition of people who appear in other than their actual looks is that the dreamer is ascribing inaccurate attributes to the person pictured.

PMID Step 4: Compare your **emotions in your dream** with your **pre-dream, waking-life emotions** to discover whether your waking-life emotions accurately reflect how you feel about the issue in this dream. Note that the issue may be a relationship issue. What differences, if any, do you find between your emotions in your dream and your waking-life emotions? It is useful to periodically review your emotions in your dreams regarding the main issue or relationship at hand.

In the dream, I am timorous, shy when I put forth that I have many articles that Dr. Charles could use. In waking life, never mind that I tell myself my writings are good. I must admit that there are times, and this is one, when my waking-life lack of confidence in my writings is revealed in my dreams. My spontaneous tears reveal that I really do feel worse than I thought, undeniably more shy than my bolder waking-life statements were before I went to sleep last night.

Another contrast is that I am very pleased for Abel and the million something. *This is exquisite. I feel it. I am very pleased for him.* Those are the emotions that I felt in my dream about Abel's success. Very different from my emotions last night when I thought about him and how I've fought so hard to feel like a million myself instead of casting myself in a deeply inferior status when it feels like someone is putting me down.

PMID Step 5: Explore your dream for possible **solutions** to problems, including changing (or affirming) your thoughts, attitudes, or behaviors. Consider your responses to each PMID model step, including Step 6, as you search for solutions and suggestions in this dream. Give primary attention to the power of your thoughts before your dream (PMID Step 2) to act as questions that your dream answers.

A suggestion: Look closely at my confidence level. In this dream, it is superior to my waking-life appraisal of my worth. Use those realizations to maintain confidence in my writing ability.

A solution: Do what I did for Dr. Charles. What I did for Dr. Charles after his criticism was to do everything in my power to learn the job better and do quality work. He changed dramatically in how he treated me. Consider the reviewers' comments as positive resources for me to improve my writings. I must learn to write better before reviewers will accept my materials.

Another solution: Use my own writings instead of looking for other experts about the unique product that our company produces. My in-progress book is the place to put materials from my articles.

PMID Step 6: Explore your dream for **family and other relationship systems perspectives,** which are influences arising from reactions to family and other major relationships, both past and current. Use these perspectives to discover whether this dream reflects your reactions during experiences with family members or other important people in your life. Compare and comment on your dreaming and your waking-life reactions to the primary relationships in this dream. (If this dream is not about a relationship, type the words "Not Applicable" in this space.)

Dr. Charles is in my dream. I reacted to him in the dream by being humble and doing my best to please him, even giving up my own articles. In waking life (I reported this under Steps 3 and 5 also), I reacted to Dr. Charles's lofty expectations of me (beginning with criticism) by working very hard to reach his high standards. In comparison, and in the context of this dream, my waking-life reactions to what the reviewers' critiques might be was defiance.

Abel is in my dream in an image that is somewhat unlike his waking-life appearance, which prompts me to deduce that I still respond to criticism based on my teenage reactions to him. In waking life when we were teenagers, I reacted to Abel by trying to emulate him. He was accepted as the superior one, it seemed to me, by just about everyone in our school. I wonder at times about whether I was born with a natural inclination, an innate tendency, to feel subordinate to people who are acclaimed as superiors. Ostensibly, Abel's superior status in comparison to mine must have weighed heavily on me, must have felt overwhelming to me. Conceivably, that is why he is a main character in my "put myself down" dreams. In comparison, and in the context of this dream, my waking-life reactions to what the reviewers' critiques might be was that I repeatedly vowed, "I will not let the reviewers' comments overwhelm me as has happened in the past."

As we read Ted's revised interpretations, we find a major change in one solution: From "I will search the library for others' writings and prepare an article from there" to "Use my own writings instead of looking for other experts about the unique product that our company produces. My in-progress book is the place to put materials from my articles." That and Ted's other new interpretations support my recommendation in the first section of this current chapter, "Review and Revise Dream Interpretations for New Insights."

Turning to page 124, "Find Indicators for When to Shut the Door on Specific Relationship Concerns," let us do the test again on whether Ted is succeeding in alleviating feelings of inferiority in the face of criticism.

Verification that the dream ties to the specific issue: Verified: Ted connects the dream with sensitivity to feeling inferior.

Retest for the three indicators:

1. Both the dream and the dreamer's interpretations contain at least one clear message that the issue may be finished.
   Indicator met: With Ted's revised interpretations, he now notices his appreciation for Abel's success: *This is exquisite. I feel it. I am very pleased for him.* Ted's laudation of Abel's success is a definite sign of his ability to overcome feeling inferior when faced with threatening circumstances. Retained from his original interpretation: Ted finds a solution in his dream that is a positive acceptance of his need to improve his writing. Do "everything in my power to learn the job and do quality work."
2. Neither the dream nor the dreamer's interpretations contain new or unused past solutions to the current issue.
   Indicator not met: The solutions that Ted finds in his dream ("Consider the reviewers' comments as positive resources for improving my writings" and "I must learn to write better before reviewers will accept my articles.") are new solutions for realizing that is what he needs to do in the specific situation regarding the reviewers' critiques of his rejected article.
3. Neither the dream nor the dreamer's interpretations give hints that the specific concern still bothers the dreamer.
   Indicator not met: Although much improved from Ted's reactions of "becoming overwhelmed," Ted's dream and his interpretations both contain hints that Ted remains sensitive to feeling inferior.

With Ted's new interpretations, we could now change the description of his dream from being an example of "When It Is Ambiguous Whether a Long-Standing Issue Has Been Overcome" to "When Progress Toward Overcoming a Long-Standing Issue Is Evident."

Regarding the indicators discussed, these are only pointers. Counselor-facilitators and dreamers need to avoid feeling worried about getting it perfectly right. As demonstrated, dreams will continue to guide us if we have left an issue before it is resolved in waking life. Maybe there will be a need to revisit past dreams. Maybe the dream theme will repeat later. There are no "have tos" or "requirements to do" here. These are simply ways to know when the dreamer realizes it is time to close one door and move forward. Other doors are then allowed to open. More people than are currently working with their dreams would be amazed and grateful if they could recognize the open door to emotional comfort that dreams have the potential to provide.

Notably, when we make conscious efforts to work with one major relationship, our dreaming minds often invite us to expand our explorations into other major relationships. It often takes several weeks to months before our dreams extend from one major relationship to others. The process by which the dreaming mind deals with only one or two major relationships at a time reminds us of gestalt philosophy, in which new issues arise as old ones are alleviated and recede into the background.

SUMMARY

This chapter is presented in two parts. First, we examine the need for reviewing earlier dream interpretations. Second, indicators and examples of dreams and interpretations are given for testing when a relationship issue is finished and the dreamer can move on. In one example, a dream shows that an issue is clearly finished. In the second example, there is only a subtle indication that the dreamer has alleviated the issue in question. In a third example, the dreamer's original interpretations indicate that the issue in question is ambiguous regarding being settled. His later thorough interpretations indicate substantial progress in overcoming a long-established stressful reaction.

SELF-STUDY QUIZ CHAPTER 11

1. This chapter makes an analogy of people's neglect to revisit their dreams and interpretations to other circumstances. What is that analogy?
2. What purposes are stated in this chapter for revisiting dreams and reviewing earlier interpretations?
3. Two ways to discover earlier misinterpretations of a dream are (circle the one correct answer)
   a. A later dream may reveal the earlier misinterpretation.
   b. You may discover the misinterpretation when you review your earlier dreams and interpretations.
   c. Neither a nor b.

   d. Both a and b.

4. This chapter states three indicators that dreams contain for when a specific issue is alleviated. What are those three indicators?
5. What is the title of the dream shown in this chapter that illustrates that a specific issue is definitely alleviated?

12

Delivery Modes for Facilitating Dream Interpretation

How They Accommodate Short-Term Counseling

DISTANCE COUNSELING AND THE PERSONALIZED METHOD FOR INTERPRETING DREAMS MODEL

The Center for Credentialing and Education (CCE) (http://www.cce-global.org/credentials-offered/dccmain) defines distance counseling.

> Distance Counseling is a counseling approach that takes the best practices of traditional counseling as well as some of its own unique advantages and adapts them for delivery to clients via electronic means in order to maximize the use of technology-assisted counseling techniques. The technology-assisted methods may include telecounseling (telephone), secure email communication, chat, videoconferencing or computerized stand-alone software programs.

ACA Code of Ethics Standard A. 12, "Technology Applications" governs distance counseling. In 2005 the ACA Code of Ethics was revised. In 2006 ACA Chief Professional Officer, D. M. Kaplan interviewed Ethics Revision Task Force members for the purpose of enlarging on substantive changes in the revised code. During 2006 ACA presented those interviews in consecutive issues of the *Counseling Today* magazine (hard copy and online at http://www.counseling.org/Publications/CounselingToday.aspx). The interview on Ethical Use of Technology in Counseling is in the October 2006 issue. In 2009, the *Journal of Counseling and Development* presented the complete set of interviews in one article (Kaplan et al., 2009). During the interviews, task force members gave priority to three A. 12 statements: Laws and Statutes, Informed Consent, and Access.

Laws and Statutes: Because distance counseling can cross jurisdictional lines, counselors need to "know and be in compliance with all laws in both their state or jurisdiction and the state or jurisdiction of the client" (p. 253).

Informed Consent: Provide details to clients on the "limitations and successes on the use" (p. 253) of the particular technology that you are using.

Access: In addition to providing accessibility for all income levels, consider "the need for clients, students, or supervisees with a disability to utilize our technology-related services" (p. 253).

Our research and exploration projects have all been via a privately owned stand-alone Web site to facilitate participants' use of the Personalized Method for Interpreting Dreams (PMID), the model featured in this book. Participants and I exchange confidential data using password-protected individual areas on the site. A discussion board and e-mail exchanges are also provided on the site, but neither is used to post confidential information.

Several benefits of distance counseling are as follows:

1. Gives both dreamer and facilitator time to think about the dream and what it means before they communicate with each other by the Internet exchange.
2. Provides flexible times for both parties to respond.
3. Encourages self-exploration because clients are most often sitting by themselves when they enter dream information and insights into the distance delivery system.
4. Encourages the possibility of freer expression when sitting in front of a personal computer than when sitting in a counseling office.
5. Provides an ongoing automatic log of exchanges between the client and the counselor-facilitator.

Distance counseling can be either synchronous (with little or no gap between counselor and client responses) or asynchronous (a time gap between counselor and client responses). I use asynchronous timing exclusively.

A current resource for distance counseling training is ReadyMinds (available at http://www.readyminds.com/training/overview.html). Another resource is Malone, Miller, and Walz's book, *Distance Counseling: Expanding the Counselor's Reach and Impact* (2007).

FACE-TO-FACE COUNSELING AND THE PMID MODEL

Although all the benefits of using the PMID model presented in this book are applicable to face-to-face counseling, there are unique differences in application between face-to-face counseling and distance counseling when using the PMID model.

Face-to-face counseling sessions, typically 50-minute sessions, limit contemplation time for responses between client and counselor. With distance counseling and asynchronous timing, there is a time gap between counselor and client responses that allows contemplation before responding.

The good news is that a time gap can be created for face-to-face settings. As the examples in this book demonstrate, the client can record his or her dreams and develop at least some meanings between counseling sessions. When the client and counselor meet, the counselor can read and use the client's writings for in-session work. Use of what a client writes between sessions thus yields many of the same benefits as distance counseling.

A major benefit of this approach is that it maximizes in-session, face-to-face time.

Encouraging people to work with their dreams between sessions is likely to stimulate clients to explore more than one dream about a specific issue, as happened with Gloria in Chapters 4 through 10. When client and counselor examine more than one dream about an issue or relationship (or a series of dreams), some of the following benefits may arise:

1. Examining a series of dreams can lead the counselor (and the client) to see progress (or lack of progress) that the dreamer-client is making with his or her dream solutions and suggestions.
2. Selecting a sequence of dreams can move the dreamer's focus away from only one extraordinary dream to interpreting a series of common dreams about the issue being studied. (A series of common dreams may contain more useful meanings for the dreamer than just one traumatic dream. For example, Gloria's "When Did I Lose Control?" dream was a common dream in which she found an extremely useful solution. Later, she had other common dreams that helped her use that solution.)
3. A series of dreams can help the counselor and the client decide what areas need the most attention.

HOW USING THE PMID MODEL CAN ACCOMMODATE SHORT-TERM COUNSELING

Many benefits of using the PMID model are presented in this book. Do these benefits include short-term counseling, as stipulated by insurance providers? Research and explorations of the PMID model show that there is potential for dedicated people to alleviate stress from relationship concerns during 8 weeks. The potential is present when the client, facilitated by a counselor on use of the PMID model, interprets a minimum of five of his or her own dreams. (Appendix A: The PMID Model Researched and Explored presents detailed results of the research and exploration projects.)

An important feature of the PMID model is that it contributes to short-term counseling by making the dreamer the primary interpreter; the counselor facilitates the process. Making the dreamer the interpreter fosters his or her ability to understand and use the model. Areas that often require attention beyond the typical duration of counseling are long-standing concerns around relationships. When a client learns how to use the PMID model with the help of the counselor-facilitator during an 8-week period, the timeframe meets short-term counseling constraints. The client has gained a method for ongoing self-help. Ongoing self-help and independent work with dreams at the conclusion of formal counseling can be especially helpful to clients who show emotional stability for independent work with their dreams.

Assessing the emotional stability of a client's need for independent work with dreams naturally rests primarily with the counselor, his or her associates, and the client-dreamer himself or herself. Appendix B presents our screening application, which is a potential assessment option for use in conjunction with the counselor's, associates', and client's appraisals. I use the term *potential* because we use our screening application as an entry assessment. It has never been used for exit evaluation.

It is important to consider the range of information that dreamers reveal with their responses to the PMID steps. The PMID model elicits events, thoughts, personal experiences, emotions, problems and solutions, and relationship systems perspectives. Obviously, all of these elements have the potential to be incorporated with theoretical orientations, whether cognitive behavior therapies or any of the other psychotherapy approaches. Incorporation, although untested to date, can potentially provide vital information for present-day counseling approaches, again conserving counseling session time.

To conclude this chapter, I pose a vital question to counselors: When your sessions end, will your clients be able to make it on their own? Consider teaching them how to understand their dreams in addition to the conventional self-discovery skills on which you instruct them.

SUMMARY

This chapter explains delivery modes (distance and face to face) for the facilitation of clients' interpretation of their dreams. With the dreamer-as-interpreter feature of the PMID model, clients can learn from their dreams between counseling sessions as well as during sessions. In the process, clients have the potential to learn how to use the PMID model in a short period (research and explorations show 8 weeks is possible). However, each client's emotional stability for working with dreams in a self-facilitated way must be evaluated before the counselor recommends independent work with dreams.

SELF-STUDY QUIZ CHAPTER 12

1. List the benefit of distance counseling that seems most productive to you. Why does the benefit that you chose seem most productive to you?
2. What percentage of benefits presented in this book for using the PMID model is applicable for face-to-face counseling? (Circle the correct answer.)
   a. 100%
   b. About 50%

  c. 0%
  d. 67%

3. With distance counseling and asynchronous timing, there is a time gap between counselor and client responses, which gives time for processing before responding. This chapter states that a time gap can be created for face-to-face settings. Simply stated, what is this procedure?
4. Benefits may arise when client and counselor examine more than one dream about an issue or relationship (a series of dreams). List one that seems most productive to you. Why does the benefit that you chose seem most productive to you?
5. Ways in which use of the PMID model can accommodate short-term counseling include (circle the best response)
   a. The dreamer-as-interpreter features of the PMID model allow clients to work on their own between sessions.
   b. Research and explorations of the PMID model show that there is a potential for dreamers to learn how to self-facilitate use of the PMID model during 8 weeks as they interpret a minimum of five dreams with guidance of the counselor-facilitator on use of the PMID model.
   c. The range of information that dreamers reveal with each PMID step—events, thoughts, personal experiences, emotions, problems and solutions, and family systems perspectives—has the potential to be incorporated within theoretical orientations, whether cognitive behavior therapies or any of the other psychotherapy approaches.
   d. All the above.
   e. None of the above.

Section III

Two Breakthrough Dream Interpretation Models of the Later 20th Century

INTRODUCTION

My invitations to Ullman and Cartwright and Lamberg came from a dream. In fact, this whole book was inspired by a dream. One night, I commented to a colleague, "When I finish updating my dream interpretation course book [an unpublished series of lessons on my Personalized Method for Interpreting Dreams (PMID) model that I wrote for a university course I taught], I am going to devote my time to my own dreams." That very night my accounting advisor (who once told me, "I did all these various jobs to get to where I am now") came to me in a dream. "The university is going to put in completely new systems, computer systems," he told me, "and you are one targeted to be the administrator."

In retrospect, I believe what my advisor meant in that dream was to completely rewrite my course book with its emphasis on the systems approach of the PMID to dream interpretation. However, when I first interpreted that dream, I thought that the word *systems* meant several dream interpretation models. Thus, I invited other contemporary dream interpretation model developers to present their models in the "completely new book."

After Montague Ullman and Rosalind Cartwright, with her coauthor Lynne Lamberg, had signed their consents, I had another dream that showed my willingness to move to another house (to present other people's models). Yet, I really wanted to stay in the house I love. In waking life, my husband and I live in a house that I love; in dream symbolism, I understood the new dream to say, "Stay with the PMID model as the primary focus in the book. That is the house you love and the model you know best how to teach."

Notice that my dreaming mind waited to present this second dream until after Ullman and Cartwright, with coauthor Lamberg had signed consents to present chapters in this book. It is my great honor to include their volunteered, formerly published writings.

ULLMAN'S GROUP MODEL AND CARTWRIGHT'S RISC MODEL

Both Ullman's (Chapter 13) and Cartwright's (Chapter 14) models are applicable to multicultures. Further, both approaches fill unique needs in the dream interpretation world and unique needs in this book.

Ullman's thrust is a group approach (*group* meaning "a gathering of people") to understanding dreams. Ullman's chapter includes a history of interest in dreams from antiquity into the 20th century when Freud, Jung, and other professionals used dreams in clinical settings. Ullman transformed work with dreams from strictly clinical use to an experiential method by which members of a group facilitate each others' understanding of dreams.

Cartwright and Lamberg present help for all ages in using the RISC Model to solve problems. Inclusion of excerpts about children's dreaming from Cartwright and Lamberg's book (1992/2000) particularly adds to the comprehensiveness of my book. My colleagues and I have yet to explore beneficial features of the PMID model for working with children's dreams.

13

Group Approach

MONTAGUE ULLMAN

INTRODUCTION

Montague Ullman (1916 to June 7, 2008), clinical professor emeritus, was "in the forefront of the movement to stimulate public interest in dreams and to encourage the development of dream sharing groups. Working with a small group process that he felt was both safe and effective he has spent … three decades leading such groups both here and abroad, especially in Sweden." (Siivola, par. 3, retrieved February 1, 2010). Ullman's literature and research support of elements contained in the Personalized Method for Interpreting Dreams (PMID) model are referenced in other chapters of the current book. Except for this introduction and the self-study quiz, this chapter is a quotation from an article written by Ullman and published in 2001.*

AN ATHEORETIC BIDIRECTIONAL EXPERIENTIAL GROUP APPROACH TO WORKING WITH DREAMS

Montague Ullman

Abstract

Despite their universality, interest in dreams has focussed almost exclusively on their clinical usefulness. Until recently there has been no serious attempt to make

* Dr. Ullman offered his group approach to this book (letter signed June 12, 2007, and a formal agreement signed September 5, 2007) by means of his article "An Atheoretic Bidirectional Experiential Group Approach to Working With Dreams" from the *Journal of the Group Department of the Postgraduate Center for Mental Health*, 5(1), Issues in Group Psychotherapy, fall 2001. The article is reproduced from http://siivola.org/monte/papers_grouped/index.htm.(Endorsement to reprint from M. Siivola, January 28, 2010.)

dreams available to the general public. Any such attempt would have to be consistent with the basic phenomenological features of dreaming consciousness and would have to take into account the vulnerability of the dreamer. The group process to be described is bidirectional. It is particularly useful in the training of clinicians for dream work, but is equally applicable to anyone with an interest in what their dreams have to say. The process is structured to generate trust and maintain the safety of the dreamer. The dreamer and the group interact in a variety of ways to facilitate the flow of relevant associations without ever being intrusive.

Key Words: Dreams, Group, Experiential

Perhaps it's time to take a look at the path our understanding of and experience with dreams has taken since the publication of Freud's classic volume one hundred years ago. That path led exclusively to the clinical use of dreams, generally by someone with a psychoanalytic background. That clinical application was inextricably interwoven with metapsychological theoretical considerations, predominantly Freudian, later qualitatively modified by Jung, and more recently by ego theory and adaptational views. Mid-century saw a dramatic increase in our knowledge of the neurophysiology and ethology of sleep and dreams through the study of sleeping subjects in the laboratory. This research, coming at a time when growth centers and consciousness raising groups came into being, stimulated considerable public interest in dreams.

Is there something missing here? I think there is, but the answer to the question depends on whether or not you can envisage a significant place for dreams in the fabric of society. In preliterate societies today, for example, there is a niche for dreams as an important intermediary between cultural, religious, and historical entities and everyday life. In antiquity, notably the classical period of Greece, this interest in one's dream life was also noted. In both instances, there was a certain symmetry between the personal and the social that served a unifying, cohesive function. The situation began to change in ancient Rome as monotheism took over and the link was finally severed in Western Europe in the middle ages with the occurrence of two historical developments, the invention of the printing press and the consolidation of the power of the Church. The first made dream books, mostly oriented to mantic practices and divination, available to the laity. The second disparaged even to the point of proscribing the circulation of such books. In the eyes of the Church, mystical visions and dreams were linked. Both could be the work of either divine or satanic influences. Since the laity could fall prey to the latter, it was felt that both dreams and visions should remain under the domain of the Church as the only power that could vouch for authentic divine influences. This concern with the vulnerability of the laity to demonic influences ultimately led to the persecution of witches.

The Industrial Revolution was the last blow to any hope that our dream life would find its own natural haven in society. Objective mastery of the external world far outstripped any realistic social investment in the subjective mastery of ourselves. Dreams had no significant social valence. With Freud the universal phenomenon of dreaming found a limited place for itself in a profession dedicated to the art of psychological healing. The public was left to shift for itself with regard to their dreams. Universal accessibility to something so insistently a part of everyone's life has remained a mirage for all but a handful of oneirophiles. In the laboratory we have learned how to deprive people of dreams by keeping people awake from the onset to the end of the successive stages of the dreaming cycle. Without giving it a second thought, we have managed to live out our lives in a dream-deprived society.

The closing decades of the last century witnessed the appearance of a truly new phenomenon, namely, people gravitating toward dream groups led both by professionals, including a scattering of psychoanalytically trained therapists, and laity. While at this point these groups are only barely visible dots on the landscape, there is every indication that this movement will grow. That growth will depend on how safe and effective these groups turn out to be. Currently, there are more people seeking such groups than there are groups to accommodate them.

The process I am going to describe began in 1974 as an effort on my part to teach candidates in training about dreams experientially rather than indirectly in a clinical seminar where only the dream and not the dreamer was present. While this was helpful in elucidating the transference and shedding light on how the dream could further the therapeutic line, there was no opportunity to demonstrate how to actively engage with the dreamer in so focussed a way as to facilitate the retrieval of the associative matrix of the dream. To speak of active engagement and focussing in relation to free association may sound like an oxymoron. It is not. As you will see when the stages of the process are described, it is simply a way of working toward relevant associations by linking that effort to a background understanding of the unique features of dreaming consciousness.

The task before me in setting out to teach dream work experientially meant transforming what is ordinarily a clinical situation into a pedagogical one with the goal of orienting the students to the richness and healing potential of their own dreams in a way that would prepare them to work with patients in individual or group psychotherapy. What I have to say about the transformation is premised on my belief that there is an art to helping a dreamer lower defensive maneuvers enough to identify what the dream is saying. It is an art, separate and distinct from any theoretical formulations. When the latter is relied on at the expense of the art, the result is intellectual rather than emotional insight. Art involves the connection of talent and craft. Only craft can be taught. Talent is innate. We are all, perhaps in varying degrees, endowed with a creative talent capable of speaking the truth to us while we dream. The experiential dream group provides us with the means to learn and master that craft. The carryover of that mastery provides tools that are useful in any form of formal therapy. This transformation from a clinical to a pedagogical stance involved a clear change in roles for myself, for the group and for the dreamer.

For myself that meant becoming a teacher pure and simple rather than a psychotherapist teaching the application of psychoanalytic theory and technique to dream work. It involved a dual responsibility. I was there to teach the process while at the same time to participate in the process in the same way that the members of the group did, including the sharing of my own dream. This is the first significant difference from formal therapy, where dream sharing is generally a one-sided affair. Dream work flourishes in a less hierarchical arrangement where everyone becomes known to each other on the level revealed in their dreams. To the extent that level of sharing is established defensive mechanisms, including transference and resistance, diminish.

For the group it means they are there as co-dreamers to create and maintain an atmosphere of trust and safety and to interact with the dreamer in a way that is helpful to the dreamer without ever being intrusive. Each assumes the responsibility for managing his or her own personal process as the focus remains on the dreamer's struggle to make contact with the dream. That help is offered in different ways at different stages of the process. The group tries to be sensitive to where the dreamer is at any given moment. It is only the dreamer who opens areas for exploration. There is further discussion of the group's function in the sections on Skills, Milieu and the Process.

It is in connection with the role of the dreamer that the process differs even more sharply from formal therapy. While the leader is there to maintain the integrity of the process, it is the dreamer who is in charge of the work being done with his own dream. If he shares a dream, he is in control of the level of sharing he feels comfortable with and is not under any obligation to go further. It is that control of the process, which also includes stopping it at any point, that is fundamental to allaying the dreamer's anxiety and defensiveness. The freedom to share is directly proportional to the lowering of anxiety. The various stages of the process unfold at the invitation of the dreamer. The group follows and never leads the dreamer. That means they don't go into areas that have not been opened up by the dreamer. The questions they put to the dreamer are to be looked upon as instruments for the dreamer to use in exploring his psyche. Leading questions take the control away from the dreamer and are taboo. You will learn more about this in the headings noted in the previous paragraph. I will say more about craft at a later point in connection with the process.

To set the stage I am going to offer a number of axioms. Axioms are propositions that appear to be self-evident. Time has wrought changes in Euclid's axioms upon which he built the structure of plane geometry when a more complex math was needed to deal with the strange quirks of gravity and sub-atomic particles. Just as plane geometry continues to hold for the ordinary dimensions of waking life, I think the following axioms hold for the mental life we lead asleep. Further axiomatic changes may occur as we learn more about dreams and their application to healing.

Axioms

1. Dreams begin in the present. Freud referred to the day residue as setting off a series of events that led to the subject matter of the dream. I prefer to seek out this triggering effect by exposing what I refer to as the Recent Emotional Context. This covers a longer but still recent period out of which feeling residues arose and lingered long enough to surface the night the dream occurred.
2. Dreams go beyond the present to link up with more remote feeling residues from the past. This linkage addresses unresolved issues that continue

to influence current behavior. This connection of past and present brings together more information than is immediately available to the dreamer when awake.

3. Dreams tell it like it is. Dreams have an intrinsic honesty. They seem to come from an incorruptible core of our being that registers the truth when it sees it. Both Freud and Jung saw dreams as containers of the truth, but they looked upon the fate of that truth in different ways. For Freud that truth underwent censorship in the interest of preserving sleep and maintaining a pre-existing emotional status quo. Manifest content was the disguised representation of whatever truth was surfacing at the time. Jung saw manifest content as the psyche's way of revealing rather than concealing the truth.
4. The neurophysiological analog of dreaming consciousness is common to all mammals thus far studied in the laboratory. This arousal mechanism is associated with cyclical bouts of dreaming and is part of the life cycle from birth on. There is indirect evidence that in other mammals it is associated with some prototypic form of consciousness (Morrison, 1993).

Based upon these axioms and integrating them with my clinical and group experience with dreams, I have come to the conclusion that dreaming consciousness is a natural healing system in a way similar to the various bodily systems. Certain assumptions underlie this point of view. While axioms command a certain consensual agreement, the following assumptions depart in various ways from the prevailing canon.

Assumptions

1. *Dreaming Consciousness as a Healing System.* All bodily systems face in two directions: internally to meet the needs of the organism in its relationship, and externally to a world experienced as extended beyond its border. Each has a unique structure and function. The endocrine system is made up of glands, the function of which is to secrete the hormones necessary to both maintain an optimal internal milieu and respond to emerging demands. Our dreams have a neurophysiological substrate at both a cortical and subcortical level. The interplay between these two levels modulates the level of arousal. Where there are adequate resources to deal with the tension involved, the state of arousal terminates naturally and sleep continues. Where the stress or tension is too great, awakening occurs. The secretions of this nocturnal organ of consciousness is the imagery that results. Most bodily systems function at an unconscious level. So do our dreams. They arise out of an unconscious domain and function in an involuntary spontaneous manner to meet normal and abnormal organismic needs. We don't command our digestive systems to respond to our food intake, nor do we consciously direct red blood cells and platelets to do their thing when bleeding occurs. Analogously, our dreams "digest" residual feelings triggered by recent events and evaluate them in regard to

their significance for our future. [They do] this by opening up our remote memory bank and exploring the degree to which a current concern links up with unresolved tensions from the past. Dreams arise spontaneously and involuntarily. No one can consciously design the opening scene of a dream.

In the course of becoming symbol-making animals, we have transformed a basic imaging mode into a vehicle for expressing in a most wondrously condensed form the tensions that arise in our more complex symbol-driven lives. After all, a single picture can capture more than a thousand words.

Regardless of how the presentational mode came about, the more interesting question is how the imagery now serves as a healing organ and in that way relates to the survival of our species? At night, while dreaming, we are in the business of manufacturing visual metaphors. Metaphor is our uniquely human way of expressing feelings that are rising up within us but are not yet clearly conceptualized. We are expressing feelings in their continuity with the past. The images of the dream are not static. They are metaphors in motion. They tell a story which, in a very creative way, speaks to where we are subjectively at a given moment in our lives. That is all they do. They are not there to argue with us, tell us what to do, make us feel good or bad about ourselves. It is the task of our waking ego to free up the feelings embedded in the imagery and thus spark across the metaphorical gap between image and reality. Feelings released in this way are authentic and authentic feelings are the connective tissue supporting the fabric of our existence. They deepen our bonds to each other. Awake we often play games with feelings. We brush them aside, suppress them or express them in ways that are inappropriate to the situation. They then become manifest in what I refer to as inauthentic feelings. They maintain distance rather than furthering closeness (e.g. neurotic guilt in contrast to genuine remorse).

2 *Dreaming consciousness and survival.* What dreaming consciousness as a system would then have in common with all other systems is that it serves the survival needs of the organism. Dreaming then is just as essential to our psychological life as the enzymes secreted by the gastro-intestinal system are to digestion. We don't accord it that degree of importance, but that is our problem. Earlier societies were more respectful of the dream. Even in the current era, where we have turned our attention to fine tuning our knowledge of the anatomy and physiology of dreaming, there has not been a commensurate advance in the depth of our understanding of the dream. It is as if in the discovery of the insulin-secreting function of the pancreas all our attention was focused on the Langerhan cells where the insulin was formed and very little to the functional importance of the insulin itself to the organism. The secretions of our bodily organs work their magic in their own way and can be explored chemically. The magic of the dream is the production of symbolic imagery which can be explored by uncovering their emotional content. The point is that, as in the case

with any other system, our dreams operate in the service of the survival of the individual which in turn is the precondition for the survival of the species.

3. *The dreamer needs help.* Some dreams are transparent. More often a dreamer needs help. The dream does not yield its secret easily. Wherever there have been dreamers there have always been others around who could be of help. The reason is twofold. The dream speaks to us in an imagistic language that differs in its logic and content from waking discourse. It is an emotional logic not constrained by time, space and causality. Furthermore, it often carries an emotional valence that has not been fully acknowledged in the waking state. We have transformed that primitive imaging capacity into highly creative symbolic forms that address specifically subterranean emotional currents at play. Our difficulty thus arises in two ways. The language is different from waking discourse and the content has often been held at arm's length when we are awake.

   The Milieu: A certain atmosphere has to prevail in a dream group if it is to serve its purpose. The dreamer seeking to discover what the dream has to say is like someone diving off a cliff into water the depth of which he does not know nor does he know what he is apt to find. The group is there to ensure his safety (the Safety Factor) and provide him with the instruments he needs to locate whatever it is that is lurking in the dark (the Discovery Factor). The first task is to generate a level of trust that makes it possible for the dreamer to risk taking the jump. The second is for the group to enter into a unique dialogue with the dreamer by posing questions to the dreamer to be used only as instruments by means of which the dreamer can light up the murkiness of his underwater search. The milieu best suited to accomplish this is one that is flat, non-hierarchical and totally nonviolent. If there is a leader, she is there to maintain the integrity of the process. In all other respects, she functions as a member of the group and has the same option as the others to share a dream or not. The sharing of a dream is a voluntary act. No one person is ever under any pressure to share a dream; whatever pressure there is [is] shared equally by all. The leader has no hidden agenda. The rationale for each stage of the process is known to all.

Certain principles guide the work of the group.

First Principle

Respect for the Privacy of the Dreamer The dream is the most personal communication of which we are capable. It is a very private affair and this element of privacy is respected at all times. Each stage of the process I use is designed to be non-intrusive. The dreamer controls the process throughout the session and works at whatever level of self-disclosure she feels comfortable with in the group. There is no pressure to go beyond that point. What the helping agency has to keep in mind is that when dreams are worked on outside of the consulting room, the dreamer's ability to reach into herself with the required degree of honesty is contingent on how safe she is made to feel. The only way of achieving that goal is for the dreamer to remain the guardian of her unconscious through her control of the level of self-disclosure.

Second Principle

Respect for the Authority of the Dreamer Over His or Her Dream Dream images arise out of the unique life experiences of the dreamer. The fit between image and meaning is something that the dreamer alone can validate. It is only the dreamer who can judge the effectiveness of the help offered. She alone has that resonant gut feeling when a truth strikes home. There is a distinct difference between intellectually accepting something that comes from the group and the spontaneous and richly generative response to a true fit.

Third Principle

Respect for the Uniqueness of the Individual Everyone's life experience is unique. Any symbolic image can be used in a highly idiosyncratic way. No a priori categorical meanings are assumed. One has to have a certain humility to do dream work and realize that there is more to learn from the dreamer than we have to offer to the dreamer. The reason is simple. Nothing in our prior learning and experience is a substitute for the work that has to be done to discover how these particular dream images emerged out of the idiosyncratic life experience of the dreamer and why they came together to shape the dream on that particular night. The work we do together uncovers the answer.

The Craft of the Dream Worker

To my knowledge, craft is not a term generally thought of in connection with dream work. To orient the reader to the sense in which I use the word, let me draw an analogy to the craft of the actor. In a way, the actor is faced with the same problem the dreamer is. Both have to bypass their waking persona to get to where they want to be. The actor's goal is to identify as closely as possible with the character she is portraying. The dreamer has to do the same with the dream characters that appear in her dream. Both need help in doing this. To some extent they can provide that help. The actor does it by the research she engages in to learn as much as possible about the life of the character, her life, her habits, her idiosyncrasies, her appearance, her vulnerability. The dreamer does it by the associations and memories she can consciously relate to the imagery. Both need more help than they alone can come up with. The actor needs the help of the many others who create the setting in which the action is to take place, and above all of the co-actor. The dreamer needs the help of the co-dreamers in the group to help her find the way back to the dream. Actors speak of "being in the moment," when with the help of the co-actor the character comes fully to life and speaks in her own true voice. For the dreamer this is known as the "aha!" response. For both actor and dreamer, it is a moment of truth. For the actor the essence of her craft is to learn how to listen and interact in a way that makes that moment happen. The art of listening and the art of interacting are also the two essential skills involved in dream work.

I will discuss in greater detail the various aspects of the dream-worker's craft as they come into play in the various stages of the process. For the moment I would like to focus on the two essential skills. Both can be conceptualized and taught but like all skills, they require practice.

Listening: Listening is a complex skill which requires not only listening to everything a dreamer says but also listening to the way it is said, listening to the accompanying feelings, listening to what is not said and, above all, listening without an a priori bias as to what is or is not important. What might seem at first like an incidental or trivial comment could assume importance as more information emerges. The dream comes out of the unique life history of the dreamer. The more one is in tune with that, rather than on foregone conclusions as to the dream's meaning, the more likely it is that the dreamer will be helped. For the neophyte this means more listening and less temptation to yield to the impulse to superimpose a ready at-hand interpretation.

Interacting: This involves the art of putting questions to the dreamer that are not invasive. By that I mean that they are not an attempt to lead the dreamer in a particular direction. A leading question has the effect of taking over control of the process and raising the anxiety level of the dreamer. Questioning should never go beyond the limits set by the dreamer. The more open-ended and simple the question is, the more effective it is in eliciting relevant information. An open-ended question points to an area to investigate and leaves the dreamer free to investigate it or not.

The Process

A more complete account of the stages and their rationale is given in the author's book (Ullman,1996).

Stage IA: The Sharing of a Dream

The process begins with someone volunteering to share a dream. Only the manifest content is shared. No associations or ideas about meaning are given at this point. Occasionally the simple act of telling the dream aloud to the group results in a sudden insight. The act of volunteering implies some readiness to lower one's defensive structure and this, in turn, results in seeing more.

Stage IB

This is the opportunity to clarify anything about the dream that was not clear and also to question the dreamer along the following lines if the information was not explicit in the dreamer's account: Are any of the characters in the dream real persons in your waking life? If so, tell briefly what the connection is (friend, relative, etc.). Are there any feelings that you were aware of in the dream? Any colors? Were you your present age? Note that no questions seeking out the dreamer's associations are asked at this point. The reason will become clear in connection with the next stage.

Stages II A & B: The Projections of the Group This is an exercise or game where the group makes the dream its own and attempts to do two things with it. Group members share with each other the feelings they associate to the imagery of the dream (II A) and then go on to explore the metaphorical possibilities of each image (II B). It is understood that whatever is said is their own projection into the dream. At this point they are neither looking at nor talking to the dreamer. The dreamer listens without actively participating and is free to accept or reject anything coming from the group. The point of the exercise is to help the dreamer begin to move closer into the dream under circumstances where it feels safe to do so.

This opening strategy which, on the face of it, seems quite random, is, in fact, very powerful. Aside from the fact that the group may come up with a feeling or give a meaning to an image that feels right on target for the dreamer, there are a number of other features that operate more subtly to further the dreamer's grasp of the dream. After going public with the dream there is the reassurance that others are taking the dream seriously, are applying it to their own lives and coming up with meaningful connections to it out of their own experience. By sharing their projections with the dreamer they are sharing a bit of their psyche with the dream just as the dreamer shared a bit of her psyche with the group.

Craft: The task of the group members now is to mobilize their own imagination to create a pool of feelings and meanings in the hope some of them would be helpful to the dreamer. We all swim around in the same social sea so that feelings or metaphors from the group might strike home for the dreamer. If they do, they have the effect of priming the pump. When they don't fit they may still bring the dreamer closer to a true fit by defining what the image is not. The art here is to be free enough to bring a wide range of feelings and metaphorical possibilities to the imagery. The dreamer's associations are, of course, the ultimate foundation for the understanding of the dream. Had the dreamer offered associations in Stage I they might have tracked and limited the spontaneously empathic and intuitive responses of the group.

At the end of this exercise the dreamer is invited to respond.

Stage IIIA: The Dreamer's Response The dreamer is free to shape the response in any way she chooses. This is the dreamer's opportunity to offer associations and ideas about the dream's meaning as well as the impact of the group's work. There is the freedom to go to whatever level of sharing feels comfortable, with the assurance that no one will exert any pressure to go beyond that level.

In this initial strategy the group's work will occasionally have helped the dreamer clarify the dream to the point where she feels satisfied and decides to stop. Further work, however, is generally necessary providing the dreamer wishes to go on.

The various strategies that follow are all designed to help the dreamer get in touch with the data that shaped the dream. These strategies are not automatically invoked but unfold at the behest of the dreamer.

Stage IIIB(1): The Search for Context This involves a dialogue between the dreamer and the group designed to clarify the source of the recent emotional residues that triggered the dream. It consists of direct questions designed to help the dreamer explore the emotional context of her life during the period immediately preceding the dream.

The dreamer is instructed to consider these questions as instruments to use in exploring her psyche. They are not questions that demand an answer. The dreamer has the freedom to respond or not. If work with the question is productive, it is the dreamer's decision to decide how much to share with the group. As the dreamer begins to trust the process, she soon learns that the more that is shared with the group the more help the group can be.

Craft: There is an art to helping a dreamer reconstruct what is in effect a diary of her emotional past. It involves a structured approach to the questions put to the dreamer and careful listening to the response. The goal is to elicit the thoughts, feelings and concerns that surfaced just prior to falling asleep as, for example: Can you recall what thoughts or feelings you had on falling asleep? Can you recall what feelings the day left you with? Did anything else happen in the recent period before the dream that left you with any particular tensions or feelings? This period may extend from a few days before the dream to one or two weeks. What we are looking for at this time are clues to whatever felt reaction may have triggered the dream.

Dreams don't come out of facts. They come out of feelings. Questions have to go beyond the facts the dreamer has disclosed in an effort to get at the feelings involved. The dreamer, for example, may have mentioned the fact that her mother called the night of the dream. The next question should be: Is there anything you can say about the feelings that call left you with?

This involves the knack of listening to any hint of where further feelings might be and helping the dreamer explore them by simple open-ended questions, e.g.: Is there anything more you can say about those feelings?

Listening carefully to any hint of where the feelings are and, when appropriate, asking follow-up questions, are skills that have to be mastered.

Stage III B(2): Playback of the Dream When the exploration of the context is over, and should the dreamer wish to go further, the next effort at eliciting data is to read the dream back to the dreamer, one scene at a time, while inviting the dreamer to say anything more about the imagery in each scene. The dreamer now has at her disposal the data that came up spontaneously in the initial response plus any additional data elicited about significant recent events and feelings. Having more data on hand, and given the opportunity to play back the imagery against all that has come out so far, the dreamer is often able to add further associations. There is another more subtle factor that tends to increase the yield. When someone other than the dreamer reads back a scene, it evokes a different feeling in the dreamer than when the dreamer deals with it privately. What may have been seen as a somewhat ephemeral creation comes back as a more real, more palpable, and now a more public creation. More of the dreamer's psyche is stimulated by experiencing it in this objectified way.

Craft: There is an art to reading a dream back to the dreamer. The dreamer may or may not have additional associations on hearing a scene read back. This is where listening and putting questions to the dreamer again come in. Has every image in that scene been clarified in its meaning for the dreamer? If not, there are several ways of helping a dreamer go further with it. One is to suggest looking at the image abstractly rather than literally and see how many metaphorical ideas may occur to her. Another is to call to her attention everything she may have said about the image previously. This gives her more to work with in her search for meaning. Finally, help her explore the image in its possible connection to what immediately preceded it and what immediately followed it.

Stage III B(3): Orchestrating Projections When the playback does not bring the dreamer to the point of closure, there is a final strategy which the dreamer may invoke, namely, an invitation to the group to offer what I refer to as an integrating or orchestrating projection. The preceding two strategies had as their goal eliciting the information needed to bridge the gap between dream image and waking reality. As more information comes to light, there is more of a chance that connections will occur to the dreamer. There are situations, however, where the information has surfaced but has not come together in a way that is sufficiently helpful to the dreamer. The final group strategy addresses this. If anyone in the group now sees a connection between what the dreamer has said and its metaphorical connection to one or more images in the dream or to the whole dream itself that the dreamer has not seen, it can now be offered to the dreamer as an orchestrating or integrating projection, orchestrating because the group member tries to bring the diverse elements together and a projection because it is the group member who makes the selection and fits it to the imagery. It may just be her projection or it may be validated by the dreamer, in which case it can be very helpful.

Craft: Based on careful listening to all that the dreamer has shared, can the group members guess what question is being unconsciously addressed by the dreamer's psyche and how the imagery and the story being told depict the answer to the question? The skill to be mastered is how to come to an orchestration that is meaningful to the dreamer based only on what the dreamer has openly shared. In practice this is not as easy as it may sound. There is often the tendency to enhance the orchestration by gratuitously adding information from one's own life or falling back on theoretical preconceptions. There is also the tendency to reframe a response to the dream so as to offer reassurance to the dreamer. The only true reassurance is the degree of contact the dreamer is helped to make with her dream. When a dreamer has fully engaged in the process, she has, in my experience, provided all the building blocks necessary for the group to be able to help her reassemble them into a meaningful fit.

Stage IV: Additional Comments by the Dreamer There follows a final stage to the process, one that no longer involves the group. After a dreamer has presented a dream, and sometime before the next meeting, the dreamer is encouraged to take a second look at the dream. Being alone and not under group pressure a dreamer may sometimes see connections that were not apparent during the group session. At the next meeting the dreamer is invited to share any additional thoughts.

Craft: There are times when, at the end of the session, there is the general feeling that while all of the material is out in the open, our efforts at putting it together fall short of satisfactory closure. Anyone in the group who is so inclined can review the material and the next time the group meets offer the dreamer what I refer to as a delayed orchestration. To do this effectively often requires note-taking. This is optional. The only note-taking I insist on is to have the dream down on paper in the dreamer's own words so that it can be read back during the Playback. I use my notes to rearrange all that a dreamer has said in [its] relation to the succession of images. Matching associations and images in this fashion often suggests new insights.

A Session

It is not easy to capture all that goes on in a dream group in the course of an hour and a half devoted to a single dream. I try to write down as much as I can of what the dreamer says and to a much lesser extent some of what else is occurring. Exchanges between members of the group and the dreamer are often too rapid to get down.

Adam is a fifty year old teacher. He had been in the group about three months at the time of the dream. He had many years of analysis before joining the group. Adam had shared a number of dreams earlier. His tight rein on his feelings made him avoid closeness with others. Aside from his love of and success with teaching, he seemed to glide through life as the "invisible man."

Adam's dream on awakening on a Wednesday morning was presented the following Saturday, August 14, 1999.

> In the dream I am about fourteen years old. I am in my parents' house. There is a knock at the front door and a current member of my department is at the door. He is delivering a paper that he typed for me. I did the writing of the paper. He told me I had forgotten to put my name on the paper. At that point, my father emerges and tells me I am not allowed to have visitors. I become angry and tell him he is unfair
>
> The person from my department is a real person. My father is dead.
>
> (Feelings in the dream?) I felt constantly controlled and hemmed in by the atmosphere around me. I felt silly I had forgotten to put my name on it. I was pleased he had brought it to my attention. It was important that my name be attached to it. My father was being intrusive again and butting in.

The Group's Projections Because the dream was short, the group members, as they made the dream their own, were invited to share their feelings as well as their ideas about the imagery.

> "Part of me was not recognized and wants recognition."
>
> "I feel controlled by my parents. They interfere with my need to express myself."
>
> "It's frightening to be known and connected to the paper although it's something I really want."

"I do this to myself as well—not letting myself be known."
"Fourteen was when I was just beginning to develop myself."
"I feel torn between the good and the bad father."
"Another man did something with my work. Can there be others who can be of help?"
"There is a sense of who I am in the paper."
"I'm exploring the relationship between creativity and egoism in contrast to being egotistical. My father was egotistical."
"It has something to do with what is a part of me."
"It's difficult for me to discover my talent. I need consensual validation with regard to my ability."
"There has to be a significant person to admire who and what we are. There is that person in the dream. My father took that away from me."
"I'm full of impressive ideas but not strong enough to follow through. My father exacerbates that by not validating me."
"The dream group is represented by the visitor. A metaphorical door was opened when he invited me to write my name."
"Both the father and the man are me. My father is the angry part of me."

The dream was returned to Adam.

Adam's Response:

"All the projections were amazingly accurate. They reached issues I am struggling with. Many memories came back. I have a friend I gave advice to. He also gave me some. It had to do with not signing the paper. I identified with him in his not being able to recognize his own ability. My father was a psychopath. I was afraid of him. I hated him and was always fearful of his violence. He had no control over his hands. He degraded any effort of mine to express myself or succeed. He was in violent competition with both my brother and myself. I really tried to be a good father to most of the younger people I meet. I have a better relation with other young people than I do with my daughter. She is not able to maintain a relationship."
"Part of me is absolutely amazed at myself. I am extremely self-destructive. I live my life as if I'm driving a truck full of dynamite. The only way to avoid danger is by keeping the hostility to myself."

Adam invited the dialogue.

Context:

(Can you recall any thoughts or feelings on falling asleep Tuesday evening?) "I was angry at my wife and blaming her."
(Anything more about Tuesday evening?) "I kept blaming my wife for my not being able to work. When we are together she wants my attention. She is

needy about spending time together. Yet I am also dependent on having someone around."

(Can you recall anything more around the time of the dream?) "At the beginning of the week I judged the summer a creative failure. I didn't develop any of the projects I had in mind. I did give a talk on TV and that made me feel better. I watched it later on TV and felt as if I were waiting for myself to make a mistake. When I finished watching it, even though I got a feeling from others that it was a success, I felt a sense of being a fraud and felt it was of no value. I had seen the tape Monday."

(Anything more at the time you were watching yourself on TV and your anger at your feeling of self-importance?) "I wanted to run out of the room even though I was getting the attention I thought I wanted."

(Anything more?) "It shows how desperate I am for validation. I did get a positive reaction from others but it's something I can't accept."

(Anything more?) "It went well and I got good reactions. What I valued was a remark from one of the undergraduates there to the effect it was the only paper he understood."

(Any other feelings on watching the tape on Monday?) "I had two kinds of feelings. I wanted to destroy my image as I watched, saying to myself you're no damn good. The subject matter was an analysis of Huckleberry Finn. I felt self-important which made me even more angry at myself."

(Anything else happen recently?) "A friend of mine died and left me to handle his estate. I felt guilty about getting anything from someone else's death. It kept me from being able to work."

The Playback: At Adam's invitation the dream was read aloud to him. Because it was a short dream it was read back in its entirety.

"I am getting very strong feelings as it was read back about the struggle between feeling powerless and feeling powerful. The feeling I had as a child was that I have to negate myself in order to be loved by myself. My father was an egomaniac. I don't want to be like him."

(Being fourteen in the dream?) "My feeling as a child was that I would never be able to get away from my parents' house. When I was that age my father ran away and joined the army. I never felt much older than fourteen."

(The current member of your department?) "I respect his work. He works well with students but he also bullies them. I used to do that but stopped. We work with ghetto kids. He physically threatened them. I thought that was silly. He wasn't capable of delivering on those threats. He is very productive. He does better than me with kids on standardized tests."

(You felt the need to bully?) "A part of me identified with the way my father bullied. When I worked at a camp coaching baseball, I became my father and I carried that over to my teaching. It wasn't fun. I stopped trying to scare people."

(About your father in the dream?) "I accepted the fact that he was better at everything than I was. He tore down everything I did and I accepted it."

(The reference to no visitors?) "I feel I can't trust anyone or let anyone know what I was feeling. It was a way of staying out of trouble with him. A lot of my guilt is connected to wanting him dead because of the hatred I felt."

(Anything more about your father in the dream?) "He is saying any attempt to develop my work is not acceptable. The only way to keep him happy is to remain anonymous. That's what I've done. I deny myself help for myself as a way of fighting my father's battle for him. I keep myself down."

Adam invited orchestrating comments:

Orchestrating Projections:

Kate: "You yearn for your father to be different, but you identify with his view of you. You were neither creative nor worthy. In other words, you were no damn good. It was intolerable for you to watch your successful performance on TV. It's as if you were doing something bad. The fact that you were successfully communicating to and connecting to others was unbearable to you. It was as if you were engaged in something bad and forbidden. You weren't allowed to have others in your life. He needed you all to himself as an outlet for his sadism."

Nora: "Your guilt is connected to wanting him dead. Part of you identifies with your father. Part of you does not. When you do identify with your father your creativity is killed. You are sacrificing your life in order to survive. It's a no-win situation."

Kate: "There is a destruction of your healthy expansiveness by leaving your name off the paper. You become your father to yourself."

Cele: "It is as if being effectively creative is experienced by you as letting some of your narcissism sneak out and be seen. It forces you to live through the accomplishments of others."

Monte: "The two significant residues were the emergence of the bully-father in you because your wife desired more time with you, and your response to the TV show where you were not open to something that might have enhanced your self-esteem. It was as if your father had taken possession of you, preventing you from daring to take possession of yourself. In a sense, he prevented you from taking full possession of yourself from the age of fourteen on. Every event from that time on was filtered through the template of that imprisoning grip of your father's possession."

Adam's Response:

"What you have said is amazing! I could not take issue with any of it. What Cele said about living through the accomplishment of other people is true. The idea of possession is accurate. I use the world to defeat myself and as a way of staying in contact with a terrible father. The sad part is that creativity is pleasurable and I don't allow it. I identify with my father in my masculinity. He had a very masculine image. Part of me still glories in that identification. That quality protects me. If I change, I have a fear I will lose my masculinity. It isn't masculinity. He was just sadistic. I protect my need to run away from other people. I felt you all knew my father in the sense that Cele did. He was omnipotent, god-like and sadistic. The problem is to move from explanation to transformation."

What follows is an amplification of my original orchestration written up in December 2000 in preparation for this paper. Adam was invited to offer a final comment.

Monte: "Two events preceding the dream precipitate the dream's depiction of the awesome internal struggle going on between your attempt to salvage any residue of self-esteem and the risk of a level of self-exposure that could threaten your very existence. The request of your wife to spend more time together evoked an attack mode (your identification with your father whom you hated and now hate in yourself) in lieu of a fairer appraisal of what was going on between your wife and yourself at the time. The other residue was your response to the TV program. You say you need consensual validation to value yourself. That is true to some extent for all of us. In your case, it really doesn't foster your self-esteem. In fact, it is counter-productive. Any genuine self-esteem would lead to a greater freedom of self-exposure and that would challenge your ability to remain invisible. It is as if you feel safer letting the self-esteem engendered in you by another remain in the other until such time as you will be in a position to reclaim it. It's as if you are a man driven to deposit all of the money you earn in a bank and then being afraid to withdraw any of it for your own immediate use."

Adam: "The dream reflects the cornerstone of my problem. I don't want to be known, even for the positive things. However, that is not the entire story. I crave recognition. It is not adult approval that I want; I want the love children should get from their parents, unconditional love.

"On some level I recognize that I can not get this form of love from intellectual work and therefore I have given up on it. That is why in the dream I do not sign my name. This is why I do not finish work I start. Part of me fears that I am seeking a regressed state. The work should get me love but that reduces me to a child's place.

"There is also the rage I feel at the angry father in the dream. I want to destroy him and the only way to do that is to destroy myself by destroying my work. Hence I do not identify with my work or myself."

Application to Therapy

There are a number of ways this group approach to dream work finds useful application to clinical practice. Perhaps the most important result is the demystification of dream work and the feeling of greater security in pursuing it. The process offers the therapist a more structured approach to the task. Taught to rely on the power of free association, the therapist often fails to realize that an active inquiry is necessary to evoke the relevant data. Before the dream is even told, for example, there should be clarity about when the dream occurred. This can be of help in alerting the therapist to possible contexts that may have given rise to the dream. Did the dream occur the night after the last session? The night preceding the present session? In therapy one begins, of course, with the patient's spontaneous associations and encourages the full play of associations to all the images. This is a necessary beginning but not sufficient by itself. Direct questioning is needed to explore more fully the recent emotional context related to the occurrence of the dream at a particular time in the patient's life. What can then also prove useful is to further follow the structure of the dialogue as described in the process to the extent it seems necessary. The patient is invited to take a second look at the dream as the therapist reads it back, scene by scene, with emphasis on the specific images that still remain obscure. The patient now has her spontaneous associations to work with as well as whatever additional light that has been shed on the recent context. The final stage of the process, the orchestration, is quite analogous to what Walter Bonime [1982] refers to as an "interpretive hypothesis," framing it as something to be considered and verified or not by the patient.

Summary

The process described in this paper evolved as a way of teaching safe and effective dream work to those who wished to use dreams in their clinical work and for those who are simply interested in their own dream life. The basic concepts can be taught and the skills can be learned by anyone. The process unfolds in stages, each of which is geared to maintaining both the safety of the dreamer while at the same time providing the help the dreamer needs to hear what the dream is saying. The inverse relationship between trust and defensiveness makes this possible.

SELF-STUDY QUIZ CHAPTER 13 (PREPARED BY EVELYN M. DUESBURY)

1. Ullman describes his group process as bidirectional. What two directions is Ullman referring to here?
2. Ullman presents four axioms about dreams. List those axioms. ("Axioms are propositions that appear to be self-evident.")
3. Of the axioms that Ullman presents, list the one that seems most remarkable to you.

4. Have you found evidence of the axiom that you listed in Question 3 during your work with your own dreams? If yes, briefly explain your dream and the evidence you found.
5. Ullman's group approach works on the premise of sharing dreams. Which members of the group are given the option to share their dreams with the group?
   a. All members, including the leader.
   b. All members, except the leader.

14

Cartwright's RISC Mode

ROSALIND CARTWRIGHT AND LYNNE LAMBERG

INTRODUCTION

Rosalind Cartwright is a professor in the Department of Behavioral Sciences at Rush University Medical Center in Chicago, where she opened the first Sleep Disorder Service in the Midwest in 1978. She has been conducting studies of dreaming for over 45 years and has published four books: *Night Life* (1977), *A Primer on Sleep and Dreams* (1978), *The Twenty-four Hour Mind* (2010), and with Lynne Lamberg, *Crisis Dreaming* (1992/2000). Cartwright was given the Distinguished Scientist award by the Sleep Research Society in 2004. (Cartwright's literature and research support of elements contained in the Personalized Method for Interpreting Dreams [PMID] model are referenced in other chapters of the current book.) Lynne Lamberg is an award winning medical journalist who specializes in mental health. She is the author or coauthor of six books, including *The Body Clock Guide to Better Health* (2001) with Smolensky. Except for this introduction, the summary, and the self-study quiz, the material in this chapter is taken from *Crisis Dreaming.*[*]

RISC THERAPY

The premise of RISC [recognize, investigate, stop, change] dream therapy is straightforward: If bad dream scripts make you awaken discouraged and downhearted, rewriting the scripts to improve the endings should lead to better moods.

RISC Dream therapy has just four steps that you can learn on your own:

[*] Cartwright and Lamberg's offered material is from *Crisis Dreaming, Using Your Dreams to Solve Your Problems* (1992/2000); reprinted by permission. The first segment is from pages 105–113.

- Recognize when you are having a bad dream, the kind that leaves you feeling helpless, guilty, or upset the next morning. You need to become aware while you are dreaming that the dream is not going well.
- Identify what it is about the dream that makes you feel badly. Locate the dimensions within your dreams that portray you in a negative light, as, for example, weak rather than strong, inept rather than capable, or out-of-control rather than in-control.
- Stop any bad dream. You do not have to let it continue. You are in charge. Most people are surprised to find that telling themselves to recognize when a bad dream is in progress often is all it takes to empower them to stop such dreams when they occur.
- Change negative dream dimensions into their opposite, positive sides. At first, you may need to wake up and devise a new conclusion before returning to sleep. With practice, you will be able to instruct yourself to change the action while remaining asleep.

The first letter of each step forms the acronym RISC to help you remember that the idea is to "risk" stepping in to change the endings of your dreams and to work toward a more positive self-image.

Troubled dreamers seeking help usually can master these four steps in just eight weeks, and often sooner. Working with a therapist may speed up the process or help you focus on aspects of your dreams you might not otherwise see, but it's reasonable to try to initiate dream repair on your own and see how far you can go.

The RISC treatment, like other techniques of psychotherapy, works both by what it does and how it does it. In most psychotherapy treatments, therapist and patient focus on changing waking attitudes and behavior. The therapist helps the patient generate the "right stuff" to talk about and work on. In the RISC program, we also seek to change waking attitudes and behavior, but we do it by spotlighting the negative aspects of the underlying identity displayed in each patient's dreams. I meet with my patients for hour-long sessions at weekly intervals, usually for eight weeks or longer.

In RISC therapy, patients do not have to search for topics to discuss. Right from the first session, the dream transcripts from their previous night in the sleep laboratory are on the table to give a compelling account of what is on their minds at night. We work as a team on the problems these dreams reveal. As therapy proceeds, I ask patients to bring in their home dream diaries so that we can work on dreams they currently are having.

Patients are not passive recipients of treatment. They serve as co-investigators to discover how their dreams relate to both their present crises and their earlier life experiences. During our sessions, they then practice creating healthier and happier conclusions for troubling dreams. "Make up a better ending," I urge them.

The way they define "better" sometimes proves surprising. One meek young man often had a nightmare in which a bus ran him down. When he changed this dream, he gave himself a machine gun so that he could attack the bus and shoot its driver. He felt much better afterward and never had the dream again. Why not? In his dream, he could retaliate aggressively against the bullies who had picked on him when he was a youngster and destroy them. His dream success rebuilt some pride he sorely needed.

The differences between RISC treatment and other types of psychotherapy become even clearer in the second through the eighth sessions, when patients bring their home dreams to the therapy hour for us to study together. Only they know what they have dreamed at home. They decide what to share with me. While they can practice the most important part of this work in my office, changing the ending of a dream, they must accomplish the task on their own at home.

Often people discover through their dreams that their present crises have reawakened distressing feelings from events earlier in life. At such times, they need therapists who are skilled enough to recognize the emotion-packed inner pictures of a damaged self and will stand by to monitor how safe it is for their patients to look at them. Therapists also must be able to help patients find images of strength to build on. In general, however, patients take a more active role in dream therapy than in most traditional forms of psychotherapy.

Altering the outcome of a dream is a tall order, but our studies show it's an achievable goal. There's an active give-and-take between the conscious and the sleeping mind. Even if you don't change a particular dream while asleep, your waking exploration of the depressive elements of your dreams, and your awareness of what you can and should change, may have a payoff. People who do their homework, who devise several possible solutions to familiar dream dilemmas, report that they often manage to incorporate some of these new waking attitudes into their dreams.

Such success reverberates with waking life. Becoming more active in dreams helps people to become more positive about the future. A successful night of dreaming produces immediate benefits for mood in the morning. Stopping a bad dream and changing it lifts the spirits. People gain a sense of empowerment from knowing they are not at the mercy of their bad dreams. Then, as they begin to change the image of a rejected, helpless self to one that is more in control, waking behavior begins to improve. They start to try out the new roles, the underdeveloped, better aspects of themselves that they first practice in dreams.

Some people have both scant memory for their dreams and scant insight into their waking feelings as well. They have a breakdown in communication between their outer lives and their inner lives. They may go through the motions of living but feel slight satisfaction with their lives. Often they have lost track of themselves in trying to please other people. Sometimes these people seek psychotherapy, but their dissatisfactions are so vague they have trouble articulating their discontent. They can't put their finger on what they want nor can they say how they feel. They lack a vocabulary for talking about themselves. For such people, dreamwork can offer rapid and remarkable rewards.

More than a decade ago, I undertook a project to help a university counseling service that had a problem: Nearly half of the students seeking help there and deemed in need of long-term individual psychotherapy failed to return or dropped out of therapy after the first few sessions. Those most likely to drop out proved to be those with difficulty expressing why they had come. All had trouble sharing their thoughts and feelings.

I wondered if potential dropouts who had the opportunity to become familiar with their inner life through their dreams—and who had practice discussing their dreams would remain in treatment longer and make better use of it. With the assistance of the counseling service's social worker, I selected 48 students considered poor risks for staying in treatment.

I offered them the opportunity to participate in a program designed to help people utilize the opportunity for psychotherapy more fully. Thirty-two of the students spent eight nights in our sleep laboratory. The other 16 went directly into treatment. My technician awakened half of those who slept in the laboratory only during REM [rapid eye movement] sleep episodes. She awakened the others only in NREM [non-REM] sleep. She asked both groups to tell what was going through their minds at that moment. Every morning, I asked those who had spent the night in the laboratory to recall whatever they could of the dreams they had told during the night. I offered no interpretations but prompted those who forgot any dreams to remember them. I asked them two questions: "Do you see any way these dreams relate to each other?" and "Do you see any way they relate to your life?"

The aim was to get these students to recognize that what was going on within was understandable and related to their problems in daily living. They did remarkably well. Those awakened during REM sleep who reported dreams more than half of the time proved most likely to remain in treatment through the first 10 sessions and to dig in and work hard at making needed changes in their lives. Even those awakened in NREM sleep who reported only a few dreams seemed to benefit from the morning-after conversations about their night thoughts. The majority of those who did not come to the laboratory first but entered treatment directly dropped out of therapy much sooner, without making progress.

The dream recallers had one complaint: Because we did not want their therapists to know which group they were in to avoid any bias in rating their treatment progress, we kept the records of their nighttime reports. However, the students wanted to discuss their dreams. When they tried to bring the subject up, the therapists discouraged them, saying, "Dreams are not my bag," and turned the hour toward dealing with reality problems. Even without a therapist's help, access to their dreams helped them to identify their emotional issues and increased their comfort in discussing their disturbing feelings.

Because sending patients regularly to a sleep laboratory is not practical, we followed this study with a small pilot study using a simpler approach. We invited eight poor-risk students to join an hour-long daily dream-modeling workshop. Instead of sleeping in the laboratory, these students first viewed a different 10-minute videotape each day for eight days. Each tape showed a morning dream discussion session with a student who had been in the REM interruption group. We encouraged the students to first look for meanings the dreamer had missed and then, for the remainder of the hour, to work in a similar fashion on one of their own dreams. This method of learning from watching others proved promising. Once their own treatment began, five of the eight stuck with it for 10 or more sessions, almost as high a proportion as those we had awakened in the laboratory during REM sleep.

Researchers in Finland adapted our study to treat a different problem in psychotherapy—getting through a dry period. They found that sending a group of patients, whose progress in treatment had been stalled, to the sleep laboratory to have their dreams collected revitalized the therapeutic process. Gaining access to their dreams made the patients more open to exploring their emotional lives.

SELF-HELP: USING RISC TO CHANGE YOUR DREAMS

Mastering the RISC method takes motivation and practice, but it is not difficult to do. These are the steps:

- With your dream diary and your day journal in hand, start by reviewing the dreams that trouble you the most and try to figure out why. As you learn to identify negative self-talk, you will become more proficient at doing so.
- Look at the message each dream displays and focus on its dimensions. Each dimension will have numerous images that illustrate its opposite pole. Initially, you may see more negative dimensions in your dreams, but as you explore in your waking life the positive side of the dimensions you habitually use, you will program yourself to incorporate more self-confident images into your dreams at night.
- When you locate a problem dream, imagine different endings. You're the scriptwriter. How else could the dream have turned out? Consider several endings. Which do you prefer?
- Think of times when you've been in a similar situation that turned out well. If you can't find many positive images in your memory bank to draw on, you will need to create new images for yourself. If you're stuck in the past, for example, mentally rewrite your dream scenarios so you are an adult, not a helpless child. If you find yourself a victim in your dreams, practice standing up for yourself in fantasy, where you can do it safely. Ponder the new possibilities at bedtime.
- Tell yourself, "Next time I dream, I want to recognize that I'm dreaming." Even more importantly, tell yourself, "Next time I have a bad dream, I want to recognize it, stop it, and change it." You always can stop a dream just by opening your eyes.

Here is an example of the RISC method in action.

Judith was a single woman in her forties who had lost her job as a traveling sales representative when her company made sweeping recessionary cutbacks. After searching unsuccessfully for months for a new job, mainly by responding to newspaper ads and sending out dozens of resumes, she was feeling depressed about the lack of opportunities and was running out of money. The longer Judith was out of work, the more she began to feel that something must be terribly wrong with her, that she was unemployable. She felt disgraced, and she was embarrassed to see her former workplace friends; she stopped calling them, and they stopped calling her.

Judith frequently dreamed that her car had broken down and that she was in a remote spot, far from help. She would awaken feeling beaten down before her day even started. After learning the RISC method, she reported this dream:

> My car was stalled at a ferry debarkation point. It was rapidly getting dark. The car was completely dead and I was standing at a distance from it, full of despair, looking at the rough waves and menacing skies, desperately wanting to go home, needing my car to do so, feeling utterly powerless and deflated.

"I woke up feeling a sense of emptiness and failure, let down, very disappointed in myself," she said. "I was thinking, 'Here comes another bad day.' But then I thought about the dimensions I kept repeating in my broken-down car dreams: dead versus alive, helplessness versus taking charge, stuck versus moving forward. I kept thinking, 'What can I do to help myself?'

"The next thing I knew," she reported, "I was back in the same dream":

> It was the next morning. My car now was in a garage. A mechanic approached me and said, "Take your car. It's fixed and we threw in a full tank of gas, free." This meant to me that the garage service was apologetic about having taken a full overnight to fix my car. I needed my car badly; it was my vehicle to getting on with my life. I was surprised and grateful.

This dream is a good example of the benefits of dream therapy. It showed Judith's gratitude for the "overnight help" she received. In the dream she turned night into day and her broken-down car into a functional one. Her dream dimensions came up on their positive side. She also saw that she didn't need to struggle entirely on her own. She recognized it was no disgrace to ask others for help, especially when they, like the man in her dream, had knowledge she lacked.

After this dream, Judith realized it was necessary to swallow her pride. Although she cherished her independence and didn't want to be in anyone's debt, she took out her address book and contacted her former co-workers and clients. She returned to a business women's lunch group she always had enjoyed and told everyone she could buttonhole that she was looking for work. Within two weeks a job offer came from what Judith thought was a surprising source: one of her former clients had long thought she was one of the better sales representatives calling on him and now wanted her to represent his company.

In one of Judith's most recent dreams, she was driving across a big bridge. In another, she was traveling down a busy highway, keeping up with traffic and enjoying the trip. She now has new images of strength to store in her memory bank. The more such images you can create for yourself, the more likely you will be to draw on them, and the more likely it is that the dream process will function well on its own when you next find yourself in a situation in which the same emotional buttons get pushed.

RISC THERAPY FOR DEPRESSION*

Some of our divorcing dreamers did not need the RISC program: they were not depressed. Some who were depressed worked through their depression on their own or with the aid of family or friends. Some benefited from other types of psychotherapy, while some, unfortunately, did not get better. Because people entered the study at different times, we have information on some from only their one-year checkup. Others, whom we first saw soon after the study began in 1988, continue to write or call from time to time to let us know how they are doing and how they are sleeping and dreaming. None of those you've met in this book have remarried to date. Those who were not depressed initially and those who participated in RISC therapy both show the most success in moving on with their lives. Their dreams reflect their progress.

Laura, [a] woman who dreamed her husband discarded [a] sock with a hole in it, was deeply depressed when she entered the divorce study. We felt then that she was bound to have trouble adjusting without help. Sadly, she did not get it. She moved to another state, where she worked as a bookkeeper and tried to provide a decent home for her children. When she came back for her one-year checkup, I asked if she were dating. She said firmly: "No way. I've no ambition to. I'll be happy when I have grandkids; that'll be enough for me."

"How are you sleeping?" I asked.

"I sleep only 20 minutes here and an hour there," she replied.

"Are you dreaming?"

"Yes, sometimes, sad dreams."

This was a dream she remembered:

> I was walking on a sidewalk on a street that bordered my old school. I was thinking I wouldn't get in a car with anyone, even to save my life. It was dark out, evening. I was hurrying, rushing because I was kind of afraid of that area. I was trying to see if there was someone coming. I was going the opposite way on the block because a car was approaching. I was my usual cautious self.

Laura saw herself in her dreams as alone and vulnerable to danger. Her dream dimensions, being alone instead of with others, in danger instead of safe, and fearful instead of self-confident, showed that her anxious, timid self-image still was undermining her recovery.

Julie, also fearful and withdrawn when she entered the study, made substantial progress toward revising her negative self-image after only six sessions of RISC therapy. At her one-year checkup, she was a much more self-confident young woman. She dreamed she recovered from a fall and from the embarrassment of being seen undressed in public.

When Harold, [a] trucker, returned for his one-year visit, he still suffered from blue moods. "If I can keep my depression at bay," Harold said, "I can think more clearly, but I think to myself, 'You come up short here, and you come up short there.' I come on strong, but I can't follow through."

* From Cartwright and Lamberg (1992/2000, pp. 148–154).

"How are you sleeping?" I asked him.

"I generally don't have any trouble, but my dreams are real vague now," he said.

He couldn't remember one to tell me. Even in the sleep laboratory, his dreams were scanty. In one he reported:

> I was fighting with somebody, wrestling. They were trying to take something away from me.

This was another:

> I kept hearing a song called "My baby just wrote me a letter."

The dimensions in these dreams were winning/losing, closeness/distance. The fragments showed Harold was still experiencing a sense of loss and disconnectedness from his family. Harold had lost touch with his inner self. He might have benefited from RISC therapy, but he chose not to pursue it. He had, however, entered psychotherapy and was learning, he said, "to do one dish at a time, instead of trying to handle the whole load of dirty dishes at once." Harold saw his children frequently, and he felt they were adjusting well to having two households.

Tony, deeply depressed when he entered the divorce study, made good progress after working on his dreams in RISC therapy. Three years after joining the study, he reported his life was much better. He was proud of his work performance and of his boys. Here is a dream that showed his progress. He called it "the happiest dream I have ever had."

> I was married with a big family. We were living in a primitive environment, but we were very happy. We had a baby girl, and I remember adoring this baby, holding her in my arms and feeding her soft, creamed corn with a tiny spoon. She was smiling, and she loved me because I was feeding her. It was almost like I was nursing her.
>
> We lived next door to some priests who told us of another baby born to a woman who didn't want her, so I started out to see if she would give us the baby. She did and we raised the two babies as sisters. There was just total love in this dream. When I woke up, I felt loved and loving.

The change from his earlier dreams of bad boys who were out of his control to the loving little baby girls was dramatic. In this dream, Tony let himself start over. Even if he could no longer father children because of his vasectomy, he saw a way he could raise them. His dream dimensions, caring versus rejection, closeness versus distance, reflect his newer, more positive outlook. This was a future-oriented dream rehearsal of successful fatherhood and love.

Jerry also benefited from the RISC program. "I've come out of my depression and faced the reality that Elaine is just not moving to join me," he reported two years after joining the study. He said he had started dating four other women and was enjoying his life as a bachelor.

"Are you sleeping better?" I asked.

"Oh, yes," he said. "And here is a dream you might like."

> Elaine was supposed to come but didn't show up. I was in this house and wanted to go to the bathroom. I went to a basement bathroom where there were wooden slats. You could be seen through them. I was sort of exposed. I needed to have a bowel movement. I took my pants down, but the commode was filled with sand. I thought, "Well, what should I do with all this shit?" There were some teenaged girls starting to come down the stairs. They looked at me and offered to help clean me up. I said, "I can do it myself."

"I laughed when I woke up," Jerry reported. "I have plenty of women offering to help me get over all this mess." The dimensions here, exposed versus private, messy versus tidy, independent versus dependent, showed Jerry was moving toward relying less on women and feeling better about himself. He acknowledged that the physical side of his life made him susceptible to dependency on women and was messy; at the same time, he said in this dream, he could clean up his act and make his own decisions about his life. Both Jerry's dreams and his good self-image speeded his recovery.

Helen was one who initially had been depressed but worked her own way out of it. In a key dream in the laboratory when she returned for her one-year visit, Helen had opened her eyes in a dense fog and found a way to climb a mountain. Two years later, Helen reported further growth.

"I am much happier and more optimistic about the future," she said. "When I first came here, I was desperate. I wanted to die. Now I know I will never kill myself. I really wanted to die, but God wouldn't let me do it. Now I don't want to."

"I had a dream that was a turning point for me," Helen related.

> I was in an old house with a ghost, a woman ghost. You could see right through her. I lived there all alone and the ghost was calling me. I lived in a closet. I think that it was the ghost of a "single-woman-living-alone" and I had to confront it and say, "That's okay."

"Now I have faced it and I am okay," Helen asserted. Her dreams showed that she had overcome her fearful earlier pattern. Her dream dimensions, substance versus shadow and confrontation versus avoidance, proclaimed that she had the self-confidence to be on her own, if she had to. She had successfully resolved the self-image crisis that her divorce precipitated.

Maggie, who dreamed during her first visit to the laboratory that she worked things out with her husband's new girlfriend, never was depressed. Two years later, she wrote to tell me she was quite satisfied with her new life. She was close to graduating from college. She had several male "friends," but was not ready to settle down with any of them. She had no trouble sleeping or dreaming. "I am more confident about who I am, and I have accepted myself," she said. "I am taking charge of my own life." She reported a recent dream:

> I was much younger and still living at home. I told my parents I was joining the Peace Corps. They were shocked and told me they always wanted me to go to Bible school, but I refused. I decided for myself to go to the Peace Corps.

"That was a good dream," Maggie said. Her dream dimensions, independence versus dependence and defiance versus compliance, mirrored her practical, helpful self and her readiness for new experiences, including new relationships with other people.

Robert, another good coper, had had a near fatal car accident in the year after leaving his hypochondriac wife. He spent several weeks in the hospital, and when he recovered, he decided it was time to live. He found a new woman, a healthy one, and eventually moved in with her. "We talk and have real communication," he told me at his one-year visit. "I take a hand with her children. I have a real sense of family now. I cut down on my drinking. I'm in better contact with my friends. I feel really good about myself. I still have pain from the accident," he said, "but when I'm free of pain, I sleep fine. I never was aware of my dreams before the lab," he recalled, "but there I got five. I'm just not a good recaller on my own." Robert didn't need to remember his dreams; everything was going well for him.

Stimulating depressed people to take charge of their lives by teaching them to play an active role in their dreams improved their outlook toward the future. … The RISC approach has many applications beyond divorce. It can even be used to ward off trouble before it gets out of hand. One example:

Barbara, a woman in her sixties, sought relief from a recurring nightmare:

> I'm a passenger on a train, going through a mountain pass. The train speeds up. I can tell it is out of control and going to crash. Just before it crashes, I wake up.

Barbara had never married and spent her entire life working in relative isolation as a librarian. She wasn't amenable to making life-style changes and thought she didn't have enough money to permit her to retire. The key dimension in this dream is the one of being out of control versus being in control. In waking life, this woman might not have identified herself as being "in crisis," but her repeated nightmares and her decision to seek therapy gave strong hints of trouble coming to the surface. Her depression was deepening. Her therapist, David Calof, suggested that the next time she had the same nightmare, she could try to change the ending. The woman accomplished this task. As she reported:

> When I realized the train was about to crash, I said to myself, "I have to do something to keep this from happening." I walked to the front of the train and discovered that the engineer's compartment was empty. Although I debated whether or not to touch the switches, I decided to try to take control of the train. Within a couple of moments, I came to a "Y" in the track. One branch continued the path I was on. The other led up and out of the valley. With a great sense of excitement, I took the path leading up and out.

Within six weeks, Calof reports, she consulted with an accountant, found a way to retire, and now travels to see places she'd long known only in books.

HELPING CHILDREN TO LEARN FROM THEIR DREAMS*

The dreams that we remember are those that stir up strong feelings. These dreams often involve a real sense of threat to the self. This threat may be an internal one. ... In the earliest dreams we remember, the threat usually is external.

When children first learn that not all adults are benign or that even parents can become hostile at times, they create monsters, giants, and witches to give form to their fears. They may dream of being chased, trapped, or attacked, while remaining powerless to help themselves. In such dreams, they are dealing with their sense of vulnerability, which for children, because they are smaller and weaker than adults, is a real issue. Some people keep these early images in their active dream repertoire and replay them in various forms later in life whenever they feel helpless.

In book after book, writer/illustrator Maurice Sendak brings us face to face with creatures who roam through dreamland. "The night Max wore his wolf suit and made mischief of one kind and another," Sendak [1963] tells us in *Where the Wild Things Are*, he was sent to bed without his supper. In his dream, Max journeys through night and day to join toothy, large-clawed monsters in a wild, wordless rumpus. He discovers that he is the most wild thing of all. Sendak's [1970] *In the Night Kitchen* follows Mickey, a young boy who tumbles out of bed and into the clutches of three hefty Oliver Hardy-lookalike bakers who mix him into their batter. The irrepressible Mickey fashions an airplane out of bread dough and makes his escape.

Common problems we all face in growing up—learning to protect ourselves from physical injury, coping with hostility, learning to live with our own upsetting feelings—fuel the creation of our early dream images. We cannot shield all children from accidents, from injuries, from pain, from war, but we can be alert to the dreams that traumatic events leave behind, the sad self-stories that need better endings.

We can encourage our children to share their dreams, and especially their nightmares. We can familiarize ourselves with how they handle the common problems that we expect to show up in the dreams. If they are falling, we can help them learn to fly or build haystacks to blunt the impact of a fall. If monsters chase them, we can teach ways to tame the savage beasts. Sendak's Max tames the wild things with the magic trick "of staring into all their yellow eyes without blinking once."

Some children relate their dreams better by acting them out or drawing them than they do by using words. In her book *Nightmare Help*, Anne Wiseman [1986] suggests using drawings to help your child master the conflicts the dream expresses. Once the monster is down on paper, you can encourage the child to draw a cage around it, for example, or add helpers to the picture. Children need to know they don't have to face their troubles all alone. Asking, "What can you do to make this dream come out better?" can help your child develop positive coping strategies.

Wiseman reports that her own son had bad dreams about their house burning down. Her husband suggested to the boy that next time he had one of these

* From Cartwright & Lamberg (1992/2000, pp. 236–239).

dreams, he put the fire out. One morning the boy came to breakfast full of excitement. He did it. He put the fire out! When his parents asked him how, he said proudly, "I peed on it." They may have traded one nighttime problem for another!

One of my patients told me she had repeated nightmares of being trapped in a burning building from age three on. These dreams started after a real incident. She and a small friend were playing with a doll and arguing about who should get to hold the toy. Her father, who was raking leaves and burning them nearby, became irritated with the children's wrangling. He grabbed the doll and threw it on the fire. Only in adulthood, after suffering from this nightmare for decades, did this woman find a solution. She learned to levitate in her dreams, to escape the fire by floating away.

For children wounded by trauma, there are few good nights and sweet dreams. They need to talk about their nightmares, to express their fears, and to learn to counteract them with images of successful coping.

Prevention is far better than treatment. Dreams are a wonderful resource for parents to use to assist their children to build a firm identity. Children need to feel their dreams are interesting and understandable and that if their dreams are frightening, they can share them and get the help they need to handle the feelings the dreams express. Regular dream checkups, much like medical and dental checkups, can help children stay well. Try this family activity: Make dream sharing part of a weekend morning breakfast. Have a scariest dream day, a happiest dream day, a best-ever dream day, and enjoy sharing the stories dreams have to tell.

While it is possible to repair a damaged self-image later in life, to activate alternate scenarios that represent the positive sides of a person's dream dimensions, and to strengthen the likelihood of using these new images to create new dreams with healthier responses to future crises, the task takes longer and is tougher than creating a strong self-image in childhood.

SUMMARY OF CHAPTER 14 (PREPARED BY EVELYN M. DUESBURY)

In this chapter, psychotherapist Cartwright, developer of the RISC model, with coauthor-writer Lamberg, fills unique needs in the dream interpretation world by sharing the RISC model for working with dreams that deal with crises. Each letter in RISC represents actions to be taken by dreamers who experience traumatic dreams. Recognize when you are having a bad dream, the kind that leaves you feeling helpless, guilty, or upset the next morning. Identify what it is about the dream that makes you feel badly. Stop any bad dream. Change negative dream dimensions into their opposite, positive sides. Children's dreaming and guidance on how parents and counselors can help children when they have nightmares are important features of this chapter. Problems that seem common to adults are often scary to our young children. Cartwright promotes helping children create alternate scenarios to scary aspects of dreams. Childhood is a critical time for attaining healthy responses to crises—critical for the child and critical for the adult who the child becomes.

SELF-STUDY QUIZ CHAPTER 14 (PREPARED BY EVELYN M. DUESBURY)

1. What words do the letters of the acronym RISC stand for?
2. Write the actions (steps) that accompany each word represented by RISC.
3. Complete the following sentence (as stated in Chapter 14): "We cannot shield all children from accidents, from injuries, from pain, from war, but we can ____."
4. Which of the following are suggestions that Cartwright makes for helping children work with their dreams?
   a. "We can encourage our children to share their dreams, and especially their nightmares."
   b. "We can familiarize ourselves with how they handle the common problems that we expect to show up in the dreams."
   c. "If monsters chase them, we can teach ways to tame the savage beasts."
   d. All of the above.
   e. None of the above.
5. Complete the following sentence: "While it is possible to repair a damaged self-image later in life, to activate alternate scenarios that represent the positive sides of a person's dream dimensions, and to strengthen the likelihood of using these new images to create new dreams with healthier responses to future crises, ________________________________."

Section IV

Conclusions

The primary aim of *The Counselor's Guide for Facilitating the Interpretation of Dreams: Family and Other Relationship Systems Perspectives* is to fill a gap that exists between current academic training for American Counseling Association (ACA) practitioners and the practitioners' needs for focused training on how to better facilitate their clients' dream interpretations.

The main theme concerns dreams about relationships, primarily dreams about family members and other major figures in the dreamer's life with whom the dreamer interacts and reacts.

The primary objectives of the book are thus to explain and demonstrate ways for counselors to assist clients who want to understand and interpret their dreams. The featured dream interpretation model, the Personalized Method for Interpreting Dreams (PMID), integrates well with contemporary psychotherapies, especially cognitive behavior therapies.

This final section contains a chapter that highlights the main teachings presented to meet the aim, theme, and primary objectives of this book.

15

Summary of the Lessons Presented in This Book

Dreaming is a natural gift we all possess. How we interpret our dreams and how we use them is a challenge to each of us.

Steven L. Duesbury

The primary aim of this book is to train counselors how to facilitate clients' interpretations of their dreams. The primary teachings about dreams and the facilitation of dream interpretations are as follows:

1. Dreams have been used as guides by cultures around the world since ancient times. Because dreams reach beyond waking-life thinking, helping people interpret their own dreams is an encompassing counseling approach (see Chapter 1).
2. During dreaming, the rational reasoning and decision-making parts of the brain are inactive. Thus, material entering the dream can extend beyond waking-life thoughts (see Chapter 1).
3. The best help that parents can give to their children when they awaken from dreams is to patiently listen to them, value their dreams, and become aware of the child's reactions, feelings, and any waking-life activities that may have prompted the dreams (see Chapter 2).
4. Preliminaries for working with adolescents' and adults' dreams begin with dream recalling, recording, and learning one's own individualized dreaming language (see Chapter 2).
5. The dreamer is the primary interpreter of his or her own dreams. Accordingly, all readers are encouraged to become familiar with their own personalized dreaming language. The counselor facilitates the process (see Chapter 2).

6. When a counselor recognizes that people's dreams often originate from their waking-life experiences, this helps the counselor better understand clients' concerns (see Chapter 2).
7. Counselors' dreams are potential adjunct resources for understanding their clients' concerns and how best to guide them (see Chapter 2).
8. The Personalized Method for Interpreting Dreams (PMID) model, which is the primary model presented in this book, is a stand-alone model. The results of four longitudinal research studies and four longitudinal exploration projects verify its completeness. In addition, pertinent information for most psychotherapy models flow from use of the PMID model (see Section II introduction).
9. The overview of the PMID model given in Chapter 3 has two purposes:
   a. It is an introduction of the PMID model for practicing counselors who use this book to learn how to facilitate clients' interpretation of their dreams.
   b. It is a one-class (3-hour) presentation to introduce the PMID model to students in graduate-level counselor education courses that are other than dream interpretation courses.
10. Actions to be taken by the dreamer to interpret dreams with the PMID model include the following steps:
    a. Connect day-before-your-dream **events** to your dream to discover the theme of this dream (Step 1 from Chapter 4).
    b. Connect day-before-your-dream **thoughts** to your dream to detect which thoughts may have prompted the responses to this dream (Step 2 from Chapter 5).
    c. Select and define **major dream phrases** and symbols from your write-up of this dream to discover the personalized meanings of the dream. Consider effects of day-before-your-dream events and thoughts and earlier experiences on the meaning of each major dream phrase (Step 3 from Chapter 6).
    d. Compare your **emotions in your dream** with your **pre-dream waking-life emotions** to discover whether your waking-life emotions accurately reflect how you feel about the issue in this dream (Step 4 from Chapter 7).
    e. Explore your dream for possible **solutions** to problems, including changing (or affirming) your thoughts, attitudes, or behaviors. Consider your responses to each PMID model step, including Step 6, as you search for solutions and suggestions contained in this dream. Give primary attention to the power of your day-before-your-dream thoughts (PMID Step 2) to act as questions that your dream answers (Step 5 from Chapter 8).
    f. Explore your dream for **family and other relationship systems perspectives**, which are influences arising from reactions to family and other major relationships, both past and current, to discover whether this dream reflects your reactions during experiences with your family or other major relationships. Compare and comment on

your dreaming and your waking-life reactions to the primary relationships in this dream (Step 6 from Chapter 9).

11. Links between dreamers' reactions to earlier relationship experiences and their reactions to current relationship experiences are often embedded in their dreams (see Chapter 9).
12. Family and other relationship systems effects can and do pass from generation to generation. When people alleviate stress, current and subsequent generations will benefit (see the introduction to Section I and Chapter 9).
13. Using the "individual's series approach to interpreting dreams" of the PMID model, the dreamer examines a series of dreams about each major relationship that may appear in his or her dreams (see Chapter 10).
14. Conscious efforts to understand our reactions to experiences with one major relationship have the potential to bring dreams about other major relationships (see Chapter 10).
15. The process of alleviating stress by interpreting dreams about stressful matters is a potential link to spiritual understanding (see Chapter 10).
16. Reviews of our original interpretations are critical to our best understanding and use of our dreams (see Chapter 11).
17. Dreams have the potential to let people know when they have successfully overcome a relationship issue. Three indicators for testing when a relationship issue has been alleviated (see Chapter 11) are
    a. The dream and the dreamer's interpretations contain at least one clear message that the issue may be finished.
    b. The dream contains no new or unused past solutions to the current issue.
    c. The dream gives no hints that the specific concern still bothers the dreamer.
18. A pertinent resource for current developments and ongoing updates on distance counseling and face-to-face counseling is the Center for Credentialing and Education (CCE) (http://www.cce-global.org/credentials-offered/dccmain (see Chapter 12).
19. Approximately 8 weeks of counseling by a knowledgeable facilitator on the use of the PMID model can result in the client's ability to use the model with limited or no facilitation. The PMID model thus has potential for short-term counseling and ongoing self-help (see Chapter 12).
20. Ullman's model, which presents a group approach to dream interpretation, and Cartwright's model, which incorporates children's dreams, add to the comprehensiveness of this book (see Chapters 13 and 14).
21. Qualitative and quantitative research methods are complementary ways to examine the effective use of dream interpretation models (see Section II introduction and Appendix A).

In completing our study, we remind ourselves that the facilitation of clients' dream interpretations has the potential to be the most encompassing counseling approach available because dreams reach further than waking thought usually extends: to the *peripheries* of the mind.

Thank you for your attention, and dream on!

References

ACA Code of Ethics (2005). Alexandria, VA: American Counseling Association.

Allen, D. M. (1994). *A family systems approach to individual psychotherapy*. Northvale, NJ: Aronson.

Ansbacher, H., & Ansbacher, R. (1956). *The individual psychology of Alfred Adler*. New York: Basic Books.

Beck, A. T., Rush, A. J., Shaw, B. R., & Emery, G. (1979). *Cognitive therapy of depression*. New York: Guilford Press.

Bonime, W. (1982). *The clinical use of dreams*. New York: Da Capo Press.

Boss, M. (1958). *Analysis of dreams*. New York: Philosophical Library.

Boss, M. (1977). *I dreamt last night …* . New York: Gardner Press.

Bowen, M. (1978). *Family therapy in clinical practice*. New York: Aronson.

Brammer, L. M., & MacDonald, G. (2003). *The helping relationship process and skills* (8th ed.). Needham Heights, MA: Allyn & Bacon.

Braun, A. R., Balkin, T. J., Wesensten, N. J., Carson, R. E., Varga, M., Baldwin, P., et al. (1997). Regional cerebral blood flow throughout the sleep-wake cycle. An H2(15)0 PET study. *Brain, 120*, 1173–1197.

Braun, A. R., Balkin, T. J., Wesensten, N. J., Gwadry, F., Carson, R. E., Varga, M., et al. (1998). Dissociated pattern of activity in visual cortices and their projections during human rapid eye movement and sleep. *Science, 279*, 91–95.

Bulkeley, K. (2000). *Transforming dreams: Learning spiritual lessons from the dreams you never forget*. New York: Wiley.

Bulkeley, K. (2002). Dream content and political ideology. *Dreaming, 12*, 61–77.

Bynum, E. B. (1984). *The family unconscious.* Wheaton, IL: Theosophical.

Bynum, E. B. (2003). *Families and the interpretation of dreams*. New York: Paraview Special Editions.

Cartwright, R., & Lamberg, L. (2000). *Crisis dreaming: Using your dreams to solve your problems*. ASJA Press. (Original work published by HarperCollins, 1992)

Cartwright, R. D. (1977). *Night life.* Englewood Cliffs, NJ: Prentice-Hall.

Cartwright, R. D. (1978). *A primer on sleep and dreaming*. Reading, MA: Addison-Wesley.

Cartwright, R. D. (2010). *The twenty-four hour mind*. New York: Oxford University Press.

Center for Credentialing and Education (CCE). Retrieved April 5, 2010 from http://www.CCE-global.org/credentials-offered/dccdomain

Corey, G. (2008). *Theory and practice of counseling and psychotherapy* (8th ed.). Florence, KY: Thomson-Brooks/Cole.

Delaney, G. (1988). *Living your dreams.* New York: HarperCollins

Delaney, G. (1993). The dream interview. In G. Delaney (Ed.), *New directions in dream interpretation* (pp. 195–240). Albany: State University of New York Press.

Delaney, G. (1996). *Living your dreams*. New York: HarperCollins.

Domhoff, G. W. (1996). *Finding meaning in dreams: A quantitative approach*. New York: Plenum.

Domhoff, G. W. (2003). *The scientific study of dreams: Neural networks, cognitive development, and content analysis*. Washington, DC: American Psychological Association.

Duesbury, E. M. (1994). Professor uses dreams as guides in working with students. *Dream Network, 13*(2), 24–25, 33.

Duesbury, E. M. (2000). *Utilizing dreams from a systemic perspective to understand and mollify relationship issues.* Unpublished master's thesis. University of Wisconsin–Whitewater.

Duesbury, E. M. (2001). Personalized Method for Interpreting Dreams (PMID)®—As applied to relationship issues. *Dreaming, 11*, 207–216.

Duesbury, E. M. (2007). *Living dreams, living life: A practical guide to understanding your dreams and how they can change your waking life*. Victoria, BC, Canada: Trafford.

Duesbury, E., Bynum, E. B., & Van Doren, D. (2002). [Anecdotal exploration of Wisconsin members of the ACA and counselor education graduate students' ability to use the Personalized Method for Interpreting Dreams (PMID) model]. Unpublished raw data.

Duesbury, E., Bynum, E. B., & Van Doren, D. (2003). [Anecdotal exploration of counselor education graduate students' ability to use the Personalized Method for Interpreting Dreams (PMID) model]. Unpublished raw data.

Duesbury, E., Bynum, E. B., & Van Doren, D. (2004). [Anecdotal exploration of counselor education undergraduate and graduate students' ability to use the Personalized Method for Interpreting Dreams (PMID) model]. Unpublished raw data.

Ellis, A. (2001). *Overcoming destructive beliefs, feelings, and behaviors*. New York: Prometheus Books.

Faraday, A. (1997). *Dream power*. Berkeley, CA: Berkeley Trade Paperback.

Foulkes, D. (1999). *Children's dreaming and the development of consciousness*. Cambridge, MA: Harvard University Press.

Freud, S. (1955). *The interpretation of dreams* (J. Strachey, Trans. and Ed.). New York: Basic Books. (Original work published 1900)

Garfield, P. (1991). *The healing power of dreams*. New York: Simon & Schuster.

Garfield, P. (1995). *Creative dreaming: Plan and control your dreams to develop creativity, overcome fears, solve problems, and create a better self*. New York: Simon & Schuster.

Gendlin, E. (1986). *Let your body interpret your dreams*. Wilmette, IL: Chiron.

Gibran, K. (1984). *The prophet*. New York: Knopf.

Goldman, L. (1992). Qualitative assessment: An approach for counselors. *Journal of Counseling and Development, 70*, 616–621.

Hall, C. (1953). *The meaning of dreams*. New York: Dell.

Hartmann, E. (1968). The day residue: Time distribution of waking events. *Psychophysiology, 5*, 222.

Hartmann, E. (1995). Making connections in a safe place: Is dreaming psychotherapy? *Dreaming, 5*, 213–228.

Hartmann, E. (2001). *Dreams and nightmares: The origin and meaning of dreams*. New York: Perseus.

Hartmann, E., Zborowski, M., Rosen, R., & Grace, N. (2001). Contextualizing images in dreams: More intense after abuse and trauma. *Dreaming, 11*, 115–126.

Hill, C. E. (1996). *Working with dreams in psychotherapy*. New York: Guilford Press.

Hill, C. E. (Ed.). (2004). *Dream work in therapy: Facilitating exploration, insight, and action*. Washington, DC: American Psychological Association.

Holowchak, M. A. (2002). *Ancient science and dreams*. Lanham, MD: University Press of America.

Jung, C. G. (1933). *Modern man in search of a soul*. New York: Harcourt Brace.

Jung, C. G. (1954). *The practice of psychotherapy* (R. F. C. Hull, Trans.). New York: Bollingen Series/Pantheon Books.

Jung, C. G. (1960). *The structure and dynamics of the psyche* (R. F. C. Hull, Trans.). New York: Bollingen Series/Pantheon Books.

Jung, C. G. (1966). *Two essays on analytical psychology* (R. F. C. Hull, Trans.). Princeton, NJ: Bollingen Series/Princeton University Press.

Kaplan, D. M. (2006, Oct.). Ethical use of technology. *Counseling Today, 11*, 43. Retrieved July 19, 2010 from http://www.counseling.org/Publications/CounselingToday.aspx

Kaplan, D. M., Kocet, M. M., Cottone, R. R., Glosoff, H. L., Miranti, J. G., Moll, C. C., Bloom, J. C., . . . Tarvydas. (2009). New mandates and imperatives in the revised ACA Code of Ethics. *Journal of Counseling and Development, 2*, 241-255.

Kelsey, M. (1981). *Transcend, a guide to the spiritual quest*. New York: Crossroad.

Kelsey, M. (1991). *God, dreams, and revelation: A Christian interpretation of dreams*. Minneapolis, MN: Augsburg. (Original work published 1974)

Kerr, M. E., & Bowen, M. (1988). *Family evaluation: An approach based on Bowen theory*. New York: Penguin.

Kramer, M. (1993). The selective mood regulatory function of dreaming: An update and revision. In A. Moffitt, M. Kramer, & R. Hoffman (Eds.), *The functions of dreaming* (pp. 139–195). New York: State University of New York Press.

Kramer, M. (2007). *The dream experience: A systematic exploration*. New York: Routledge.

Kramer, M., Roth, T., Arand, D., & Bonnet, M. (1981). Waking and dreaming mentation: A test of their interrelationship. *Neuroscience Letters, 22*, 83–86.

Krippner, S., & Dillard, J. (1988). *Dreamworking: How to use your dreams for creative problem-solving*. New York: Bearly.

LaBerge, S. (2004). *Lucid dreaming*. Boulder, CO: Sounds True.

Lowry, R. (2009a). Concepts and applications of inferential statistics. Retrieved October 31, 2009, from http://faculty.vassar.edu/lowry/webtext.html

Lowry, R. (2009b). Wilcoxon signed-rank test [Software computations]. Retrieved October 31, 2009, from http://faculty.vassar.edu/lowry/wilcoxon.html

Mahrer, A. R. (1989). *Dreamwork in psychotherapy and self-change*. New York: Norton.

Malone, J. E., Miller, R. M., & Walz, G. R. (2007). *Distance counseling: Expanding the counselor's reach and impact*. Ann Arbor, MI: Counseling Outfitters.

Maquet, P., Peters, J., Aerts, J., Delfiore, G., Degueldre, C., Luxen, A., et al. (1996). Functional neuroanatomy of human rapid-eye-movement sleep and dreaming. *Nature, 383*, 163–166.

Mattoon, M. A. (1984). *Understanding dreams*. Dallas, TX: Spring.

Meichenbaum, D. (1977). *Cognitive behavior modification: An integrative approach*. New York: Plenum Press.

Merriam-Webster OnLine. Retrieved April 5, 2010 from http://www.merriam-webster.com/dictionary/

Morrison, A. (1993). Animal dreams. In M. A. Carskadon (Ed.), *Encyclopedia of sleep and dreaming* (pp. 37–38). New York: MacMillan.

Nofzinger, E. A., Mintun, M. A., Wiseman, M., Kupfer, D. J., & Moore, R. Y. (1997). Forebrain activation in REM sleep: An FDG PET study. *Brain Research, 770*, 192–201.

Okocha, A. G., & Duesbury, E. M. (2005–2006). [Research of a general population's ability to use the Personalized Method for Interpreting Dreams (PMID) model]. Unpublished raw data.

Perls, F. (1969). *Gestalt therapy verbatim*. Moab, UT: Real People Press.

Plesma, D. (2003). Assessing family issues related to the presenting problem. In D. M. Kaplan & Associates, *Family counseling for all counselors* (pp. 87–119). Greensboro, NC: CAPS, co-published with the American Counseling Association Foundation.

Polster, E., & Polster, M. (1973). *Gestalt therapy integrated*. New York: Brunner/Mazel.

Radha, S. (1994). *Realities of the dreaming mind*. Spokane, WA: Timeless Books.

ReadyMinds. Counselor Training. Retrieved March 6, 2009, from http://www.readyminds.com/training/overview.html

Rochlen, A. B., & Hill, C. E. (1999). Exploring a terrifying dream. In S. Krippner & M. Waldman (Eds.), *Dreamscaping: New and creative ways to work with your dreams* (pp. 56–67). Los Angeles: Lowell House.

Rosner, R. I., Lyddon, W. J., & Freeman, A. (Eds.). (2004). *Cognitive therapy and dreams*. New York: Springer.

Savary, L. M., Berne, P. H., & Williams, S. K. (1984). *Dreams and spiritual growth*. New York: Paulist Press.

Schredl, M. (2003). Continuity between waking and dreaming: A proposal for a mathematical model. *Sleep and Hypnosis, 5*(1), 38–52.

Schredl, M. (2006). Factors affecting the continuity between waking and dreaming: Emotional intensity and emotional tone of the waking-life event. *Sleep and Hypnosis, 8*(1), 1–5.

Seafield, F. (1865). *The literature and curiosities of dreams*. London: Chapman and Hall.

Sendak, M. (1963). *Where the wild things are*. New York: Harper & Row.

Sendak, M. (1970). *In the night kitchen*. New York: Harper & Row.

Shafton, A. (1995). *Dream reader: Contemporary approaches to the understanding of dreams*. Albany: State University of New York Press.

Siegel, A. (1998). Nighttime remedies, helping your child tame the demons of the night. *Dream Time, 15*(1&2), 1, 32–35.

Siegel, A. (2002). *Dream wisdom: Uncovering life's answers in your dreams*. Berkeley, CA: Celestial Arts.

Siegel, A., & Bulkeley, K. (1998). *Dreamcatching: Every parent's guide to exploring and understanding children's dreams and nightmares*. New York: Three Rivers Press.

Siivola, M. Biographical note for Dr. Montague Ullman, par. 3. Retrieved February 1, 2010 from http://www.siivola.org/monte/biographical_note.htm

Smolensky, M., & Lamberg, L. (2001). *The body clock guide to better health*. New York: Henry Holt and Company.

Strauch, I. (2005). REM dreaming in the transition from late childhood to adolescence: A longitudinal study. *Dreaming, 15*, 155–169.

Strauch, I., & Meier, B. (1996). *In search of dreams: Results of experimental dream research*. Albany: State University of New York Press.

Synesius of Cyrene. (1930) *On dreams* (A. Fitzgerald, Trans.). New York: Oxford University Press. Retrieved March 6, 2009, from http://www.geocities.com/Athens/Acropolis/5164/sdreams.html. (Original work published 5th century AD)

Ullman, M. (1996). *Appreciating dreams: A group approach*. Thousand Oaks, CA: Sage.

Ullman, M. (1999). Dreaming consciousness: More than a bit player in the search for answers to the mind/body problem. *Journal of Scientific Exploration, 13*, 91–112.

Ullman, M. (2001). An atheoretic bidirectional experiential group approach to working with dreams. *Journal of the Group Department of the Postgraduate Center for Mental Health, 5*(1), 7–30. Issues in Group Psychotherapy, Fall 2001. Retrieved February 1, 2010, from http://www.siivola.org/monte/papers_grouped/index.htm

Van de Castle, R. L. (1994). *Our dreaming mind*. New York: Ballantine.

Van Doren, D., & Duesbury, E. M. (2000). [Research pilot to examine ability of counselor education graduates and graduate students to learn how to interpret their dreams utilizing the Personalized Method for Interpreting Dreams (PMID) model]. Unpublished raw data.

Van Doren, D., & Duesbury, E. M. (2001). [Anecdotal exploration of Wisconsin members of ACA and counselor education graduate students' ability to use the Personalized Method for Interpreting Dreams (PMID) model]. Unpublished raw data.

Van Doren, D., & Duesbury, E. M. (2005–2006). [Research of the Personalized Method for Interpreting Dreams (PMID) model's usefulness for ongoing personal and professional development]. Unpublished raw data.

Wiseman, A. (1986). *Nightmare help*. Berkeley, CA: Ten Speed Press.

Wolff, W. (1952). *The dream—Mirror of conscience*. New York: Grune & Stratton.

Wolman, B. B., & Ullman, M. (1986). *Handbook of states of consciousness*. New York: Van Nostrand Reinhold.

Appendix A: The PMID Model Researched and Explored

INTRODUCTION

As reported in Section II of this book, I developed the Personalized Method for Interpreting Dreams (PMID) model during thesis research, an endeavor that achieved recognition as the thesis of the year at University of Wisconsin–Whitewater in 2000. My colleagues and I refined the model during three more research projects (Okocha & Duesbury, 2005–2006; Van Doren & Duesbury, 2000, 2005–2006) and four explorations (Duesbury et al., 2002, 2003, 2004; Van Doren & Duesbury, 2001).

QUALITATIVE DATA COLLECTED FOR THE PMID PROJECTS

The primary qualitative data were participants' dream narratives and their corresponding interpretations. Participants also wrote paragraphs about major relationships that appeared in their dreams. They entered their dream data on my privately owned Web site. I provided facilitative feedback on their use of the PMID model. Qualitative data were analyzed for all projects.

QUANTITATIVE DATA COLLECTED FOR THE PMID PROJECTS

Primary quantitative data were obtained from participants' periodic feedback instruments (PFIs) and emotional change instruments (ECIs). (Formats of the PFI and ECI are shown in Appendix B.) The PFI contains six statements related to the six PMID steps. Participants used the PFI to self-rate their abilities to do each PMID step. The rating scale is 1–7, with 7 the highest agreement. The ECI contains a series of questions designed to increase the dreamer-participants' awareness of differences between their dreaming emotions and their pre-dream waking-life emotions regarding the people about whom they dream. These two instruments were used for all projects from 2002 onward.

LIMITATIONS

Because selection of volunteers for our projects was nonrandom, findings cannot be generalized to other populations. In addition, the sizes of the samples may appear to be a restraint on the scope of the studies.

Because intuitive awareness is so often needed for effective use of the PMID, it is a limitation for use of the PMID and probably for a high percentage of dream interpretation models. Individuals with low intuitive awareness will therefore be unable to make full use of the model.

An obvious restraint on the scope of the findings in these studies is that although participants were encouraged to review their original interpretations for new insights and resubmit revised interpretations, many did not submit reinterpretations. One participant's reinterpretation is presented in this Appendix to demonstrate the productiveness of reviewing original interpretations.

An obvious limitation of dream interpretation in general is the possibility of misinterpretation. Studying more than one dream about critical issues, reviewing dreams and interpretations before acting, and consulting with a professional counselor trained in dream work all help dreamers forestall misinterpretation. Another obvious limitation on research of all dream interpretation models is that people must have dream recall. Although all people dream as a biological necessity, some have little or no dream recall.

Tables A1 through A8 show the qualitative and quantitative methodologies and outcomes from the eight projects.

TABLE A1 Thesis Research, 7-Year Case Study

Participant: White American woman, case study participant.

Qualitative

Data: Selection of 70 dreams and interpretations from participant's 7-year diary of approximately 2,500 dreams. Number of dreams selected per year:

Year 1	Year 2	Year 3	Year 4	Year 5	Year 6	Year 7
18	11	3	10	16	7	5

Methodology: I presented participant's raw dream data to my thesis committee. The committee advised me to "tell us how she did it. … That is, what procedures did you find implicit in Rose, the participant's dream meanings to support your theory of how best to find personal meanings to dreams?"

Outcome: In the process of satisfying the thesis committee's expectations and with the committee's guidance, I developed my initial step-by-step model for finding personal meanings in dreams, the Personalized Method for Interpreting Dreams (PMID), from participant Rose's dreamwork. See Appendix E for some of the participant's dreams and PMID Model interpretations.

Quantitative

Quantitative outcomes are presented in text Tables 4.1, 5.1, 6.1, 7.1, 8.1, and 9.1. They are also presented below in concise displays.

Methodology: After completing the thesis, I engaged independent dream specialist R. L. Van de Castle, PhD, to examine and rate the participant's use of the PMID model for interpreting her 70 dreams (eight series [sets] of relationship dreams).

Outcomes: Van de Castle's ratings of the participant's percentage rate of successfully implementing each PMID step for her several dreams during yearly time periods.

	Step 1	Step 2	Step 3	Step 4	Step 5	Step 6
Year 1	66.7	61.1	100.0	88.9	94.4	66.7
Year 2	55.5	45.5	90.9	100.0	81.8	72.7
Year 3	66.7	66.7	66.7	100.0	100.0	33.3
Year 4	50.0	80.0	90.0	70.0	100.0	90.0
Year 5	81.3	87.5	81.3	100.0	100.0	56.3
Year 6	42.9	71.4	85.7	100.0	100.0	14.3
Year 7	100.0	100.0	100.0	100.0	100.0	60.0

Outcomes: Van de Castle's Rating of the Series as a Whole	Percentage
Reflected positive change in emotions about the main relationship in each series	100.0
Reflected help to understand issues with the main character of the series	100.0
Reflected that the participant recognized suggestions she was not consciously aware of prior to the dream	100.0
Reflected that the participant acted on suggestions that she found in her dreams	100.0
Reflected that the participant reduced emotional stress about the main character of the series during her work with the series	100.0
Significant degree of reduction: mother, dad, husband, and mother-in-law	
Moderate degree of reduction: child, childhood friend, mentor, and sexual issues	

Note: From Duesbury, E. M. *Utilizing Dreams From a Systemic Perspective to Understand and Mollify Relationship Issues.* Unpublished master's thesis, University of Wisconsin–Whitewater, 2000.

TABLE A2 Pilot Research, 3 Months

Participants: Ten counselor education graduates and current counselor education graduate students. Race: White. Nationality: American. Gender: female. Age range: 28 to 53

Qualitative

Data: Pre-PMID dreams and interpretations (50) and post-PMID dreams and related PMID interpretations (9)

Methodology: Participants were required to submit seven dreams and their interpretations before the PMID model was revealed to them. In retrospect, seven was an excessive number to require because most of the research period was taken up by submitting pre-PMID dreams and interpretations. Participants who met the seven-dream pre-PMID requirements were given access to individual password-protected areas on a privately owned Web site. Instructions were available on the Web site for how to use the PMID model and how to enter dreams and interpretations. No limit was placed on number of dreams and PMID interpretations submitted. I, as coinvestigator, gave facilitative feedback on participants' use of the PMID model.

Outcomes: Four participants met our requirement of 7 pre-PMID dreams (28 dreams). Numbers of pre- and post-PMID dreams and related interpretations volunteered by those four participants were as follows:

	Participant A	Participant B	Participant C	Participant D
Pre-PMID	7	7	7	7
Post-PMID	1	3	3	2

Methodology: Investigators examined all pre- and post-PMID dreams and interpretations (59 total) for relationship issues.

Outcomes: Relationship issues found in participants' dreams and interpretations

- Spouse: distrust of, disagreements with, divorced, deceased
- Marriage: breakup, new marriage
- Significant other: difficulty in gay relationships, breakup, emotional ties to former partner
- Parents: restrictive, reluctance to rely on family and friends, alcoholic family members
- Sexual molestation

A synopsis of one of the nine post-PMID dreams and interpretations submitted by participants is presented next to demonstrate level achieved in use of the PMID model.

Dream Title: "Mom's House"

One night after thinking about difficulties with a coworker (PMID Step 2), Florence, the participant, dreamed: *I am walking across town to my mom's house.* The participant understood that her dream directed her to study family of origin experiences for how to understand and alleviate stress with the coworker (PMID Step 5) and to understand whether her current reactions had any originations from her earlier reactions in relationship experiences (PMID Step 6).

Quantitative

Quantitative outcomes are presented in text Tables 4.1, 5.1, 6.1, 7.1, 8.1, and 9.1. They are also presented below in concise displays.

Data: The four qualifying participants' pre-PMID dreams and interpretations (28) and post-PMID relationship dreams and interpretations (9)

Methodology: As coinvestigator, I examined the qualifying participants' pre-PMID and post-PMID interpretations regarding whether the interpretations met the criteria for each PMID step.

	Percentage
Outcomes: Pre-PMID interpretations (28)	
Connected day-before events to dreams (Step 1)	28.6
Connected day-before thoughts to dreams (Step 2)	3.6
Defined at least three dream phrases (Step 3)	0.0
Recognized dreaming emotions (Step 4)	32.1
Found suggestions or solutions in dreams (Step 5)	21.4

Explored dream reactions to others (Step 6)	17.9
Outcomes: Post-PMID interpretations (9)	
Connected day-before events to dreams (Step 1)	88.9
Connected day-before thoughts to dreams (Step 2)	66.7
Defined at least three dream phrases (Step 3)	33.3
Recognized dreaming emotions (Step 4)	44.4
Found suggestions or solutions in dreams (Step 5)	100.0
Explored dream reactions to others (Step 6)	11.1

Note: From Van Doren, D., & Duesbury, E. M. [Research pilot to examine ability of counselor education graduates and current graduate students to learn how to interpret their dreams utilizing the Personalized Method for Interpreting Dreams (PMID) model]. Unpublished raw data, 2000.

TABLE A3 Exploration, 4 Months

Participants: Five Wisconsin members of the American Counseling Association and counselor education graduate students. Race represented: White American. Gender: four females and one male. Age range: 27–46

Qualitative

Raw Data: Participants' pre-PMID dreams and interpretations (13 of 15 were relationship dreams) and post-PMID relationship dreams and PMID interpretations (33); total relationship dreams: 46

Methodologies: Participants were required to submit three dreams and their interpretations before the PMID model was revealed to them. After meeting the three-dream pre-PMID requirements, participants were given access to individual password-protected areas on a privately owned Web site. Instructions were available on the Web site for how to use the PMID model and how to enter dreams and PMID interpretations. No limit was placed on number of dreams and PMID interpretations submitted. As coinvestigator, I gave facilitative feedback on participants' use of the PMID model.

Outcomes: Number of dreams and related pre- and post-PMID dreams and interpretations volunteered by individual participants were as follows:

	Participant A	Participant B	Participant C	Participant D	Participant E
Pre-PMID dreams and interpretations	1	3	3	3	3
Post-PMID dreams and interpretations	2	17	8	3	3

Quantitative

Quantitative outcomes are presented in text Tables 4.1, 5.1, 6.1, 7.1, 8.1, and 9.1. They are also presented below in concise displays.

Data: Participants' self-ratings of their abilities to do each PMID step on a scale of 1 to 7, with 7 the highest agreement (form similar to the later copyrighted PFI)

Methodology: Each participant was requested to provide self-ratings at two times during their use of the PMID model. The first time was after entering his or her second dream and related interpretations. The second time was at the end of the project.

	Percentages	
Outcomes: Medians of Participants' Self-Ratings	After 2 Dreams (5 Participants)	At 4 Months (4 Participants)
Connected day-before events to dreams (Step 1)	71.4	92.9
Connected day-before thoughts to dreams (Step 2)	71.4	92.9
Defined at least three dream phrases (Step 3)	71.4	71.4
Recognized dreaming emotions (Step 4)	71.4	92.9
Found suggestions or solutions in dreams (Step 5)	71.4	85.7
Explored relationship experiences (Step 6)	71.4	92.9

Data: Independent dream specialist's rating on participants' pre-PMID dream interpretations and post-PMID use of the PMID model.

Methodology: Dream specialist R. L. Van de Castle, PhD, was engaged to rate participants' pre-PMID and 24 of 33 post-PMID interpretations.

Outcomes: Medians of Van de Castle's Ratings	Percentages
Pre-PMID Interpretations (13)	**Pre-PMID Medians**
Connected day-before events to dreams (Step 1)	76.9
Connected day-before thoughts to dreams (Step 2)	7.7
Defined at least three dream phrases (Step 3)	0.0
Recognized dreaming emotions (Step 4)	92.3
Found suggestions or solutions in dreams (Step 5)	15.4
Explored dream reactions to others (Step 6)	69.2
Post-PMID Interpretations (24 of 33)	**Post-PMID Medians**
Connected day-before events to dreams (Step 1)	100.0
Connected day-before thoughts to dreams (Step 2)	100.0
Defined at least three dream phrases (Step 3)	66.7
Recognized dreaming emotions (Step 4)	95.8
Found suggestions or solutions in dreams (Step 5)	100.0
Explored dream reactions to others (Step 6)	87.5

Note: From Van Doren, D., & Duesbury, E. M. [Anecdotal exploration of Wisconsin members of the ACA and counselor education graduate students' ability to use the Personalized Method for Interpreting Dreams (PMID) model]. Unpublished raw data, 2001.

TABLE A4 Exploration, 3 Months

Participants: Eleven Wisconsin members of the American Counseling Association and counselor education graduate students. Races represented: Asian (1), White American (9), Hispanic (1). Gender: Nine females and two males. Age range: 24–55

Qualitative

Raw Data: Participants' relationship dreams and related PMID interpretations (81)

Methodology: Participants were given access to individual password-protected areas on a privately owned Web site. Instructions were available on the Web site for how to use the PMID model and how to enter dreams and PMID interpretations. Participants were requested to submit five dreams and related PMID interpretations, with no maximum limit placed. As coinvestigator, I gave facilitative feedback on participants' use of the PMID model for the first five PMID interpretations and periodically thereafter. Participants were encouraged to review facilitative feedbacks and revise their original interpretations if needed to conform to the PMID model steps and for any new insights gained.

Outcomes: Numbers of dreams and related interpretations volunteered by individual participants were as follows:

Participant A	Participant B	Participant C	Participant D	Participant E	Participant F
6	5	8	7	5	12
Participant G	**Participant H**	**Participant I**	**Participant J**	**Participant K**	**Total**
5	9	7	8	9	81

Quantitative

Quantitative outcomes are presented in text Tables 4.1, 5.1, 6.1, 7.1, 8.1, and 9.1. They are also presented below in concise displays.

Data: Participants' PFI's[a]

Methodology: Participants were requested to complete PFIs at three dates: start of the project, 8 weeks after the start, and 3 months after the start. The Wilcoxon signed rank test, a nonparametric test, was used to analyze the PFI results. (A nonparametric test can be applied to test significance for small samples. An Internet Web site (Lowry, 2009b) was used to compute paired rankings at the start with those at 8 weeks and paired rankings at 8 weeks with 14 weeks.

Outcomes: A significant positive difference was found between participants' PFI ratings at the beginning of the project and their ratings at 8 weeks.

PFI Statement 1 (event connections)	$W- = 2, W+ = 64, N = 11, p \leq .00293$
PFI Statement 2 (thought connections)	$W- = 0, W+ = 55, N = 10, p \leq .00195$
PFI Statement 3 (dream phrases defined)	$W- = 2, W+ = 53, N = 10, p \leq .005859$
PFI Statement 4 (emotions compared)	$W- = 2, W+ = 43, N = 9, p \leq .01172$
PFI Statement 5 (solutions or suggestions)	$W- = 1, W+ = 54, N = 10, p \leq .003906$
PFI Statement 6 (reactions in relationships)	$W- = 5.50, W+ = 60.50, N = 11, p \leq .00977$
Totals from each participant	$W- = 1, W+ = 65, N = 11, p \leq .001953$

Participants' PFI ratings remained stable at 14 weeks at the significant positive levels achieved by 8 weeks.[a]

Outcomes: Medians of participants' PFI self-ratings were as follows:

	Start	8 Weeks	Final
PFI Statement 1 (event connections)	4.0	7.0	7.0
PFI Statement 2 (thought connections)	3.0	7.0	7.0
PFI Statement 3 (dream phrases defined)	2.0	6.0	7.0
PFI Statement 4 (emotions compared)	3.0	6.0	6.0

PFI Statement 5 (solutions or suggestions)	2.0	6.0	6.0
PFI Statement 6 (reactions in relationships)	3.0	6.0	7.0

Data: Participants' emotional change instruments (ECIs)[b]

Methodology: Participants were requested to complete ECIs at two times: 10 weeks after the start and 14 weeks after the start.

Outcomes: At 10 weeks, 7 of the 11 participants reported positive changes in dreaming emotions about one or more relationship. At 14 weeks, all 11 reported positive changes in dreaming emotions about one or more relationships.

Note: From Duesbury, E., Bynum, E. B., & Van Doren, D. [Anecdotal exploration of Wisconsin members of the ACA and counselor education graduate students' ability to use the Personalized Method for Interpreting Dreams (PMID) model]. Unpublished raw data, 2002.

[a] The PFI contains six statements related to the six PMID steps. Participants used these statements to self-rate their abilities to do each PMID step on a scale of 1–7, with 7 the highest agreement. See PFI in Appendix B.

[b] The ECI contains a series of questions designed to increase dreamers' self-awareness of differences between their dreaming emotions and their pre-dream waking-life emotions regarding the people about whom they dream. See ECI in Appendix B.

TABLE A5 Exploration, 3 Months

Participants: Five counselor education graduate students. Races represented: African American and White American. Gender: female. Age range: 31–50

Qualitative

Raw Data: Participants' relationship dreams and related PMID interpretations (36)

Methodology: Participants were given access to individual password-protected areas on a privately owned Web site. Instructions were available on the Web site for how to use the PMID model and how to enter dreams and PMID interpretations. Five dreams and related PMID interpretations were requested, with no maximum limit placed. As coinvestigator, I gave facilitative feedback to individual participants on their use of the PMID model for the first five PMID interpretations and periodically thereafter. Participants were encouraged to review facilitative feedback and revise their original interpretations if needed to conform to the PMID model steps and for new insights gained.

Outcomes: Number of dreams and related PMID interpretations volunteered by individual participants were as follows:

Participant A	Participant B	Participant C	Participant D	Participant E
5	10	10	5	6

Quantitative

Quantitative outcomes are presented in text Tables 4.1, 5.1, 6.1, 7.1, 8.1, and 9.1. They are also presented below in concise displays.

Data: Participants' periodic feedback instruments (PFIs)[a]

Methodology: Participants were requested to complete PFIs at three dates: start of the project, 8 weeks after the start, and 3 months after the start.

Outcomes: Medians of participants' PFI self-ratings were as follows:

	Start	8 Weeks	3 Months
PFI Statement 1 (event connections)	5.5	5.0	6.0
PFI Statement 2 (thought connections)	2.0	5.0	6.0
PFI Statement 3 (dream phrases defined)	2.0	5.0	5.0
PFI Statement 4 (emotions compared)	3.0	5.0	6.0
PFI Statement 5 (solutions or suggestions)	2.0	5.0	5.0
PFI Statement 6 (reactions in relationships)	4.0	5.0	6.0

My examinations of participants' PMID interpretations indicated that some participants' ratings, especially at the beginning, were overstated. For this reason, no analysis beyond the medians presented here was made on PFI ratings for this project.

Data: Emotional change instruments (ECIs)[b]

Methodology: Participants completed ECIs at two times: 10 weeks after the start and at 14 weeks after the start.

Outcomes: At 10 weeks, two of the five participants reported a positive change in dreaming emotions about one or more relationships. At 14 weeks, four of the five participants reported a positive change in dreaming emotions about one or more relationships.

Note: From Duesbury, E., Bynum, E. B., & Van Doren, D. [Anecdotal exploration of counselor education graduate students' ability to use the Personalized Method for Interpreting Dreams (PMID) model]. Unpublished raw data, 2003.

[a] The PFI contains six statements related to the six PMID steps that participants used to self-rate their abilities to do each PMID step on a scale of 1 to 7, with 7 the highest agreement. See PFI in Appendix B.

[b] The ECI contains a series of questions designed to increase dreamers' self-awareness of differences between their dreaming emotions and their pre-dream waking-life emotions regarding the people about whom they dream. See ECI in Appendix B.

TABLE A6 Exploration, 3 Months

Participants: A total of six, including five counselor education undergraduate students and one counselor education graduate student. Race represented: White. Gender: Five females and one male. Age range: 21–39

Qualitative

Raw Data: Participants relationship dreams and their related PMID interpretations (29)

Methodology: Participants were given access to individual password-protected areas on a privately owned Web site. Instructions were available on the Web site for how to use the PMID model and how to enter dreams and PMID interpretations. Participants were requested to submit five dreams and related PMID interpretations, with no maximum limit placed. As coinvestigator, I gave facilitative feedback on participants' use of the PMID model for the first five PMID interpretations and periodically thereafter. Participants were encouraged to review facilitative feedbacks and revise their original interpretations if needed to conform to the PMID model steps and for any new insights gained.

Outcomes: Number of dreams and related PMID interpretations volunteered by individual participants were as follows:

Participant A	Participant B	Participant C	Participant D	Participant E	Participant F
5	4	3	5	8	4

Quantitative

Quantitative outcomes are presented in text Tables 4.1, 5.1, 6.1, 7.1, 8.1, and 9.1. They are also presented below in concise displays.

Data: Participants' periodic feedback instruments (PFIs)[a]

Methodology: Participants were requested to complete PFIs at three dates: start of the project, 8 weeks after the start, and 3 months after the start.

Outcomes: Medians of participants' PFI self-ratings:

	Start	8 Weeks	3 Months
PFI Statement 1 (event connections)	5.5	5.0	6.0
PFI Statement 2 (thought connections)	5.5	5.0	6.0
PFI Statement 3 (dream phrases defined)	2.5	4.5	5.5
PFI Statement 4 (emotions compared)	2.5	5.0	6.5
PFI Statement 5 (solutions or suggestions)	2.0	3.5	6.0
PFI Statement 6 (reactions in relationships)	6.0	5.0	5.0

My examinations of participants' PMID interpretations indicated that some participants' ratings, especially at the beginning, were overstated. For this reason, no analysis beyond the medians given here was made on PFI ratings for this project.

Data: Participants' emotional change instruments (ECIs)[b]

Methodology: Participants completed ECIs two times: at 10 weeks and at 14 weeks.

Outcomes: At 10 weeks, three of the six participants reported a positive change in dreaming emotions about one or more relationships. At 14 weeks, four of the six participants reported a positive change in dreaming emotions about one or more relationship.

Note: From Duesbury, E., Bynum, E. B., & Van Doren, D. [Anecdotal exploration of counselor education undergraduate and graduate students' ability to use the Personalized Method for Interpreting Dreams (PMID) model]. Unpublished raw data, 2004.

[a] The PFI contains six statements related to the six PMID steps, which participants use to self-rate their abilities to do each PMID step on a scale of 1 to 7, with 7 the highest agreement. See PFI in Appendix B.

[b] The ECI contains a series of questions designed to increase dreamers' self-awareness of differences between their dreaming emotions and their pre-dream waking-life emotions regarding the people about whom they dream. See ECI in Appendix B.

TABLE A7 Research, Open-Ended for 1 Year

Participants: Five people who had participated in earlier projects. These were four counselor education graduates and one person who applied when Wisconsin members of the American Counseling Association were invited. Races represented: Asian and White American. Gender: four females and one male. Age range: 35–58

Qualitative

Raw Data: Participants' relationship dreams and their PMID interpretations (46 earlier dreams and interpretations, 10 current dreams and interpretations)

Methodology: Participants were given access to individual password-protected areas on a privately owned Web site. No minimum or maximum requests were made. As coinvestigator, I gave facilitative feedback to participants on their use of the PMID model.

Outcomes: Number of dreams and related PMID interpretations volunteered by participants during their participation in earlier projects (46) and during the current project (10) were as follows:

	Participant A	Participant B	Participant C	Participant D	Participant E
Earlier projects	8	6	10	17	5
Current project	0	0	2	7	1

Dream and Related PMID Interpretations

One current dream and participant's (Participant C) related PMID interpretations are presented next to demonstrate ongoing success with the PMID model. Italicized words distinguish them from the facilitator's words.

Dream Title: "Dirty Dilemma"

I return to my parents' house. I look for their sauna to just relax and enjoy the warmth of the water. Finally find it. But the water runs out when I step in and leaves filth settling in the bottom of the sauna. I look around for another place in my parents' house. It's larger than I recall and darker than I recall. I discover another sauna. Again the water runs out when I step in and a dirty film is left. I feel repulsed. Then I notice some bare electrical cords. Now I am alarmed.

PMID Step 1: Day-before-your-dream **events** that connect to this dream.

Yesterday I met with a former lover, one who had turned sour in the past, but now seems new and refreshing.

PMID Step 2: Day-before-your-dream **thoughts** that connect to this dream.

Last night thought about the relationship—how my old lover sees me now.

PMID Step 3: Major dream phrases (and symbols) defined in the context of this dream.

1. ***My parents' home:*** *[In the context of this dream] my concepts formulated during my growing-up years.*
2. ***Difficulty finding the sauna:*** *Wanting to get clean. Here, wanting to have a pleasant experience with a former lover, but I encounter difficulties.*
3. ***Dirty water:*** *Water can relate to emotions, so dirty water might signify unclean emotions, something I don't want to encounter and want to avoid.*
4. ***Bare electrical cords:*** *Dangerous encounter.*

PMID Step 4: Dreaming **emotions** compared with waking-life emotions about issue in this dream.

In the dream, I was wanting the sauna—I was attracted to the feelings of love—then repelled by the icky water and dangerous electrical cords. Water can signify emotions. In waking life, I worry that I will look foolish any way I go. If I am wanted by him, I will screw it up and it will be bad. Or it will be okay, and I will look emotional and silly. Or I will be rejected by him and look foolish.

PMID Step 5: Solutions or suggestions for changing (or affirming) thoughts, attitudes, or behaviors. Look for answers to your day-before-your-dream thoughts.

The only way to avoid the disaster symbolized by my dream is to avoid becoming drawn into another close relationship with my former friend. But my dream doesn't name my former friend, so I won't chuck the relationship just yet.

PMID Step 6: Dreaming and waking-life **reactions** to each person in this dream.

If my dream had named the former relationship instead of appearing in subjective images, I would say that I reacted in my dream by avoiding a return to our former close relationship. In my waking life before this dream, I agreed to meet him, but only in a group of mutual friends for now. My reactions to my parents are perhaps shown in my dream by my reactions to the filth I see in the house. Perhaps the filth I see represents my unconscious reactions to their guidelines from childhood and adolescence?

Quantitative

Quantitative outcomes are presented in text Tables 4.1, 5.1, 6.1, 7.1, 8.1, and 9.1. They are also presented below in concise displays.

Data: Participants' periodic feedback instruments (PFIs)[a]

Methodology: Participants were invited to submit PFIs6x months after the beginning of the study. Those outcomes were compared to each participant's earlier year PFIs.

Outcomes: Raw scores of participants' earlier and current PFIs

	A	B	C	D	E
			Previous PFIs		
Years Since Previous PFI	3	3	2	4	3
PFI Statement 1 (event connections)	7.0	7.0	6.0	7.0	7.0
PFI Statement 2 (thought connections)	7.0	7.0	6.0	7.0	7.0
PFI Statement 3 (dream phrases defined)	7.0	7.0	6.0	5.0	7.0
PFI Statement 4 (emotions compared)	7.0	6.0	5.0	7.0	7.0
PFI Statement 5 (solutions or suggestions)	7.0	6.0	6.0	6.5	5.0
PFI Statement 6 (reactions in relationships)	7.0	5.0	5.0	6.0	7.0
			Current PFIs[b]		
PFI Statement 1 (event connections)	7.0	6.0	6.0	4.5	
PFI Statement 2 (thought connections)	7.0	6.0	6.0	4.5	
PFI Statement 3 (dream phrases defined)	7.0	4.0	7.0	5.0	
PFI Statement 4 (emotions compared)	6.0	5.0	6.0	3.0	

PFI Statement 5 (solutions or suggestions)	6.0	7.0	6.0	1.5
PFI Statement 6 (reactions in relationships)	7.0	4.0	5.0	1.5

Participants' comments on their use of the PMID model:

Participant A: "I continue to use this valuable tool sporadically in my own life and occasionally with clients in my counseling practice."

Participant B: "I rated myself lower in the areas of definition and analyzing relationships only because I have been lax in my use of the method. While actively using the PMID model, I found it to be extremely useful in these areas as well. I now have a much greater awareness and reverence for my dreams and use the information they hold in my waking life. Thank you for your gift to me."

Participant C: "I wish I had been able to enter more dreams … between finishing my internship and being promoted and transferred. … [But] thank you. I do pay attention to what my subconscious tries to alert my conscious mind to at night."

Participant D: "I am low in the number levels because I haven't been consistent in practicing dream recollection. … For me it boiled down to having self-discipline to stick to it long enough to see results. I will have to work on this on my own now that the research project is done."

Note: From Van Doren, D., & Duesbury, E. M. [Research of the Personalized Method for Interpreting Dreams (PMID) model's usefulness for ongoing personal and professional development]. Unpublished raw data, 2005–2006.

[a] The PFI contains six statements related to the six PMID steps, which participants use to self-rate their abilities to do each PMID step on a scale of to 7, with 7 the highest agreement. See PFI in Appendix B.

[b] Participant E did not offer a current PFI.

TABLE A8 Research, 6 Months

Participants: Seventeen, including 16 from a general population in the Midwest and 1 from Europe. There were 13 female and 4 male participants. Female participants, ranging in age from 26 to 57, included Asian, American Indian, White American, and White European and were involved in 11 different occupations (marketing, student, homemaking, food service, university administrator, hospitality, tourist consulting, support services, librarianship, teaching, and counseling). Male participants were White Americans ranging in age from 30 to 54 and were involved in three different occupations (food service provider, public relations consultant, and media). Fourteen participants had education beyond high school. Eight participants, seven females and one male, representing one culture (American Indian) and one race (White) and having a median age of 41, were still active at the end of the project.

Qualitative

Raw Data: Participants' dreams and their related PMID interpretations (222, 200 being from the 8 participants who continued active to the end of the 6-month project)

Total relationship of dreams submitted was 122, 103 being from the 8 continuing active participants.

Methodology: Participants were given access to individual password-protected areas on a privately owned Web site. Instructions were available on the Web site for how to use the PMID model and how to enter dreams and PMID interpretations. No minimum or maximum limits were made. As coinvestigator, I gave facilitative feedback to individual participants on their use of the PMID model for the first five PMID interpretations and periodically thereafter. Participants were encouraged to review facilitative feedback and revise their original interpretations if needed to conform to the PMID model steps and for new insights gained.

Outcomes: Number of dreams and related PMID interpretations volunteered by the eight participants who continued to the end of the 6-month project were as follows (numerator is number of relationship dreams; denominator is total number of dreams submitted):

Participant A	Participant B	Participant C	Participant D	Participant E	Participant F	Participant G	Participant H
4/5	13/38	29/44	22/67	6/7	13/17	2/4	14/18

Outcomes: To illustrate participants' use of the PMID model, one dream narrative, the original PMID interpretations, my feedback as facilitator on the participant's use of the PMID model, and the participants' revised interpretations are presented next. James (Participant E) interpreted this dream about 7 weeks after the research began. (James's words are italicized to distinguish them from the facilitator's words.)

Dream Title: "The Orange Corvette" (Permission to use given by James, the dreamer)

I am waiting outside in the rain for my wife, Jenna, to pick me up in her car. It's raining heavily and the sky is dark and gray. I don't recognize the street or the town I am in. It feels depressing. After several minutes, Jenna shows up late to pick me up. I am surprised when I see her pull up in an orange Corvette since this isn't her normal car. As she drives up, she is all smiles.

When I ask her about the Corvette, she tells me that it was her Great Uncle Johnson's car, and he gave it to her when he passed away. She only drives it on rare occasions.

As I jump into the car, I notice that the sky is now bright and blue. The rain and gloominess have faded away.

I have plans this evening to see my friend, Martin, but Jenna makes a request that she and I have dinner first before I see Martin. I feel conflicted because I had agreed to meet Martin at a specific time, and if I have dinner with Jenna I will be very late. Plus, I feel guilty because Martin is going through a difficult time because his nephew recently committed suicide. Despite my feelings of guilt, however, I agree to go to dinner with Jenna. I awaken just as we're driving on our way to dinner.

Facilitator's feedback on James's dream recording: Fine work in recording your dream in first person and present tense and recording the emotions you felt during your dream in the dream narrative.

PMID Step 1: Record the events you had before your dream (most often, day before) that appear either objectively or figuratively in this dream.

Two nights ago, Jenna told me that she would be home around 8:00 p.m. after she attended a social engagement related to work. Later in the evening, she called to inform me that she wouldn't be home until later because her new boss had showed up late to the event and she needed to schmooze with him and some coworkers. She arrived home around 11:00 p.m.

Just over a week ago, Martin informed me that a young nephew had just committed suicide. Martin was very upset, confused, and shocked by his nephew's death. I sent him a card expressing my condolences to him and his family.

Facilitator's feedback on Step 1: Fine connections of pre-dream events to your dream.

Note to readers: Notice that the event James connected to this dream happened two nights and just over a week ago, respectively, before the dream. For the majority of dreams in this study, dreamers cited events from 1 day before. For four of James's other six dreams, he cited day-before-the-dream events.

PMID Step 2: Record the thoughts you had before your dream (most often, day before) that seem to connect to this dream either objectively or figuratively. Write "I thought" statements to help clarify which day-before-the-dream thoughts brought this dream.

Two nights ago, I returned home from working out at my health club eager to see Jenna. I called her, and she informed me that her plans had changed and she would not be home at 8:00 p.m. as planned, but closer to 11:00 p.m. due to a work commitment. I was very disappointed by her reply and felt that her work commitment was more important to her than spending time with me. I was short with Jenna on the phone as well as when she returned home later that night.

Facilitator's feedback on Step 2: Although the events (PMID Step 1) happened two nights and just over a week ago, respectively, before your dream (instead of the night before your dream, as is the usual case for PMID Step 1), consider whether you were still thinking about those events the day and night before you went to sleep and dreamed this dream. Then write out a thought here. "Yesterday/last evening a predominant thought(s) I had was/were … ." Then you have a thought that your dreaming mind responded to and brought this "answering" dream.

Note to readers: Participants tend to write events (Step 1 criteria) again (as James has done) instead of tracing their thoughts to their dreams. One common task of the facilitator is to remind participants of their need to specifically address "thoughts" in Step 2. James does have a thought implied in his Step 2 response (*[I] felt like her work commitment was more important than spending time with me*). The facilitator's responsibility was to remind James of the critical function of Step 2.

PMID Step 3: Select all major dream phrases (and symbols) in your dream and write your personal definitions for each in the context of this dream.

- ***Orange Corvette:*** *I'm not certain what the orange Corvette represents. Perhaps it is hope of brighter days, better times.*
- ***Sky is bright and blue:*** *Feeling of happiness, joy.*
- ***Sky is dark and gray:*** *Feeling of depression.*
- ***Waiting outside in the rain:*** *Feeling of loneliness.*

Note to readers: Notice that James's definitions for the last three dream phrases are helpful to him in interpreting the emotions he felt in his dream. This type of connection is common from PMID Step 3 to the remainder of the steps. Also notice that James could have increased his understanding of the personal meanings in his dream if he had considered the context of the dream (his pre-dream events, thoughts, and previous experiences). Yet, he did well in selecting dream phrases and choosing ones that were important to him.

Facilitator's feedback on PMID Step 3: Fine PMID work with the dream phrases you have listed and defined. Good that you have listed the dream phrase "orange Corvette," although you weren't sure at the time what it meant. Now the orange Corvette has your attention and you can update your definitions if you wish. In my view, this is a rich dream that you may want to explore further, so I propose some more dream phrases (given in bold below) from your dream narrative for you to consider defining in the context of this dream:

- **Jenna driving her Great Uncle's orange Corvette:** (James, could you tell me a bit about Jenna's great uncle? I am curious just why it is his car. And why a Corvette? And why orange? By the way, one universal meaning of the color orange is "balance.")
- **The orange Corvette isn't Jenna's normal car:**
- **My plans to see Martin conflicting with Jenna's plans for our eating out:** (James, do I understand it was the same night when Jenna was later than planned when you had thoughts of calling Martin, but didn't call him.)
- **Overrule my feelings of guilt re Martin and go with Jenna:**
- **Jenna driving a Corvette instead of her own car:** (Can you think of any meaning? Possibly she is like her great uncle, except what?)

Note to readers: Two other dream phrases the facilitator could have suggested are "only driving it on rare occasions" and "to pick me up."

PMID Step 4: Compare your dreaming emotions with your waking-life emotions about the main issue or relationship in this dream. What differences, if any, do you find between your dreaming emotions and waking-life emotions? Also, periodically review your dreaming emotions about the main issue or relationship.

[Most of] my dreaming emotions and waking emotions are somewhat similar. I am anxious and depressed in my dream while I am waiting for Jenna to pick me up in her car. I also feel bad for Martin and his loss. In my waking life, I am anxious, hurt, and angry when Jenna informs me that she will be arriving home late. I feel sad for Martin and have thoughts about calling him that night to see how he is doing, but I don't call him, which makes me feel a little guilty.

[However,] in my dream I immediately forgive Jenna for being late and am happy to see her. In my waking life, I am still angry when I see Jenna later in the evening. I pout about it.

Facilitator feedback on PMID Step 4: Excellent PMID work in exploring your waking-life and dreaming emotions about the main issue or relationship in this dream.

PMID Step 5: Explore your dream for possible solutions or suggestions on changing thoughts, attitudes, or behaviors.

In my waking life, I often lose perspective during moments when those close to me (like Jenna) disappoint me. I am overcome by feelings of sadness, depression, anger, hurt, etc., when someone close to me lets me down. In my dream, I was able to recognize that Jenna was late to pick me up because the weather was bad and she had to go to a special, more distant location to pick up the orange Corvette, since it was in storage.

I recognized these facts and was able to forgive her for being late and enjoy the happy moment with her. In my waking life, I was not able to shift my hurt feelings so quickly and recognize that it was really important on a professional level for Jenna to schmooze with her new boss. Instead, I focused on feelings of being let down and disappointed.

I can learn from my dream that my feelings in the moment often are felt without a full understanding of the facts of the situation.

Facilitator's feedback on PMID Step 5: Very fine PMID work. See my comments under Step 6 (reactions in relationship experiences) for whether this dream could contain even wider-reaching helpfulness.

Notes to readers: The solutions James finds in his dream are to recognize the facts, forgive Jenna for being late, and "enjoy the happy moment with her." If he had been aware of and used those solutions before this dream, it would have "picked him up" from feeling depressed. Also notice that James is aware of his sensitivity to "when those close to me disappoint me." That isn't a new realization for him. Yet for James, the reminder of this sensitivity is also a solution presented by his work with this dream.

PMID Step 6: With whom is your primary relationship in this dream? Compare your dreaming and waking-life reactions to each person in this dream. In addition, note any influences from the past indicated in this dream.

It's not surprising that I reacted so strongly to Jenna's change of plans two nights ago. The majority of my childhood was spent wondering when my mother, who worked as an international correspondent, would return home. I often remember being disappointed when I learned that one of her meetings was going longer than planned. Similarly, Jenna's occupation on the staff of a sports magazine requires her to be out late at night during the week. She often arrives home later than planned, which stirs up feelings of anxiety, hurt, anger, etc., within me. These feelings are identical to those I experienced as a child when my mother changed her plans and returned home hours, or in some cases days, later than planned.

Facilitator's feedback on PMID Step 6: Understandably, you didn't state a primary relationship for this dream. Your believing earlier experiences with your mother being late affected your current reactions to your wife might suggest that your mother is the primary relationship. But because your wife is in the dream—and because your reaction to her being late was the primary impetus for this dream—consider naming your wife as the primary relationship.

Martin is in your dream, so you might write a bit about your reactions to him here. Fine work in writing about your emotional reactions to him under Step 4. There is naturally crossover between Step 4 and Step 6. However, Step 6 asks, "What did you do?" in contrast to the Step 4 question, "What emotions did you feel?"

James, when (or if) you modify any of your original interpretations, either leave your dream as originally recorded or just type "See original." Retain your original title, but add something like Revision No. 1 to the title. For any PMID step interpretations that you leave unchanged, just type, "See original."

Note 1 to readers about PMID Step 6: A past influence is revealed in James's dream, which brings a memory of one aspect of Jenna's great uncle's personality that Jenna shares, but only "*drives,*" that is, displays, "*on rare occasions.*" James's dream invites him to notice those similarities to help him understand his wife's actions during her social/work engagement and subsequent late arrival at home.

Notice that James takes responsibility for changing his own reactions instead of expecting others to change their behaviors. The PMID concept is that it is easier (and better because of the possibility of becoming stuck in blaming and counter-defensiveness) to change oneself than to try to change others, even when others may be at fault.

Note 2 to readers about PMID Step 6: Dreamers' discussions about reactions to persons who are neither depicted nor symbolized in the dream are usually discouraged because such discussions may divert the dreamer from the main meaning of the dream. PMID Step 6 states, "Note any influences from the past indicated in this dream." James's previous searching had already made him aware of the sensitivity from childhood to *when those close to me … disappoint me.* James wisely understands that his emotional reactions to earlier experiences may be affecting his reactions to the event that prompted this dream. He will need to explore future dreams for verification of whether his childhood reactions to his mother's behavior affect his current reactions to his wife's behavior.

James's modifications to his original interpretations. James added new insights to Steps 2, 3, and 6. (PMID steps are abbreviated to save space.)

Step 2: Day-before-your-dream **thoughts** that connect to this dream.

Yesterday I had a predominant thought about the event that occurred the prior evening [when Jenna came home late].

Step 3: Major dream phrases (and symbols) defined in the context of this dream.

- ***Jenna driving a Corvette instead of her normal car:*** *Jenna is like her great uncle Johnson in her vivacious and outgoing personality. However, Jenna is more grounded and has deeper personal relationships and friendships than her great uncle Johnson had.*
- ***Jenna driving her great uncle's orange Corvette:*** *Jenna's personality is very similar to her great uncle Johnson's, very vivacious, outgoing, and loving to enjoy life.*
- ***My plans to see Martin conflicting with Jenna's plans for us eating out:*** *My internal conflict between choosing an option I desire (having dinner with Jenna) versus choosing an option I feel morally obligated to do (seeing Martin).*
- ***Orange Corvette:*** *Jenna's personality: bright, lights up a room, flashy.*

James included his original PMID Step 3 work by adding this note: *See my original interpretations for Step 3 for the rest of the dream phrases and definitions for this dream.*

Step 6: Dreaming and waking-life **reactions** to each person in this dream.

In addition, Jenna's presence provides a positive energy in my life. When Jenna and I are together, I feel some warmth and brightness. I feel alive! Similarly, in my childhood, when my mother was present, I generally felt comforted and happy.

My compassionate reactions to Martin indicate a strong inward nature. Jenna's outgoing, vivacious nature demonstrates an admirable outward nature. Jenna and I have a yin/yang balancing effect on one another. Jenna's outgoing nature helps to draw me out of my shell and into the social world. My introspective nature helps to draw Jenna into herself and her thoughts and emotions.

James included his original PMID Step 6 work by adding this note: *See my original Step 6 interpretations for the rest of my responses to this step.*

In summary, the qualitative perspectives of this investigation as illustrated by James's case study of his dream and interpretations show the efficacy of the problem-solving capacity of the PMID model.

Methodology: Further information about the usefulness of my facilitative feedbacks was collected from the following statement at the end of the 6-month PFI: "Facilitative feedbacks from [one of the coinvestigators] were more helpful than I could have done on my own." Participants were expected to respond Yes or No to that statement. All eight participants responded Yes. (See Appendix B for full PFI statements.)

Quantitative

Quantitative outcomes are presented in text Tables 4.1, 5.1, 6.1, 7.1, 8.1, and 9.1. They are also presented below in concise displays.

Data: Participants' periodic feedback instruments (PFIs).[a]

Methodology: Participants were requested to complete PFIs for three dates: retrospective to start of the project, at 8 weeks after the start, and at 3 months after the start.

Outcomes:

Eight participants completed all three PFIs. To test significance when normality cannot be assumed (a population of less than 10), a nonparametric test should be applied. The Wilcoxon signed rank test, critical values of *W* (sum of the signed ranks), is a nonparametric test appropriate for small samples (Lowry, 2009a). The Wilcoxon signed rank test was used to compare participants' PFI ratings at the start of the study with their ratings at 2½ months and to compare participants' PFI ratings at 2½ months with their 6-month PFI ratings. Results were as follows:

Wilcoxon Signed Rank Tests: Critical Values of *W* for Samples Smaller Than 10[b]

	PFI 1 (PMID 1)	PFI 2 (PMID 2)	PFI 3 (PMID 3)	PFI 4 (PMID 4)	PFI 5 (PMID 5)	PFI 6 (PMID 6)
Level of significance, paired rankings at start with 2½ months	$W = 33$ $n_{s/r} = 8$ p $p \leq .05$	$W = 34$ $n_{s/r} = 8$ $p \leq .02$	$W = 30$ $n_{s/r} = 8$ $p \leq .05$	$W = 28$ $n_{s/r} = 7 \leq$ $p \leq .02$	$W = 26$ $n_{s/r} = 7 \leq$ $p \leq .05$	$W = 28$ $n_{s/r} = 7$ $p \leq .02$
Level of significance, paired rankings at 2½ months with 6 months	$W = 5$ $n_{s/r} = 4$ Nonsignificant	$W = 21$ $n_{s/r} = 6 \leq$ .05	$W = 28$ $n_{s/r} = 7 \leq$ .02	$W = 6$ $n_{s/r} = 4$ Nonsignificant	$W = 11$ $n_{s/r} = 5$ Nonsignificant	$W = 21$ $n_{s/r} = 6$ ≤.05

Following are the medians of the eight participants' PFI ratings:

	Start	2½ Months	6 Months
PFI Statement 1 (event connections)	2.5	6.0	6.0
PFI Statement 2 (thought connections)	2.0	5.0	6.0
PFI Statement 3 (dream phrases defined)	2.0	4.5	6.0
PFI Statement 4 (emotions compared)	2.0	6.0	6.0
PFI Statement 5 (solutions or suggestions)	3.5	5.5	6.0
PFI Statement 6 (reactions in relationships)	4.0	5.5	6.0

Data: Emotional change instruments (ECIs).[c]

Methodology: ECIs were offered to active participants for completion at two times: 3½ months after the start and at the end of the research (6 months).

Outcomes: At 3½ months, six of the eight continuing participants completed ECIs. Three reported a positive change in their dreaming emotions about one or more relationships. At 6 months, seven of the eight continuing participants (an injury curtailed the eighth participant's final reporting) completed ECIs. Five reported a positive change in dreaming emotions about one or more relationshipd.

As coinvestigator, I examined all the ECIs completed by the eight continuing participants. My examinations agreed with all but one ECI rating by one participant. Results: Emotions in dreams differed from waking-life emotions for 46 dreams, with 43 more positive in dreams than in waking-life appraisal of emotions about the dream issues, 5 more negative than in waking life (2 dreams contained both positive and negative differences).

Note: From Okocha, A. G., & Duesbury, E. M. [Research of a general population's ability to use the Personalized Method for Interpreting Dreams (PMID) model]. Unpublished raw data, 2005–2006.

[a] The PFI contains six statements related to the six PMID steps, which participants use to self-rate their abilities to do each PMID step on a scale of 1 to 7, with 7 the highest agreement. See PFI in Appendix B.

[b] Computed from Lowry, 2009b.

[c] The ECI contains a series of questions designed to increase dreamers' self-awareness of differences between their dreaming emotions and their pre-dream waking-life emotions regarding the people about whom they dream. See ECI in Appendix B.

PARTICIPANTS' VOLUNTEERED COMMENTS

Next are representative volunteered comments made by participants in the various projects:

- "Although I feel I have truly excelled [in some areas], I am not as clear on making the connections from past to present; perhaps I'm not ready or perhaps it's too painful. I will continue. This course has changed my life!"
- "Wish I hadn't had so many pressing concerns at home, so would have had more time. I did learn from this project."
- "This has been a wonderful learning experience for me. I am so elated to finally understand and be able to symbolize what my dreaming spirit is trying to teach me."
- "I look ahead to using this model over extensive times to see patterns over several dreams."
- "This project has opened many new doors for me. The PMID model is something I would love to help with and work with in my future."
- "The structured method [and] the repetition of guiding feedback have opened an avenue of understanding through what used to be confusing territory."
- "I have renewed faith in the power of dreams to guide us."
- "PMID has helped me to take my dreams from when I used to try to find literal meanings [that] made little sense to now understanding the symbolism they contain."
- "Not only do I remember my dreams more, but I am also constantly looking at what it is the dreams are saying. By interpreting my dreams through PMID I have a new understanding of myself, which now allows me to move on to relationship issues."
- "I feel I have gained tremendous insight into relationship issues and have gotten much better at connecting my dreams to waking-life situations and relationships."
- "I am still a work-in-progress. I still feel I can learn more about the dream world. I have only touched a tip of the mountain. I will investigate further."
- "I have come to recognize my biggest stressor from noticing the repetition of a waking-life situation in my dreams."
- "This project and this PMID have really opened my eyes to the real problems and some really good solutions, some I may not have come up with myself."
- "I have definitely learned a lot about how dreams can help me with many of my waking-life emotions."
- "Wish I would have done this in a less busy time. Nevertheless, the dream work is really helping me. What is great is that I can continue working with my dreams the rest of my life."
- "It is amazing that my dreams in a way show me whether the change in my emotions are positive or negative ones."

- "I have thus far found that working with my dreams is one of the most effective ways of working with my life and dealing with situations that arise and relationships that occur."
- "I have very much enjoyed being a part of your study on dreams and the uses of PMID interpretations."
- "My dreams have been reflective of my personal challenges with my relationship, first and foremost, with myself, which have a huge impact on all my other relationships (or lack thereof) and the emotions I choose to express or identify at times."
- "I can definitely see a connection between waking and dreaming life. Dreaming life, more accurately than not, reflects waking-life emotions and situations."
- "The dreams often show unexpected emotions, like complicity in the relationship when I go to bed feeling angry and not understood, or vice versa, as the subconscious tells me that I am not looking at the full picture."
- "I never really took stock of my dreams before, but they certainly do say a lot when you don't expect them to."
- "In the dreams, it seems to me that fairly often I was more calm and reassured in any given situation than I think of myself as being when awake. That idea has led me to stop and take a breath now and then while awake, and remain calmer, deep down, at certain times."
- "I really appreciate the insight that comes not only from looking further into my dreams and waking-life thoughts, but also from the valuable feedback."
- "It [this study] has been very helpful in my everyday life."
- "The structured PMID has helped me catch the dream meanings much more quickly."
- "Though it can be a bit startling to realize just how much you now know about me, I can get past that realization and see how much I have also learned about myself."
- "During these months I have been motivated to work on my dreams despite the effort and amount of time it takes, as doing this research has been infinitely more fulfilling than any kind of therapy, holistic or not, and I feel I have made great strides into coming closer to my subconscious."
- "I [have] never recorded my thoughts [before], and it took a long time to be able to make the connections. In my recent experience, if you work straight away when the thoughts are still current, you can learn much more and explore the dream at greater depth. I often recorded dreams reasonably early after having them and understood some of the symbolism, but never recorded the thoughts and missed out on a whole new level of dream interpretation. I have learned much."
- "The PMID has proven to be an insightful, yet practical, tool for looking onward."
- "This has really been helpful in giving me insight into my inner thoughts and feelings."
- "The emerging cognitions about my most important relationships have helped me understand the stress I have imposed upon myself. Paying

attention to emotions isn't something I have done much of, so sometimes [it] was stressful, but [it] will be very beneficial in the long run."

- "Having used your feedback, I do now include emotions in the dream itself and have found that this does indeed make it easier to recall aspects of the dream when reviewing it later."
- "I can really see where recording and then analyzing dreams using PMID and focusing on relationships can in the long run improve most relationships."
- "More than any other class I have taken as a graduate student, our dream interpretation class has made a real and positive impact on my personal and professional life. Thank you for your guidance and support in the start of my journey of understanding the messages of my dreams."
- "I haven't recalled dreams about the same person more than once yet, but, even so, just by stepping back and looking at a couple of the relationships I have dreamt about, I have still been able to use the information to make some changes that I believe have then affected those relationships."
- "I am feeling much more confident about my abilities to use dreams to understand and or improve my waking life. … This is all very new to me, and I was quite leery of my abilities. I'm actually finding the PMID process to be not easy but also not difficult and a good structured way to approach analyzing dreams WHEN I can recall them. That—recollection of dreams—is proving to be the most difficult part of the process for me."

Author's note: The next two comments are representative of others. I include them for reinforcement to counselors that (a) it is important to fully understand how to use the model before facilitating others' use of it; (b) as in so much of counseling, a good working relationship with the client is crucial; and (c) it is also crucial to facilitate your clients' finding their own answers instead of making interpretations for them.

- "The personal comments and feedback were extremely helpful!"
- "The facilitator's feedback allowed me to look at things I missed or really did not cue into."

Author's note: Many participants' comments made at the beginning of the studies contrasted with their comments made at the conclusion of the studies:

- Beginning of the project: "As of right now, I feel I have very little insight into my dreams and their connections to my life."
- Conclusion of the project: "I feel that I have gained tremendous insight into relationship issues and have become much better at connecting my dreams to waking [life] situations and relationships."
- "At the beginning, if zero was a score I could have used it, as I never really paid attention to my dreams unless they scared me. Now I am more aware of my dreams than ever before. They certainly do hold keys that I was fully unaware of previously."

Appendix B: Instruments Used Before and During Facilitation of Clients' Dream Interpretations

INTRODUCTION

Three instruments were developed for use with the Personalized Method for Interpreting Dreams (PMID) model:

Screening instrument. Application for counselor's appraisal of each applicant's emotional ability to work with his or her dreams.
Periodic feedback instrument (PFI). Six statements, each related to the six PMID steps, that participants use to self-rate their abilities to do each PMID step. Scale of 1–7, with 7 the highest agreement.
Emotional change instrument (ECI). A series of questions designed to increase the dreamer's self-awareness of differences between their dreaming emotions and pre-dream waking-life emotions regarding the people about whom they dream.

These three instruments are presented next.

SCREENING INSTRUMENT

Personal Information

Date Applied: ____________________

User Name: ____________________

Password: ____________________

First and Last Name: ____________________

Address: ____________________

Country: ____________________

Phone: ____________________

E-mail: ____________________

Gender: ____________________

Birthday: ____________________

Occupation: ____________________

Highest Level of Education Completed:
Degree/Major:
Marital Status:
Ethnicity:
Emergency Contact Person:

Self-Rating *(Scale 1–7, with 7 high)*

Question and Rating

1. My current ability to understand my dream symbols:
2. My ability to solve puzzles:
3. My ability to learn new skills:
4. My interest in this research is to try to help me relieve stress:
5. I wonder if my past relationships affect how I function in my current relationships:
6. Overall, I'm very happy with my level of success in life:

Multiple Choice (Mark Yes [Y] for All That Apply for Each Statement)

1. I currently
   - Am not involved with working with my dreams
   - Would like to learn how to find personal meanings in my dreams
   - Use a dream interpretation method that seems to be helpful
   - Use a dream interpretation method that does NOT seem to be helpful
   - Am involved in dream study with an individual counselor
   - Am involved in dream study with a group counselor
   - Am involved with self-help dream interpretation on a regular basis
2. I recall my dreams
   - Every night
   - Two or more times a week
   - About once a week
   - Rarely
   - Rarely, but I would like to recall them more
3. I am
   - A dream researcher myself and interested in what others are doing
   - A dream researcher and am searching for more effective dreamwork methods
   - Interested because I teach dream studies or related areas
   - I am a counselor or therapist
   - An individual interested in learning how to interpret my dreams
4. I am a
   - Self-starter
   - Procrastinator
   - Procrastinator unless I am involved in a learning and creative activity

5. My friends describe me as
   - Reliable
   - Energetic
   - Honest
   - A loner
   - Interested in self-improvement
   - Competitive
   - Logical and reasoning
   - Intuitive
   - Patient
   - Creative
   - Prompt
6. I describe myself as
   - A happy person
   - Motivated to work out my problems
   - A person who has difficulty getting started with projects and other responsibilities
   - A person who does things that keep me interested
   - A person who has, at times, had weeks or months of being unable to take care of my daily tasks
   - A brooding person
   - Not as good as other people
7. Lately I have thought a lot about
   - Wishing I were dead, but I would not kill myself
   - Wishing I were dead and how I would kill myself
   - Life in the hereafter
   - Other similar topics
8. Lately, I often feel
   - Lonely
   - Blue
   - Happy
   - Useless
   - Energetic
   - That I don't care what happens to me
9. It seems to me that
   - Most people don't care what happens to me
   - Life is worthwhile
10. My future seems
    - Bright
    - Hopeless
    - Empty and meaningless
    - Uncertain but hopeful
11. I am familiar with the following dream interpretation methods:
    - Jungian
    - Perls
    - Freudian

PMID
Other

12. I am currently taking medications:
    Yes No
13. I am
    In a long-term intimate relationship with a spouse
    In a long-term intimate relationship with a partner
    In an intimate relationship with a significant other person
    Not currently in a long-term intimate relationship
    Have never been in a long-term intimate relationship

Essay (Write in the Blanks)

1. The activity I most enjoy is
2. The relationship that I seem to dream the most about (living or passed on) is
3. Other major relationships that I seem to dream the most about (living or passed on) are
4. The one greatest success I am currently experiencing is
5. Other sources of success I am currently experiencing are
6. The one greatest frustration I am currently experiencing is with
7. Other sources of frustration I am currently experiencing are
8. Summing it all up, the reasons I want to participate in this project with particular focus on relationship issues are

PERIODIC FEEDBACK INSTRUMENT (PFI)

(Each statement is associated with the related PMID step)
On a scale of 1–7 (1 = *strongly disagree* and 7 = *strongly agree*), using the Personalized Method for Interpreting Dreams (PMID), I rate my ability to

1. Connect my waking-life events (most often those occurring the day before) to my dreams.
2. Connect my waking-life thoughts (most often those occurring the day before) to my dreams.
3. Develop personal definitions for dream phrases (and symbols) in the context of this dream.
4. Identify when my dreaming emotions and waking-life emotions are similar and when they are different about the main issue in the dream.
5. Discover problem-solving suggestions.
6. Compare my reactions in relationship experiences as reflected in this dream with my waking-life reactions in similar circumstances.

EMOTIONAL CHANGE INSTRUMENT (ECI)

1. Of the dreams and PMID interpretations I have submitted at this point, I noticed a difference in my dreaming emotions from my waking emotions about a situation for at least one of my dreams and interpretations. ___Yes ___ No. If yes, title(s) for the dream(s) is (are): ______________________ ____ (Number of titles ____).
2. The number of dreams and PMID interpretations I have submitted at this point is ____.
3. Of the dreams and PMID interpretations I have submitted at this point, I recorded emotions I felt during the dream for ____ of those dreams. If one or more, continue to Item 4.
4. Of the dreams and PMID interpretations I have submitted at this point, I dreamed more than once about at least one relationship. ____ Yes ____ No. If yes, continue to Items 5 and 6.
5. The relationship(s) I dreamed about more than once at this point is (are) ____ ____________.
6. I have noticed a positive change in my dreaming emotions about one or more relationships. ____ Yes ____ No. If yes, continue to Item 7.
7. Title(s) of my dreams in which I noticed a positive change in my dreaming emotions about one or more relationships is (are) __________________ ____ (Number of titles ____).

Created by Evelyn M. Duesbury, 2002.

Appendix C: Caveat on Bad or Worrisome Dreams

EDWARD BRUCE BYNUM

By now, you have become aware that dreams and working with your own dreams can be powerful catalysts for understanding the deeper dynamics and realities of your emotional life, especially as it flows into the important parts of the lives of those for whom we feel love, anger, jealousy, kinship, rivalry, pain, and joy within our most important moments. While these moments of insight and feeling usually have a grounding and satisfying effect, we must also be aware that they can be disturbing at times on an intimate level.

When this occurs, it is important to consider exploring these feelings with others. It may even be useful at times to consult a professional counselor. Although not usual, this need does occur even with normal but highly stressful dreams. An example would be a dream series in which we wake up frightened or alarmed by what seems to occur repeatedly. This may be around an incident, trauma, or tragedy that befell you or a family member. It may be about what seems to be a memory or fragment of a memory of something that is trying to come to the surface. It is important in these situations to remember that a dream may be emotionally true but not factually true. A dream may present a symbolic situation to you rather than an actual lived moment or series of past situations.

The unconscious is the great treasure house of not only our loves, hopes, and expectations but also our primal fears, anxieties, and social-cultural traumas that have not actually physically occurred to us but rather have impacted us on a psychological level. All the painful images painted each night on the nightly news of prisoner abuse, degradation, and torture give rise to a bottomless ocean of negative counter images in our collective dreams. Therefore, when you have negative and fearful dreams that repeat themselves, dreams in which you awaken repeatedly in a panic, or dreams in which there is a sickening sensation and a sense of foreboding and dread that follows you through the day, consider speaking with a professional counselor who is well versed in these intimate matters (Duesbury, 2007, pp. 66–67).

Appendix D: The Vital Importance of Taking Periodic Refreshing Breaks From Intensive Work With Relationship Dreams

INTRODUCTION

The purpose of this appendix is to encourage all you who study and use this book to take periodic inspirational breaks from your work with relationship dreams. As with any consuming activity, we can often advance more rapidly and be more productive when we occasionally take time out for relaxing inspiration.

What do you do for relaxing inspiration? Your dreams may use symbols to remind you of activities or nonactivities that inspire you and move you onward. Although I soundly support that it is vitally important for all who work with relationship issues to take periodic breaks from that work, I resisted sharing exactly what I do for relaxation and inspiration. I resisted until the following two dreams persuaded me to share:

Dream Title:
"Resistance to Showing Personal Material on the University's Screen"

(Tuesday, May 26, 2009)

I am standing with a man outside a university classroom. We are watching a man inside the classroom who is projecting large, impressive pictures onto a screen in the front of the class. The man with me suggests that I ask to use the projection equipment and show my pictures, but I say, "Oh, no. That wouldn't be [and I use a word like ethical or accepted protocol]. Mine is for personal use. I just wouldn't ask them to bend the rules for me."

Again he says to ask them. And I still insist I just wouldn't do that.

In the next scene, the man who has been telling me to ask to use this equipment and I are outdoors. We see a fellow crossing a grassy field toward what I know is where some authorities are. I know that he is going to ask for permission for me to use the equipment. I still am very resistant to what I believe to be taking advantage of the university to show personal pictures.

PMID (Personalized Method for Interpreting Dreams) Step 1: Connect your **previous-day** (often the day before) **events** to the dream to discover the theme of this dream. The events may appear in either symbolic or literal terms in your dream. Write down the appropriate events and record when they occurred.

Yesterday, I worked on a proposal for this book to send to a publisher. The main event and theme of my dream seem to be my work on the proposal.

PMID Step 2: Connect your **previous-day** (often the day before) **thoughts** to your dream to detect which thoughts may have prompted this dream's responses. Like events, your thoughts may appear in your dream in either literal or symbolic terms. Write "I thought" statements and record when you thought them.

Yesterday, while working on my book proposal, I wondered if there is any other material I need to include in the book. This thought seems to be the main one that my dream answers. A probable thought-question is, "Are there any additional materials that are important to include in my book?"

PMID Step 3: Select and define **major dream phrases** and symbols from your write-up of this dream to discover the dream's personalized meanings. Consider effects of your events and thoughts of the day before your dream and earlier experiences on the meaning of each major dream phrase and symbol. The general definition for phrases as used in this step is "a string of words." The strings of words can be phrases, clauses, or whole sentences.

1. **University classroom:** At the time of this dream, I had considered *The Counselor's Guide for Facilitating the Interpretation of Dreams: Family and Other Relationship Systems Perspectives* to be a textbook only. (At this writing, the main target of this book is practicing counselors. The secondary audience is master's-level counselor education students.)
2. **Projecting large impressive pictures onto a screen in the front of the classroom:** In the context of my events and thoughts yesterday, this is something I need to picture or include in my book.
3. **Suggests that I ask to use that equipment and show my pictures:** In the context of this dream, the "equipment" or instrument symbolized here is the book, which is a vehicle for teaching important lessons.

4. **Mine is for personal use:** Some material I consider too private to show in the "university" book that I am writing.
5. **Wouldn't ask them to bend the rules for me:** Whatever the material, the topic is something that I consider outside the protocol for a university book.
6. **Again he says to ask them:** Significance, as represented by repetitive requests.
7. **Still insist I just wouldn't do that:** Depth of my resistance represented by repetitive turndowns.
8. **Grassy field:** For me, grass represents growth. I think of fields as large areas. Putting those two ideas together could mean expansive growth.
9. **Know that he is going to ask for permission for me to use the equipment:** The material is significant beyond my personal resistance.
10. **Still am very resistant to what I believe is taking advantage of the university to show personal pictures:** Intensity of my resistance, although in waking life at the time of this dream I am unaware what my dream means for me to show in *The Counselor's Guide for Facilitating the Interpretation of Dreams: Family and Other Relationship Systems Perspectives.*

PMID Step 4: Compare your **emotions in your dream** with your **pre-dream, waking-life emotions** to discover whether your waking-life emotions accurately reflect how you feel about the issue in this dream. Note that the issue may be a relationship issue. What differences, if any, do you find between your emotions in your dream and your waking-life emotions? It is useful to periodically review your emotions in your dreams regarding the main issue or relationship at hand.

In my dream, I feel very resistant to using *The Counselor's Guide for Facilitating the Interpretation of Dreams: Family and Other Relationship Systems Perspectives* to show something that is personal to me. Yet, in my waking life at the time of this dream I am unaware of the information to which my dream is pointing. So, I don't know what my waking-life emotions are on the matter. However, I believe my dream is letting me know ahead of time so that I will understand and be willing to share.

PMID Step 5: Explore your dream for possible **solutions** to problems, including changing (or affirming) your thoughts, attitudes, or behaviors. Consider your responses to each PMID model step, including Step 6, as you search for solutions and suggestions in this dream. Give primary attention to the power of your thoughts before your dream (PMID Step 2) to act as questions that your dream answers.

In response to yesterday's thought, "I wondered if there is any other material that is important to include in the book," my dream demands that I include some significant personal material that I consider beyond protocol to share in a university book.

How I Used This Dream

I decided that my series of dreams that led me to attaining a counselor education master's degree would fit the category of personal material that I resist sharing. One night after I started writing an appendix about those dreams, I had another dream that changed my mind.

Dream Title: "Meditation—For Personal Inspiration"

(Wednesday, June 10, 2009)

I am standing in a bedroom where I periodically stay. I am talking with a man whose viewpoint is objective. That is, he is rational minded. I am telling him about my dreams that led me to earning a counselor education degree. That degree eventually led to my writing this book. He doesn't seem to catch on. (He may be an administrator of some kind.) I keep relating my dreams that led me to earn the counselor education degree, but he says he is surprised that the woman who rents rooms in this house would leave this room open for me when I don't use it all the time, when I just come periodically.

I hear students in the room across the hall and realize there are students in all the other rooms.

The room where we are standing and where I periodically stay is a lovely, spacious room. The man is uncertain why this is the room that the woman keeps open for me. He concludes, "Well, this room is on the side of the house that is in the shade, so that could be the reason she leaves this open for you."

I hadn't thought about that before.

He adds, "You should be very gratefu to this woman for leaving this room open for you."

I feel embarrassed and think, Oh my goodness, I must be sure to thank her and make her know how I appreciate her extreme thoughtfulness.

PMID Step 1: Connect your **previous-day** (often the day before) **events** to the dream to discover the theme of this dream. The events may appear in either symbolic or literal terms in your dream. Write down the appropriate events and record when they occurred.

Yesterday, I set up this appendix with an intention to include the dreams that led me to earn a counselor education degree. I set up the appendix as a response to my "Resistance to Showing Personal Material on the University's Screen" dream. The theme of this new dream seems to be "Personal Information to Share With Readers of This Current Book."

PMID Step 2: Connect your **previous-day** (often the day before) **thoughts** to your dream to detect which thoughts may have prompted this dream's responses. Like events, your thoughts may appear in your dream in either literal or symbolic terms. Write "I thought" statements and record when you thought them.

The thought I had yesterday that I believe most prompted this dream is about how exciting it will be to gather the dreams that led me to earn my degree and inspired my further work with dreams.

Thus, the main likely thought–question that this dream seems to answer is, "Are the dreams that led me to earn a counselor education degree the private material that my 'Resistance to Showing Personal Material on the University's Screen' dream means for me to share with *The Counselor's Guide* readers?"

PMID Step 3: Select and define **major dream phrases** and symbols from your write-up of this dream to discover the dream's personalized meanings. Consider effects of your events and thoughts of the day before your dream and earlier experiences on the meaning of each major dream phrase and symbol. The general definition for phrases as used in this step is "a string of words." The strings of words can be phrases, clauses, or whole sentences.

1. **Standing in a bedroom area where I periodically stay:** In the context of this dream, this is the room where I go for meditation.
2. **Man who is objective:** The reasoning, objective function of my brain.
3. **Relating my dreams that led me to attaining a counselor education degree and that resulted in my writing this book:** The topic I had selected for this appendix.
4. **Doesn't seem to catch on:** It just doesn't make rational sense that my dreams that led me to earn a counselor education degree are vitally important for the readers of my book to know about.
5. **Keep telling him my dreams that led me to earning a counselor education degree:** I was so focused on the dreams that led me to earning the degree as the appropriate ones to share in this appendix that I couldn't concentrate on any other topics.

6. **Says he is surprised that the woman who rents rooms in this house would leave this room open for me when I don't use it all the time, when I just come periodically:** The room in our home where I go for meditation is a guest bedroom. When we don't have guests, I use it for my meditation room. Here, my dream is "telling on me." I've been so busy working on this book that I've decided that there are days that I can skip my regular meditation time.
7. **Woman proprietor:** I share a common association of the feeling and intuitive nature of the right hemisphere of the brain as feminine in all people, male and female. I think of meditation as using mostly the intuitive function.
8. **All the other rooms filled with students:** Working on this book is my primary work at this time. I'm writing it for practicing counselors and students in training.
9. **Room where I stay periodically is a lovely, spacious room:** The room in our home where I go for meditations is a lovely, spacious room.
10. **Room is on the side of the house that is in the shade so that could be the reason she leaves this open for you:** The room in our home where I go for meditations is located in a hillside, so it is truly "in the shade."

PMID Step 4: Compare your **emotions in your dream** with your **pre-dream, waking-life emotions** to discover whether your waking-life emotions accurately reflect how you feel about the issue in this dream. Note that the issue may be a relationship issue. What differences, if any, do you find between your emotions in your dream and your waking-life emotions? It is useful to periodically review your emotions in your dreams regarding the main issue or relationship at hand.

In my dream, I feel embarrassed that I have not thanked the woman who keeps a room open for me to use for my periodic inspiration break. In waking life, I admit I have not felt embarrassed that I have neglected to be grateful for having a place open for my inspiration breaks. My dream tells on me here. It is true that for several weeks I have been so busy that I have skipped daily meditation at times and cut several meditations short.

PMID Step 5: Explore your dream for possible **solutions** to problems, including changing (or affirming) your thoughts, attitudes, or behaviors. Consider your responses to each PMID model step, including Step 6, as you search for solutions and suggestions in this dream. Give primary attention to the power of your thoughts before your dream (PMID Step 2) to act as questions that your dream answers.

The answer to the current dream is No. My earlier dreams that led me to earning a counselor education degree are not the private material that my "Resistance to Showing Personal Material on the University's Screen" dream means. My thoughts yesterday about those earlier dreams brought this current dream to assure me it is not logical that my counselor education pathway dreams are vital to show to my readers.

The material that I believe this current dream reveals as the private material to show you is what I do for relaxation and inspiration. But, it is personal information that I rarely share. At the same time, however, I soundly support and encourage each of you to work from your highest perspective when doing the work of this book, no question on that. My dreams tell me how important it is to take inspirational breaks from intensive work on personal concerns. What do I do for relaxing inspiration? I go to a quiet place, read some inspirational writings, and then meditate.

Perhaps meditation is what you now do or will do for inspiration. Whatever you do, be grateful for the power of your dreaming mind to help you alleviate the stress of worries about relationships and thus promote your personality growth. You can come back to your dreams refreshed and ready for new insights.

Appendix E: Article Published in *Dreaming*

INTRODUCTION

The formal PMID model originated from my thesis (Duesbury, 2000). In December 2001, *Dreaming* published a brief form of my thesis. Though the PMID steps have been substantially updated, I present the article to show the PMID model's origin. A significant feature of this article is that it demonstrates values of interpreting relationship dreams over time.

PERSONALIZED METHOD FOR INTERPRETING DREAMS (PMID)—AS APPLIED TO RELATIONSHIP ISSUES*

Evelyn Duesbury

Abstract

The purpose of this study was to develop a dreamwork model that would help individuals deal with relationship issues. Seventy dreams, involving seven major relationships, were selected from the woman participant's dreams. A dream interpretation model, the Personalized Method for Interpreting Dreams (PMID)® was developed. Well-founded concepts in the PMID are: 1) dreams reflect emotions; and, 2) pre-dream thoughts, current circumstances, and personal definitions build dream meanings. The newest dreamwork concept of the PMID is the systemic perspective that relationship issues are best understood by discovering how relationship experiences influence our thoughts, emotions and behavior in other relationships. With a dreamwork systemic approach, the individual gathers together and studies series of dreams about major relationships in his or her life, primarily the family. Results of the thesis study show that the participant's use of the model was a factor in reducing stressful relationship issues.

When I began this study I expected that dream content, correctly understood, would accurately reflect changes in emotion over time. I also expected that the use of dream interpretations would reflect suggestions for understanding and reducing relationship issues. However, I did not anticipate the extent of interconnected influences found from one relationship to another, the systemic effects.

* Reprinted from Duesbury, E., (2001). *Dreaming, 11*, 203–216. With permission.

Family systems models have emerged based on the concept that "individual behavior is better understood when viewed within the dynamic context of one's family relationships" (Brown & Lent, 1992, p. 261). Yet, there may be few, if any, dreamwork case studies on record that facilitate an individual's dealing with the web of interconnected relationships in the individual's life. Since dreaming is common, dreamwork may be the most universal self-facilitated technique available.

A dreamwork systems approach for utilizing dreams to resolve relationship issues is mindful of recent family systemic models, except instead of having the family together in a counseling session an individual gathers together his/her dreams about various major relationships, primarily the family.

Support for the Qualitative Case Study Approach. The research design is a qualitative descriptive approach. An in-depth case study demonstrated the utility of this approach. Case studies, especially qualitative case studies, have been prevalent throughout the field of education for over thirty years (Merriam, 1998). Goldman (1992) holds that qualitative studies help participants be aware of and understand themselves; usually integrate several components of a situation; tend to operate within a developmental framework; are conducive to intimate counselor-client relationships; and, are flexible and adaptable to varied populations.

Support for Dreamwork as Helpful in Undergoing Personal Change. Dreams are perhaps best known for their usefulness in helping us understand ourselves and solve emotional and interpersonal problems (Delaney, 1993). Dreams reveal old memories and connect them to recent experiences (Hartmann, 1999). Probably the best way to undergo remarkable personal change is to work with your own dreams (Mahrer, 1989). Working with our dreams helps us become involved in our own personality growth (Savary, 1990).

Support for Utilizing a Systemic Dreamwork Approach to Understand and Reduce Relationship Issues. Dreamwork approaches to personal relationship issues can be immensely helpful since dreams reflect emotional concerns and since the majority of our emotional concerns are with personal relationships (Faraday, 1974). Many studies have been conducted about the dream's accuracy in reflecting the dreamer's emotions, and changes in emotions (Jung, 1966; J. A. Hall, 1977; Wolman & Ullman, 1986; Ullman, 1990; Kramer, 1993). Our dreams confront us with the current order and disorder in our relationships with others and also reflect origins of relationship issues in earlier experience (Wolman & Ullman, 1986). The dreaming mind makes suggestions for resolving problems (Jung, 1960; Wolff, 1972; Greenberg & Pearlman, 1993; Van de Castle, 1994; Hill, 1996). Dreams reflect repeated patterns of interaction with major relationships in people's lives and shed light on oneself and one's culture (Bynum, 1993). So dreams can help us understand the complexity of various relationships such as with marriage, friends, family and situations at work and elsewhere (J. A. Hall, 1977).

Recent family systems therapists (Becvar & Becvar, 1982; Bowen, 1985; Brown & Lent, 1992; Bynum, 1993; Allen, 1994) have demonstrated the effectiveness of a systemic method for alleviating relationship issues. So, it seems beneficial to incorporate systems concepts and family dreamwork concepts into a model for helping individuals utilize dreams to relieve relationship issues with family members and other major people in the person's life.

Method

The participant was a White American woman, Rose. She interpreted her dreams and in the process monitored her dreams for emotional states of mind and changes in emotional states of mind about unsettling issues with relationships. She used dream suggestions of how to change underlying thoughts, attitudes and behavior to help her consciously understand and alleviate distressing emotional issues involved with her relationships. When other major relationships and relationship issues were implicated or depicted in an original series, she worked with dreams about the other relationship(s).

The theme, major relationships, was used for selecting series of dreams. Criteria for choosing a particular relationship were that the relationship was predominantly depicted in the participant's dreams and reflected unresolved emotional issues. In all, eight series of dreams were selected, including husband, mother, dad, son, mother-in-law, a mentor, childhood best friend, and a series of dreams exclusively about sexual issues.

A dream interpretation model, the Personalized Method for Interpreting Dreams (PMID) was developed and used during the process. The steps of the PMID are:

[Note: Wording of these steps has since been modified based on later research and exploration projects. See other chapters in this book for the current forms.]

Step 1: Connect the dream contents to current events and circumstances (most often same day) to identify the context or category of the dream.

Step 2: Connect pre-dream thoughts (most often same day) to dream contents by treating the dream as a responsive answer to pre-dream thoughts.

Step 3: Develop personally experienced-based definitions, or associations about each dream symbol: each dream character, place, object or circumstance.

Step 4: Explore dream for evidence of current emotions. Also, explore dream for changes in emotions over time about a relationship or issue being studied.

Step 5: Explore dream for possible suggestions of how to change thoughts, attitudes or behaviors leading to understanding of and reduction of relationship issues.

Step 6: Examine dream for interconnectedness of conceptions about the main dream character with other relationships depicted or implicated in the dream.

Results

For purposes of concise yet detailed reporting the Joel series is highlighted to demonstrate the results of the study....

The six steps of the PMID were used to address the five research questions developed for this study. To guide the reader's review of the results, the research questions and the PMID steps that address each research question [are] provided next.

Research Question 1: Assuming a dreamwork approach is appropriate, what dream interpretation method can be used for self-facilitation? All six steps in the PMID address this question. That is, all the steps were designed for individual use.

Research Question 2: Can a dream interpretation method be personalized to each individual dreamer? PMID Step 3, develop personally experienced-based definitions, or associations about each dream symbol: each dream character, place, object or circumstance specifically addresses this question. Yet all six steps generally address Research Question 2 since all six steps reflect information, emotions, understanding and relationships unique to the dreamer.

Research Question 3: Will the use of dream interpretations reflect change in emotion over time? PMID Step 4, explore dream for evidence of current emotions; also, explore dream for changes in emotions over time about a relationship or issue being studied, addresses this question.

Research Question 4: Will the use of dream interpretations help the dreamer understand relationship issues? PMID Step 5, explore dream for possible suggestions of how to change thoughts, attitudes or behaviors leading to understanding of and reduction of relationship issues, addresses this question. PMID Step 6, examine dream for interconnectedness of conceptions about the main character of a dream with other relationships depicted or implicated in the dream also addresses this question. All the steps generally address Question 4 since all the steps contribute to the development and understanding of meanings not previously understood by the dreamer.

Research Question 5: Will the use of dream interpretations help the dreamer alleviate relationship issues? PMID Steps 5 and 6 address this question. Table I lists the relationship issues identified by the participant in her series of dreams about her husband, and Table II shows how the participant used her dreams and PMID interpretations to reduce relationship issues about her husband.

These following two dreams and PMID interpretations demonstrate Rose's PMID use.

Dream 2. Horses and Rings and Our Son in Joel's Trousers

Joel and I, and Shane are at a horse race. (Shane is his present age.) Shane and I are participating.... The idea is to put your hand under some part of the horse as he starts—perhaps between the harness straps or something near its hindquarters. Somehow the right hand is under its hindquarters as it takes off.

I do this and I am aware the horse in the lane to the left has started before the one in front of me. Now the horse in front of me starts and is held—or perhaps the reason he didn't get started so quick is that he is caught a bit on my ring (the gold band...)

TABLE I Relationship Issues With Husband

Dream Number	Relationship Issue	Dream Title
Dream 1	Feelings of being restricted in the marriage relationship	Joel Heavier on Me than I Realized
Dream 2	Marriage vows vs. spiritual vows; Husband's role vs. son's role	Horses and Rings and Our Son in Joel's Trousers
Dream 3	Difficulty with husband's devotion to his mother	Joel's First Wife
Dream 4	Sexual distress	Man with the Baggy Pants
Dream 5	Communications with husband	Mine in Arizona
Dream 6	Status of overcoming sexual issues	The Maroon Cat is Now a Child
Dream 7	No issues, just comfortable with marriage	Joel and I Going to Marry

I tell Joel and Shane how one could really get a finger hurt by doing this. And Joel says that is why he just doesn't try it because of that danger....

Now Shane notices the diamond and wedding rings from Joel—on my left hand. The diamond is set up just a bit higher than I recalled; it is very pretty, dainty, small, sparkling.... Shane is pleased. He puts his arm around my shoulders in congratulations for having the wedding rings back on. I tell him I am surprised to see them. I wasn't conscious of putting them on again. I tell him how I must have done it while cleaning the dresser where I have kept them. He says, "God did it."

I am pleased he is happy, but I feel uncomfortable yet with the rings and I feel certain I would not even have unconsciously put the rings back on. I think how the white (silver) and yellow gold do not match....

Shane says he is going to get something.... I think he has asked me to go with him, but I hesitate, since I do not want to overstep myself. But yes, now he beckons me to come along. Joel is interested in perhaps some field of corn here.

I gladly walk along with Shane. We go around the outside of the tall rows. A horse or fellow is trying to get going in the muddy area around the corner and sprays mud on someone standing there. I believe Shane tries to help. It seems this isn't a situation where you would think mud would spin out. But now mud spins out onto Shane's trousers. I think how he is wearing jeans so will be easy to clean. But as I look I see he has on dress trousers with a plaid design. I think how maybe I'll wash them for him.

As we walk on toward the gate Shane talks about some girl. He doesn't say she was angry, but he talks of the power of her tennis strokes and that showed she was angry. Oh, my mind was wandering there at first. Who did he say the young woman was? I ask him, "Did you say it was Charlene?" He says or does something that makes me realize I've overstepped my bounds by asking.

We come to the gate and Shane goes up into a tower type thing just outside the gate, I believe, to wash the mud off his trousers.

TABLE II Participant's Use of Her Dreams and PMID Interpretations

Participant's Understanding of Problem-Solving Suggestions Contained in Her Dreams	How Participant Used Problem-Solving Suggestions Contained in Her Dreams
Dream 1: Put yourself in your husband's position, to understand him.	Listened to him, watched him as he interacted with others, inquired about his work and play.
Dream 2: Take gold ring off that you put on to replace your wedding rings. (I thought the gold ring could represent my spiritual commitment.)	Removed the gold ring. Recognized from the dream that the gold ring held me back. Dream prophesied weddings rings would be returned to my hand; son said, "God did it."
Dream 2: Notice that you are putting your son in your husband's place. In the dream he wears his dad's trousers.	Acknowledged that I was burdening my son and leaving my husband on the sidelines. Insight from the dream changed my attitude.
Dream 3: Recognize that you are unconsciously perceiving your husband and his mother's relationship as a spousal relationship. Notice that his devotion to her is in the realm of service to others regardless of religious denomination (In the dream he helped a Protestant minister and a Catholic Priest carry their bags into the hotel where he and his mom were staying.)	Asked my husband about his belief system: He answered "what I learned from my family and acquaintances—even to generations past." So, the very significant message of this dream is one that would have helped me very much had I understood it some time ago. His allegiance to his mom stems from his belief system that is highly influenced by his mom; service to others is the basis of their close relationship, and the basis of his close attention to her.
Dream 4: Change unconscious unhealthy thoughts about your husband's sexual intentions toward you. Distortion is in your attitude about sex instead of your husband's attitudes.	Explored dreams about sexual issues. Uncovered early religious experiences and experiences in my parental home that influenced my resistance to sexual interaction with my husband.
Dream 5: Work within the confines of your own mind instead of trying to talk more to my husband in an attempt to relieve tension between you caused by materials you gave him to read.	I changed my plans to talk more with him about the upset that resulted from the materials I had given to him. I worked to train myself to think before I acted, in this and other interactions.
Dream 6: Notice the progress you made when you, with your husband's help, treated your feminine sexuality as a natural faculty of your human nature.	Studied the lessons of the dream: Avoid getting caught in negative attitudes that "sophisticated" women are not sexually active, feed my mind with wholesome thoughts about my sexuality, and learn from my husband's cleansing attitudes about sexuality.

- Step 1: Connect the dream contents to current event(s) and circumstances (most often same day) to identify the context or category of the dream.

  When the pressure of the marriage was greatest, I replaced my wedding rings with a gold ring. The gold ring was so people would not question us about our marriage. Also, I told myself the gold ring represented my spiritual marriage.
- Step 2: Connect pre-dream thoughts (most often same day) to dream contents by treating the dream as a responsive answer to pre-dream thoughts.

My pre-dream thoughts were about how I like being alone while Joel is away with his mother on a six-week trip. A question posed by my thoughts to my dreaming mind could be, "What would being alone do for me?" I understood the dream's responsive answer to be: "Leaving your husband on the sidelines and attempting to race ahead via your idea of a spiritual marriage will only inhibit your spiritual progress."

- Step 3: Develop personally experienced-based definitions, or associations about each dream symbol: each dream character, place, object or circumstance.

Joel: Represents himself in the dream.

Shane: Our son represents himself in the dream.

Horse race: Horses connote power to me. Three same night dreams reflected power loss.

The gold ring: The ring I used to replace my wedding rings.

My horse is held, perhaps caught on the gold ring: My idea of a spiritual marriage, the gold ring, causes me to lose power of some kind.

Joel doesn't participate: Joel was worried about my spiritual pursuits and didn't take part.

Wedding rings (white gold) returned to my wedding ring finger: Prophecy that I will wear the rings again, although at the time of the dream I had no plans of doing so.

Diamond is set up just a bit higher than I recalled: Represents a prophecy that Joel and my commitment to each other will become "a bit higher" than it has ever been.

Right hand: In the dream the gold replacement ring was on my right hand. In waking life I wore the ring on my left-hand, on my wedding ring finger. From a physiology standpoint, the gold ring on my right hand could represent control by the left hemisphere of my brain. I associate the left hemisphere of the brain with logical reasoning tasks. So, the gold ring that the dream moved to my right hand could be the dream's work to show that the idea to wear the gold ring was my logical reasoning decision; it was not born of an Infinite idea.

Dress trousers with plaid design that Shane is wearing: The type trousers Joel wears. I don't ever recall seeing Shane wear plaid trousers. Symbolizes I put our son in the position of "wearing the pants" in the family, in his dad's place.

Mud on Shane's Joel trousers: The dirt that I was throwing on Shane's conception about his dad when for the first time I did not speak well of Shane's dad to Shane.

Young woman was with the power tennis strokes: Shane's former girlfriend. Shane was still healing from her anger when I told him of my plans to leave his dad. I was so honed in on my issues that I was not tuned into the pain he was feeling from the power of the young woman's anger.

Overstepped my bounds: Overstepped my bounds into Shane's private life.

- Step 4: Explore dream for evidence of current emotions. Also, explore dream for changes in emotions over time about a relationship or issue being studied.
  I feel some relief from the pressure of our relationship compared to Dream 1, but I still feel resistance to wearing my wedding rings and consequently resistance to the marriage relationship.
- Step 5: Explore dream for possible suggestions of how to change thoughts, attitudes, or behaviors leading to understanding of and reduction of relationship issue.
  Stop wearing the gold ring. Recognize burdens I place on my son from over-reliance on him.
- Step 6: Examine dream for interconnectedness of conceptions about the main dream character with other relationships depicted or implicated in the dream.
  The dream reflects how my over-reliance on our son for support not only placed unfair burdens on him it also left Joel standing on the sidelines. My work with a series of dreams about Shane contributed to helping me relate to my son from a healthier perspective and to treating Joel as my partner instead of someone standing on the sidelines of my life.

Dream 3. Joel's First Wife

We seem to be in an upper story of a hotel. Joel has helped two "men of the cloth" move in. It seems two of them were Catholic. Now he is helping a Protestant minister move in.

Now the minister comes out with his wife and family.... Their clothes seem back... to an earlier style of clothing....

Now there is a tall woman here. She is Joel's first wife. She is well groomed but plain and is unsmiling. She is wearing a nice dress. She and Joel haven't been together for a while, but somehow the couples that have been married will be in the same hotel room, so Joel and she will be sleeping together it seems.

There is at least another couple—may be others who have been married to another person, too, it seems, but the attention for me is Joel and his first wife.

Now Joel is here. He shows me what he is wearing. It is a bib overall. The bib is not quite as high as a regular overall. He points out the shirt he has on under it. It is a green plaid shirt. Joel wants to make certain I know the shirt is one I gave to him. He has a kind of "peppy" smile on his face, like he does when he wants everyone to be happy. It is a sort of gesture to let me know he is paying "homage" to me.

I have a sort of pained or hurt feeling that he will be with her, but it isn't a feeling that it is unfair or that he is doing something he should not do. I don't have a feeling of "ownership" of him—not an agony feeling, but a surprising hurt.

- Step 1: Connect the dream contents to current event(s) and circumstances (most often same day) to identify the context or category of the dream.

  Yesterday I wrote in my dream journal I feel good I do not feel bothered about Joel taking a trip with his mom.
- Step 2: Connect pre-dream thoughts (most often same day) to dream contents by treating the dream as a responsive answer to pre-dream thoughts.

  My dream disputes my waking thoughts and shows I still feel bothered by Joel's relationship with his mom.
- Step 3: Develop personally experienced-based definitions, or associations about each dream symbol: each dream character, place, object or circumstance.

  Era of the clothing worn in the dream: When we were first married. That is when I began to think that Joel's first allegiance was to his mom.

  Joel's first wife: Joel's mom. When I first worked with this dream I suddenly realized, in an intuitive flash, "Oh, Joel's first wife is his mom." Joel's mom was a tall, slender lady when we were married. She was always well groomed and neat.

  Joel and his first wife haven't been together for a while: Joel's mom died two months ago.

  Clergy: Belief system.

  Catholic and Protestant clergy: Belief system not dependent on one particular religion.

  Joel helps the clergy with their luggage: Joel's belief system is service-oriented.

  Staying in a hotel: Reflects the trip Joel and his mom took together.

  Sleeping together: Similar ideals and beliefs.

  Bib overall: A little boy. Young boy's clothing (from my growing up years).

  Joel wears a bib overall. Joel pays respect to his mom by acting like his mom's little boy.

  Joel wears the green plaid shirt that I gave to him: Joel pays respect to me, also.
- Step 4: Explore dream for evidence of current emotions. Also, explore dream for changes in emotions over time about a relationship or issue being studied.

  Pained or hurt. The dream aptly reflects how the hurt felt to me. Although I consciously thought my emotions had changed, the dream shows I still feel hurt, yet don't feel it is unfair.
- Step 5: Explore dream for possible suggestions of how to change thoughts, attitudes or behaviors leading to understanding of and reduction of relationship issue.

  Explore Joel and his mom's belief system. When I finally understood the dream I did explore Joel's belief system. Joel's allegiance to his mom stems from his belief system that was highly influenced by his mom. It astounds me I did not understand the dramatic impacts of his mom's service-oriented belief system on Joel long ago. Of course, Joel's mother takes on a "significant other" role that goes even beyond her nurturing parental role.

- Step 6: Examine dream for interconnectedness of conceptions about the main dream character with other relationships depicted or implicated in the dream.

  Joel's mom is reflected in the dream. This dream helped me realize that my feelings about Joel were clouded by yet unresolved feelings that Joel's first devotion is to his mother and it inspired me to explore a series of my dreams primarily about Joel's mom.

Rose worked through a series of dreams about her mother-in-law. Resolution of stress about her mother-in-law eased Rose's relationship with Joel. One of Rose's last dreams she presented about her mother-in-law shows Rose pulling weeds out of her mother-in-law's flower bed. Every time Rose pulls a weed something else pops up—a flower.

In the last dream Rose presented about her husband, Rose was "happily looking forward to marrying her husband," although in waking life they had been married for some time....

Systems effects were reflected, for example, when Carlie came in a dream about Rose's terror at her son's moving out of her reach in the individuation process. There Carlie plays on first team basketball in Rose's place, revealing Rose was unconsciously repeating the feeling of being replaced in her current friendship with her son. Dream help comes when Rose picks up a handful of rich black dirt that just falls apart as she holds her hand open, which she understood to assure her the falling apart of her son from her close mothering was productive. From her farm background she knows that black dirt is a most productive soil, unlike clay soil that sticks together. In a later dream about her son, Rose is watching a television play about a woman and a young man officer who had been comrades for an involved mission for what seemed to be their whole lives to this point. Now at this point they are going on to separate missions. They aren't leaving each other; it means their relationship as it has been is ended, though. Then in the dream Rose recognizes herself as the woman. When she woke she realized the young man officer symbolized her son....

Limitations of the Study: The time frame of the study (seven years) may make it appear that it took seven years for the participant to understand and alleviate any relationship issues. Upon closer observation, the participant's effective use of dream interpretations could have been demonstrated in, for example, a one-dream study or a one-year study. I chose to extend the study until all of Rose's current major issues with each of the major relationships covered by this study seemed to be reduced.

The extent to which the findings of this study can be applied to other people's dreamwork to resolve relationship issues may pose some limitations since not all people are motivated to the level of commitment shown by the participant.

Discussion

Using the PMID in a self-directed way, the participant completed all six steps of the Personalized Method of Interpreting Dreams (PMID) for most dreams. Her account of personal circumstances (PMID Step 1) and pre-dream thoughts (PMID Step 2) relate primarily to her activities and thoughts the day prior to each dream. Her personal experiences (PMID Step 3) defined dream [phrases and] symbols. Over the course of the Joel series of dreams, Rose's dream interpretations reflect great positive changes in her emotions (PMID Step 4) about her husband. Strong evidence that use of dream interpretations resulted in Rose's understanding of relationship issues is demonstrated by her ability to recognize dream suggestions (PMID Step 5) she was not consciously aware of prior to the dream. Rose's examination of the interconnectedness of her experiences in other relationships (PMID Step 6) helped Rose reduce stress about her relationship with the main dream characters. For, example, Rose's dream interpretations helped Rose understand that losing her best friend in childhood affected how she was interacting in current friendships.

When the dream interpretation data are examined over the course of the study we find they reflect that relationship issues were reduced. However, reduction of issues is difficult to trace to its source(s) because of confounding variables. So, did the use of dream interpretations have any effect on reducing relationship issues? The participant attests that she acted on the above suggestions. That is, she took the gold ring off, she "read" the story of possible sexual abuse by reading and interpreting her dreams about sexual issues, she worked to continue treating her sexuality as a natural human faculty, and she interpreted series of dreams about interconnecting relationships. She also worked to improve her thoughts. She attests that her work with dreams contributed greatly to her present feelings of comfort with major relationships. Yet, for purposes of this study, we need to gather some evidence from the data itself for whether the use of dream interpretations reduced relationship issues. One approach is to tie understanding with reduction of issues.

In psychoanalytic therapy a cure may result when clients understand associations between past experiences and current psychological functioning (Erikson, 1963). Existential therapy helps people gain awareness and self-consciousness of their relationship to their self. Self-consciousness leads to insight. Insight is curative because now the individual sees the possibility of doing something about problems (May, 1983). There is no reality for a human being unless he/she is conscious of it. "Only this truth has the power to change human beings" (May, 1969, p. 14). In gestalt therapy self-awareness of sensation and expression by itself is curative (Polster & Polster, 1973). The self-enhancement gained from becoming aware of and interpreting dreams can lead to change in the dreamer (Kramer, 1993). Repeated dream interpretations over time leads to insight and insight leads to behavioral change (Spiegel & Hill, 1989). Findings do show that the use of dream interpretations helped the participant understand relationship issues. It seems obvious that understanding leads to behavior modification and behavior modification leads to problem reduction.

Another approach to determine whether the use of dream interpretations alleviated relationship issues is to tie change in emotions with reduction of emotional stress. Change in thoughts, attitudes and behavior precede emotional change. Automatic thoughts "profoundly affect your mood" (Seligman, 1995, p. 135). Cognitions are based on attitudes developed from previous experience (Beck, Rush, Shaw, & Emery, 1979). Beliefs about a negative event affect how a person feels following the event (Ellis, 1963). All the dream interpretations presented in this study show suggestions for changing ([or affirming]) thoughts, attitudes or behavior. The dream interpretations also show emotional reaction improved about the relationships examined over the course of the study. Since suggestions were made for change of thoughts, attitudes or behavior, and emotions improved over time, it can be inferred that the participant made at least some of the suggested changes to an extent that emotional reaction improved. If the participant made changes suggested by dream interpretations that resulted at least in part in the improved emotional reaction reflected in dreams, reduction of relationships issues is a result, at least in part, to the use of dream interpretations.

The credibility of the participant's interpretations naturally impacts the credibility of this study. Ernest Hartmann, dream researcher, professor of psychiatry and editor-emeritus of *Dreaming* magazine read narrative forms of most dream interpretations contained in this study. He described these dream interpretations as "a brilliant job of using dreams as psychotherapy and being (her) own therapist through the use of dreams" (E. Hartman, personal communication, January 27, 1997).

How the Findings Relate to Prior Studies and Findings: The most notable finding of this study is that use the PMID helped the participant understand and alleviate relationship issues connected with seven major people in her life. The PMID utilizes six characteristics of dreams as reflected in the six steps of the method: pre-dream events and circumstances together with thoughts initiate the dream, symbols [whole phrases taken directly from the dream narrative] are largely derived from personal associations, emotional content of dreams reflect changes over time, dreams contain problem-solving suggestions, and relationship issues with one relationship are more fully understood by understanding influential conceptions about other major relationships in the dreamer's life. Findings that relate to each of those characteristics are discussed next.

The findings that dreams reflect previous-day activities are consistent with day-residue studies (Hartmann, 1968; Marquardt, Bonato & Hoffmann, 1996) and with mood measurement studies (Kramer, 1993). Waking events incorporated in dreams are often closely linked to past events and circumstances, a finding that corroborates Hartmann's (1999) contentions. In addition, the present study found that previous-day events and circumstances set the context of the dream, a finding consistent with Freud (1955).

The findings that dreams reflect pre-dream waking thoughts is consistent with studies conducted by Kramer, McQuarrie, and Bonnet (1981) and studies conducted by Kramer, Roth, Arand, and Bonnet (1981). In addition, the present study found that pre-dream waking thoughts trigger dreams, a finding that parallels literature discussions (Seafield, 1865; Freud, 1955; C. S. Hall & Van de Castle, 1966; Faraday, 1974).

Flowers and Zweben's (1998) study utilized Delaney's (1993) Dream Interview method and confirmed that dream symbols derive from the dreamer's personal associations. An assumption of Hill's (1996) model is that dreams are uniquely individual. Hildebrant (cited in Van de Castle, 1994) was so certain that dream symbols come from the chambers of one's memory that he claimed it would be possible to explain every dream image if enough time were available to trace the image to the person's memory (Van de Castle). Once the dreamer understands the dream code, his/her personal associations, dream symbols, are "neither mysterious nor inaccessible" (Cartwright & Lamberg, 1992, p. 5). The present study agrees with these findings and assertions.

Hall and Van de Castle (1966) and Kramer (1993) found that emotions are reflected in dream content, a finding that is confirmed in the present study. That dreams reflect changes in emotion corresponds with the literature review (Jung, 1966; Kramer, 1993).

Jung relied extensively on the problem-solving powers of the dreaming mind (Jung, 1966). The present study relied extensively on problem-solving suggestions in dreams and found interpretations of dream suggestions were helpful to the participant.

The finding that dreams reflect interconnecting relationship issues with major relationships is consistent with Bynum's (1993) ongoing study of family dreams. Although recent theories encourage exploration of family systems to understand conflicts in family members' lives, the exploration of an individual's dreams from the systemic perspective of interconnected relationships is rare.

An important dreamwork concept relied on in this study is the series method of fitting combinations of dreams together until the dreams fall into a meaningful picture of the dreamer (C. Hall, 1966). The investigator followed the participant's psychological development by exploring series of her dreams, which is consistent with Jung, cited in J. A. Hall (1977). Another finding about the series method is that dreams provide internal correctives to possible arbitrariness of a single dream interpretation, which is consistent with Jung, cited in J. A. Hall (1977) and Faraday (1974).

Dream interpretation, using the PMID, was found to be effective for self-facilitation by the participant. The Hill (1996) dream interpretation model was found to be effective for self-guided dream interpretation sessions, although, using the Hill method, volunteer participants reported preference for therapist-facilitated dream interpretation sessions (Heaton, Hill, Petersen, Rochlen, & Zack, 1998).

The time frame involved in achieving relief from separate issues was often reasonably short. That finding is congruent with Flowers (1993) and Flowers and Zweben's (1998) findings that dreamwork is very useful for short-term counseling.

Significance of the Present Study: The present study extends beyond the above studies and literature discussions in its utility of dreams from a systemic perspective to understand and reduce relationship issues. The procedure in the PMID for exploration of an individual's dreams from the systemic perspective of interconnected relationships is not a procedure in any of the contemporary dream interpretation methods I explored during this study. Further, I did not find any other dream interpretation method that exclusively combines pre-dream events and circumstances, pre-dream thoughts, emotional content, personal associations, dream solutions with interconnectedness of major relationships.

Implications for Counseling: Hartmann (1995) envisages when the dreamer is in therapy, "the therapist can help in making further integrative use of the dream as well as other material that arises in the therapeutic relationship" (p. 224). Although the participant in this case study worked alone, a person may be too steeped in emotional issues to understand and interpret relationship dreams. If so, counselor-facilitation of dream interpretations would be more helpful than the individual's self-facilitation.

Whether the person works alone to interpret dreams or with a counselor, an implication of this study is that the counseling process could be accelerated by clients' use of the PMID to record dream information and develop at least some meanings before the session. Then counselors could use those pre-writings in session to help the clients.

Several benefits seem likely from the client's pre-write. First, the client's thought processes during the dream selection and writing in a form understandable to the counselor will force clients to delve deeper for meanings than just informally thinking about each dream. Second, the selection of a sequence of dreams for each series of dreams would help the counselor (and the client) notice either changes or stalemates in the client's consciousness. Third, the selection of a sequence of dreams would move away from focusing on only one dream when perhaps a few "everyday" dreams would contain more useful meanings for the dreamer and the counselor than one traumatic dream. Fourth, the series of client-written dreams would help the counselor decide what areas to address with the client. Fifth, client participation maximizes counselor session time.

The present study found that issues were often understood and reduced in a reasonably short time utilizing the PMID. A counseling implication of this circumstance is to coordinate counselor-facilitated short-term counseling sessions with development of self-facilitated dream interpretation. Implementation of self-facilitated dream interpretation, utilizing the model developed in this study, could result in achieving dual goals of brief counselor-facilitated sessions and ongoing self-reflection.

Conclusions

Outcomes of this study in relation to the five research questions posed are all positive. The PMID was found to be effective for self-facilitation (Research Question 1). All six steps in the PMID were found to be uniquely personal to the participant (Research Question 2). Use of dream interpretations reflected change in affect over time (Research Question 3), and the use of the dream interpretations helped the participant understand and reduce her relationship issues (Research Questions 4 and 5).

A particularly important finding of this study is that a systemic perspective can be applied to an individual's interpretation of dreams to understand and alleviate relationship issues. Inferences of that finding include that the individual who is distressed about relationship issues is the one who takes responsibility for change in thoughts, attitude, or behavior instead of approaching others in the system to effect changes in self, others and the system. "If individuals change the way that they relate to other family members, this forces family members to change the way they relate to individuals" (Allen, 1994, p. 229). If systemic changes can be accomplished by individual change, it seems an excellent way to avoid risks of entrenching dysfunctional homeostatic patterns by approaching others about family problems.

The model could help other individuals in several aspects. First, the model seems especially appropriate for individual use because of its fundamental concepts about thoughts, circumstances, personal associations, emotions and problem resolution qualities in dreams. Second, the model is a self-monitoring vehicle since it tracks affects over time. Self-monitoring is "an excellent way of supplementing other sources of information" (Brown & Lent, 1992, p. 727). Third, the PMID aims to teach people how to understand and alleviate their own relationship issues. "The aim of all help is self-help and eventual self-sufficiency," (Brammer & MacDonald, 1996, p. 6). Fourth, use of the model promotes ongoing self-reflection through dreamwork. We do not help people very much if we only help them solve immediate problems and then they must find someone to help them each time new issues arise (Brammer & MacDonald, 1996).

Acknowledgments

I am deeply grateful for the supportive guidance and expertise from members of my thesis committee: Anene Okocha, Ph.D., David Van Doren, Ed.D., and Brenda O'Beirne, Ph.D., Counselor Education Department, University of Wisconsin-Whitewater.

REFERENCES

Allen, D. M. (1994). *A family systems approach to individual psychotherapy.* Northvale, NJ: Jason Aronson, Inc.

Beck, A. T., Rush, A. J., Shaw, B. F., & Emery, G. (1979). *Cognitive therapy of depression.* New York: The Guilford Press.

Becvar, R. J., & Becvar, D. Stroh. (1982). *Systems theory and family therapy*. University Press of America, Inc.

Bowen, M. (1985). *Family therapy in clinical practice.* New York: Jason Aronson.

Brammer, L. M., & MacDonald, G. (1996). *The helping relationship, process and skills* (6th ed.). Needham Heights, MA: Allyn and Bacon.

Brown, S. D., & Lent, R. W. (1992). *Handbook of counseling psychology* (2nd ed.). New York: John Wiley & Sons, Inc.

Bynum, E. B. (1993). *Families and the interpretation of dreams: Awakening the intimate web*. New York: The Haworth Press, Inc.

Cartwright, R., & Lamberg, L. (1992). *Crisis dreaming, using your dreams to solve your problems.* New York: HarperPerennial.

Delaney, G. (1993). The dream interview. In G. Delaney (Ed.), *New directions in dream interpretation* (pp. 195–240). Albany, NY: State University of New York Press.

Duesbury, E. M. (2000). Utilizing dreams from a systemic perspective to understand and mollify relationship issues (Unpublished master's thesis). University of Wisconsin–Whitewater.

Ellis, A. (1963). *Reason and emotion in psychotherapy*. New York: Lyle Stuart.

Erikson, E. (1963). *Childhood and society*. New York: W. W. Norton & Company.

Faraday, A. (1974). *The dream game*. New York: Harper & Row.

Flowers, L. K. (1993). The dream interview method in a private outpatient psychotherapy practice. In G. Delaney (Ed.), *New directions in dream interpretation* (pp. 241–288). NY: State University of New York.

Flowers, L. K., & Zweben, J. E. (1998). The changing role of "using" dreams in addiction recovery. *Journal of Substance Abuse Treatment, 15*(3), 193–200.

Freud, S. (1955). *The interpretation of dreams*. (J. Strachey, Trans. and Ed.). New York: Basic Book, Inc., Publishers.

Goldman, L. (1992). Qualitative assessment: An approach for counselors. *Journal of Counseling & Development, 70*, 616–621.

Greenberg, R., & Pearlman, C. (1993). An integrated approach to dream theory and clinical practice. In G. Delaney (Ed.), *New directions in dream interpretation* (pp. 289–306). Albany, NY: State University of New York Press.

Hall, C. S. (1966). *The meaning of dreams*. Harper & Row.

Hall, C. S., & Van de Castle, R. L. (1966). *Content analysis of dreams*. New York: Appleton-Century-Crofts, Division of Meredith Publishing Company.

Hall, J. A. (1977). *Clinical uses of dreams: Jungian interpretations and enactments*. New York: Grune & Stratton, Inc.

Hartmann, E. (1968). The day-residue; time distribution of waking events. *Psychophysiology, 5*(2), 222.

Hartmann, E. (1995). Making connections in a safe place: Is dreaming psychotherapy? *Dreaming, 5*(4), 213–228.

Hartmann, E. (1999). The nature of dreaming, an excerpt from *Dreams and nightmares: The new theory on the origin of meaning of dreams*. (E. Hartmann, 1998), *Dream Time, 16*(1 and 2), 4–5 and 27–28.

Heaton, K. J., Hill, C. E., Petersen, D. A., Rochlen, A. B., & Zack, J. S. (1998). A comparison of therapist-facilitated and self-guided dream interpretation sessions. *Journal of Counseling Psychology, 45*(1), 115–122.

Hill, C. E. (1996). *Working with dreams in psychotherapy*. New York: The Guilford Press.

Jung, C. G. (1960). *The structure and dynamics of the psyche* (R. F. C. Hull, Trans.). New York: Bollingen Series/Pantheon Books.

Jung, C. G. (1966). *Two essays on analytical psychology* (R. F. C. Hull, Trans.). Princeton, NJ: Bollingen Series/Princeton University Press.

Kramer, M. (1993). The selective mood regulatory function of dreaming: An update and revision. In A. Moffitt, M. Kramer & R. Hoffman (Eds.), *The functions of dreaming* (pp. 139–195). New York: State University of New York Press.

Kramer, M., McQuarrie, E., & Bonnet, M. (1981). Problem solving in dreaming: An empirical test. In W. P. Koella (Ed), *Sleep 1980*, Fifth European Congress on Sleep Research, Amsterdam, 1980 (pp. 174–178). Basel: S. Karger.

Kramer, M., Roth, T., Arand, D., & Bonnet, M. (1981). Waking and dreaming mentation: A test of their interrelationship. *Neuroscience Letters, 22*, 83–86.

Mahrer, A. R. (1989). *Dreamwork in psychotherapy and self-change*. New York: W. W. Norton & Company, Inc.

Marquardt, C., Bonato, R., & Hoffmann, R. (1996). An empirical investigation into the day-residue and dream-lag effects. *Dreaming, 6*(1), 57–65.

May, R. (1969). *Existential psychology*. New York: Random House.

May, R. (1983). *The discovery of being*. New York: W. W. Norton & Company

Merriam, S. B. (1998). Qualitative research and case study applications in education. San Francisco: Jossey-Bass Inc.

Polster, E., & Polster, M. (1973). Gestalt therapy integrated. New York: Brunner/Mazel Publishers.

Savary, L. M. (1990). Dreams for personal and spiritual growth. In S. Krippner, (Ed.), *Dreamtime and dreamwork: Decoding the language of the night* (pp. 22–134). Los Angeles: Jeremy P. Tarcher, Inc.

Seafield, F. (1865). *The literature and curiosities of dreams.* London: Chapman and Hall.

Seligman, M. E. P. (1995). *The optimistic child.* Boston/New York: Houghton Mifflin Company.

Spiegel, S. B., & Hill, C. A. (1989). Guidelines for research on therapist interpretation: Toward greater methodological rigor and relevance to practice. *Journal of Counseling Psychology, 36*(1), 121–129.

Ullman, M. (1990). Guidelines for teaching dreamwork. In S. Krippner, (Ed.), *Dreamtime and dreamwork: Decoding the language of the night* (pp. 22–134). Los Angeles: Jeremy P. Tarcher, Inc.

Van de Castle, R. L. (1994). *Our dreaming mind.* New York: Ballantine Books.

Wolff, W. (1972). *The dream-mirror of conscience.* Westport, CT: Greenwood Press.

Wolman, B. B., & Ullman, M. (1986). *Handbook of states of consciousness.* New York: Van Nostrand Reinhold Company.

Appendix F: Answer Key for Chapter Quizzes

IMPORTANT NOTE TO COUNSELORS WHO TEACH FROM THIS BOOK

Because all answers are available in this appendix, consider only grading for credit those questions that require personal dreams and responses to one or more Personalized Method for Interpreting Dreams (PMID) steps.

ANSWERS, CHAPTER 1 QUIZ

1. 100%
2. True
3. Any of the following are correct responses:
   - Healing, finding food, or spiritual enrichment (Australian Aborigines)
   - Freedom from slavery in Egypt and Babylon, for example, as a result of Joseph's and Daniel's interpretations of rulers' dreams
   - Medical discoveries, early Greeks; diagnostic purposes, ancient Chinese
   - Connection to dreamer's previous lives and later adulthood dreams to future lives, the Hindu Upanishads
4. Allows material beyond waking-life thoughts to enter dreams
5. Any two of the following are correct responses:
   - Identify emotional stressors
   - Identify emotions with greater accuracy than the waking mind does
   - Contain suggestions for resolving problems
   - Incorporate experiential information beyond what we grasp in our waking thoughts
   - Make broader connections to our past experiences than our waking cognitions make
   - Provide self-discovery

ANSWERS, CHAPTER 2 QUIZ

1. Patiently listen as their children relate their dreams.
2. Dreams that revolve around interactions with friends, siblings, parents, and teachers. Adolescents most often have coming of age dreams.
3. The student's personal preference from the following four activities suggested in Chapter 2:
   - Tell yourself before you go to sleep that you will recall your dreams.
   - Say to yourself several times, "I will remember a dream when I wake up."
   - When you wake up in the morning, lie very still. Keep yourself in a relaxed, almost drowsy state, and wait for dream recall to emerge into your mind.
   - If no recall comes after you have been lying still for a while, turn slowly to another position and keep waiting for recall.
   - When you have recall, while continuing to lie still, rehearse or describe the dreams in your mind.
   - Also be alert for dream recall during the day, especially during relaxed moments.
   - Trust the process. Be confident in your ability to remember dreams. All people dream. It is a matter of biological necessity.
4. The student's personal preference from the following four activities suggested in Chapter 2:
   - Keep a pad and pencil, or a tape recorder if you prefer, near your bed. These will remind you to recall your dreams and record them as soon as you wake.
   - Record your dreams in *first person* and *present tense* to foster the immediate and intimate feelings of the dream.
   - Include your dreaming emotions in your dream narrative. Emotions are integral parts of the dreaming experience.
   - Record every recalled detail of the dream, regardless of its seeming relevance or importance. Details that seem insignificant are often keys to later insights.
5. d.

ANSWERS, CHAPTER 3 QUIZ

1. Chapter 3 is
   - An overview of the Personalized Method for Interpreting Dreams (PMID) for practicing counselors who use this book for learning how to facilitate clients' interpretation of their dreams.

   - A one-class, 3-hour presentation to introduce the PMID model to students in graduate-level counselor education courses that are other than full-semester courses.
2. Any of the following are key findings from research and explorations of the PMID model:
   - Most participants did dream about relationships.
   - A high percentage of active participants (*active* meaning contributing to the conclusion of the project) reported that they were able to understand and use the PMID model within 8 weeks.
   - Almost all active participants reported positive changes in emotions about one or more relationships in a period of between a few weeks to 2 months while using the PMID model.
   - While researching a general population, investigators compared participants' self-reports of positive emotional change to content in their dreams and found almost 100% corroboration.
   - Most active participants in all projects rated their use of the PMID steps prior to learning the PMID model to be low, but after several weeks of using the PMID model they rated their ability to do all six steps high.
3. Coaching dream interpretation when you have little understanding of your own dreams is like coaching an athletic team when you have yet to play the game yourself. How well would you do? How long would top management keep you on staff?
4. Either one of the following:
   - Intrarelational conflicts that might result from face-to-face meetings can be avoided.
   - Blaming self or others, which assigns meaning and not blame, is avoided.
5. The student's personal preference from the six PMID steps.

ANSWER, CHAPTER 4 QUIZ

Evaluate for whether the dreamer's Step 1 connection events connect to the dream and are clearly explained. Time of the events (preferably the day before the dream) is to be included.

ANSWER, CHAPTER 5 QUIZ

Evaluate for whether the dreamer's Step 2 connections are thoughts, are stated as thoughts, connect to the dream, and are clearly explained. Time of the thoughts (preferably the day before the dream) is to be included.

ANSWER, CHAPTER 6 QUIZ

Evaluate for whether the dreamer's Step 3 definitions are clearly explained and held tight to the dream being interpreted. Has the dreamer addressed each of the five questions?

ANSWER, CHAPTER 7 QUIZ

Evaluate for whether the dreamer has complied with Step 4 in its entirety and compared dreaming emotions to waking-life emotions and connected those emotions to the main issue or relationship in the current dream. (Research showed that although often exaggerated, emotions during dreaming are often more accurate than the dreamer's waking-life emotions.)

ANSWER, CHAPTER 8 QUIZ

Evaluate for whether the dreamer's Step 5 responses clearly show that he or she has explored probable suggestions or solutions in this dream—at least considered them, even if the dreamer is unable at the time of the dream to discover suggestions or solutions. Look for whether the dreamer considered the other PMID steps in developing suggestions or solutions. Comment on whether the dreamer recognizes pre-dream thoughts as questions that the dream responds to or answers. However, make no deductions for these last two items. It often takes considerable practice before people become adept at noticing such ties.

ANSWER, CHAPTER 9 QUIZ

Evaluate for whether the dreamer's Step 6 responses indicate that he or she has explored for relationship systems perspectives and for whether the dreamer has explored the dream for effects (either shown directly or implicated in the dream) from his or her reactions (what she or he does) in family or other major relationships experiences. Notice whether the dreamer considers only her or his reactions to what others do instead of blaming. The ability to take responsibility for changing one's own reactions instead of trying to change others or blame others or self often provides the best opportunities to alleviate stress and move onward.

ANSWERS, CHAPTER 10 QUIZ

1. Credit for two or more titles being listed.
2. Credit for both a theme or topic and dates of dreams listed.

3. Credit for either a "yes" answer or a "no" answer.
4. Credit for either a "yes" answer and listing of new information gained or a "no" answer.
5. Credit for either a "yes" answer and listing of unanswered questions or a "no" answer.

ANSWERS, CHAPTER 11 QUIZ

1. When people neglect to revisit their dreams and interpretations, at least the major ones, it seems analogous to counselors keeping running records of their work with clients and then never referring to those records again.
2. Refresh former meanings, discover new insights, and review for misinterpretations.
3. d.
4. Three indicators that a specific issue is alleviated:
   a. Both the dream and the dreamer's interpretations contain at least one clear message that the issue may be finished.
   b. Neither the dream nor the dreamer's interpretations contain new or unused past solutions to the current issue.
   c. Neither the dream nor the dreamer's interpretations give hints that the specific concern still bothers the dreamer.
5. "Why Is It Taking the Man So Long to Die?"

ANSWERS, CHAPTER 12 QUIZ

1. The answer to the first part is a choice from the list given here of distance counseling benefits. The answer to the second part of this question is the reader's personal reasoning for why the one chosen seems most beneficial.
   a. Gives both dreamer and facilitator time to think about the dream and what it means between times.
   b. Provides flexible times for both parties to respond.
   c. Encourages self-exploration because clients are most often sitting by themselves when they enter dream information and insights into the distance delivery system.
   d. Encourages the possibility of freer expression when sitting in front of a personal computer than when sitting in a counseling office.
   e. Provides an ongoing automatic log of exchanges between the client and the counselor-facilitator.
2. a.

3. The client can record his or her dreams and develop at least some meanings between counseling sessions.
4. The answer to the first part of this question is a choice from the following list of benefits from examining more than one dream about an issue or relationship (a series of dreams). The answer to the second part is the student's personal reasoning for why the one chosen seems most beneficial.
   a. Can lead the counselor (and the client) to see progress (or lack of progress) that the dreamer-client is making with his or her dream solutions and suggestions.
   b. Can move the dreamer's focus away from only one extraordinary dream to the interpretation of a series of common dreams about the issue being studied. (A series of common dreams may contain more useful meanings for the dreamer than just one traumatic dream. For example, Gloria's "When Did I Lose Control?" dream was a common dream in which she found an extremely useful solution. Later, she had other common dreams that helped her use that solution.)
   c. Can help the counselor and the client decide what areas need the most attention.
5. d.

ANSWERS, CHAPTER 13 QUIZ

1. One direction is "training of clinicians for dream work." Another direction is "anyone with an interest in what their dreams have to say."
2. The four axioms are as follows:
   a. Dreams begin in the present.
   b. Dreams go beyond the present to link up with more remote feeling residues from the past.
   c. Dreams tell it like it is.
   d. The neurophysiological analogue of dreaming consciousness is common to all mammals thus far studied in the laboratory.
3. The answer to this question is the student's personal choice.
4. Yes or no, according to personal experience. If yes, give credit for the student's responses regarding dreams and evidence.
5. a.

ANSWERS, CHAPTER 14 QUIZ

1. Recognize, identify, stop, change.
2. *Recognize* when you are having a bad dream, the kind that leaves you feeling helpless, guilty, or upset the next morning. *Identify* what it is about

the dream that makes you feel bad. *Stop* any bad dream. *Change* negative dream dimensions into their opposite, positive sides.

3. Be alert to the dreams that traumatic events leave behind, the sad self-stories that need better endings.
4. d.
5. The task takes longer and is tougher than creating a strong self-image in childhood.

Index

R

S

T

U

W

"I ain't sure what you're talking about, Willie Mitchell. Like I said, that Flip-Flop got a mind of his own. I don't know what he's up to half the time."

"*Was* up to," I said. "He's not going to hurt anyone ever again."

"Well, that's probably a good thing."

"How did you know A.G. was my son Jake?"

"You must think I'm dumb as the rest of those niggers in Sunshine," he said. "Jake look just like you. Walk and talk just like you. I used to see him around the baseball field watching me and your other boy Scott. I knew who he was soon as I saw him out here in these woods."

I stared at him in silence for a moment. The longer we sat, the more his smile and bravado seemed increasingly difficult for him to sustain. Something was boiling inside him, trying to get out.

"I want you to tell me why you did all this, James Lee. If it weren't for me you'd still be in Parchman right now."

He pursed his lips. James Lee the con artist was being sublimated.

"You see, Mr. D.A., when I was growing up in Sunshine, I didn't have nuthin'. Well, you know how it was. Lucretia Payne, my Muh-Dear, she worked in people's houses. Bowin' and scrapin' all the time. You know she died right before I got out of the joint. I didn't even get to go to the funeral."

"I'm sorry. Lucretia was a nice lady. She stood up for you."

"She was the only one ever did. But your boy Scott, the one on my team, he had you and his mama and his brother backin' him, and all your family's money and land, and the rest of us ain't got shit."

"You were always smart," I said. "I tried to steer you in the right direction. I don't know what else I could have done."

"You see, Mr. D.A., that's just the point. It ain't what you and your pretty wife and your rich sons did or didn't do for me. It's who you are, and who I ain't. It's what your boys are, and what I ain't and won't never be."

"I don't understand what that means."

"And I don't expect you to, Willie Mitchell. You and your people came into this world on top. And I didn't. No matter how hard I study or work, I ain't never catchin' up with people like you."

"So, killing Susan and trying to kill my son and me is going to make up for all the unfairness that's been visited on you? That's not right, James Lee."

"I know it, Coach Banks. But I didn't really do all that, what you're talking about. Flip-Flop was one bad dude. Doctors could study him for years and not figure him out. He ain't had no conscience, no feeling bad about anything he did. I don't figure he minded dying too much, if you say he's dead. And all this meth selling you talking about, there's at least a hundred homemade meth labs out in these woods, and there's lots of people usin' and sellin'. It's hard to keep up with all the people slinging dope in Tallabusha County. Anybody will tell you that."

"What are we going to do about our situation here, James Lee?"

"You goin' to arrest me, take me into the Sheriff's office, and they gon' charge me with something. It really don't matter what."

"Maybe."

"Or what? That's all you goin' to do, Coach. It's what you been doin' all your life. You Mr. Law and Order, Mr. Dudley Do-Right. You got it in your blood to play by the rules. And I'll go in peacefully. I promise."

"Good to know," I said. "You got a lawyer?"

"Oh, yeah. I got one in Cedar Grove. Office right by the courthouse where I picked up your boy that day. He's good. Knows all those evidence rules. He takes care of my friends out here when they get in trouble. He likes to party, and I send him goodies every two weeks. The man can go through some stuff. Likes the girls we got out here, too. Even the colored ones. He's an equal opportunity lawyer."

"I expect you know Sheriff Burr and all his deputies."

"A few."

"And you probably know someone on every jury that's picked to try a case in Tallabusha County."

"It's a small population. Everybody know everybody."

"Probably hard to get twelve people on a jury who don't have some connection to you, like a family member who's out here in these woods living off the dope you sell. You probably have people lining up to replace Flip-Flop, people who wouldn't mind threatening a juror."

"That's the thing about people, Willie Mitchell. You can't ever keep 'em under control. No telling what some of 'em will do. Like Flip-Flop. Stone cold."

"You ready to go?"

"I guess. We got time to stop and get something to eat on the way in to the Sheriff's office? I'm hungry, and they won't be serving breakfast in the jail until seven. I know the cook. He used to hang out here."

"Stand up slowly," I said. "Back away from the table, and keep your hands on your head."

"Yes, sir, Mr. D.A. You won't have no trouble from me."

James Lee Payne stood and took a couple of steps back. I walked around the table and stopped a couple of feet from him, my Glock pointed at his chest. The roaring in my ears returned, this time louder than ever.

"Ready?" I asked.

"Yes, sir. You want me to lead the way?"

"Not necessary," I said, and shot James Lee Payne in his cold heart.

Chapter Fifty-Eight

I sat down at the table until the roaring in my brain subsided. I thought of the things I needed to do, starting with making sure James Lee was dead. I felt his neck for a pulse. I may have detected something, but wasn't sure. I didn't want to take any chances, so I shot him again, this time in his temple. I picked up the two spent brass shells, stuck them in my pocket, and hustled back to Jake's truck, my Glock still in my hand. I wanted to be ready if Q-Man's people bushwhacked me between the house and the road.

I drove back to Jake's trailer. Flip-Flop's body lay on the floor where I left him. He looked dead, but I put a round into his head to be certain. I picked up my three ejected brass rounds off the trailer floor. With all five spent brass rounds accounted for and in my pocket, I drove off in the darkness toward Sunshine. I checked the time: 3:30 a.m.

I pulled out my pre-paid phone and punched in the number of my longtime friend and doctor in Sunshine, Dr. Nathan Clement, who had treated our family for years. I told him Jake was in bad shape and on his way to Sunshine. I gave him April's number and asked him to call to let her know he would be waiting for Jake and her at my house. I told him I would explain everything, as soon as I arrived, that Jake was seriously ill with a very weak pulse and God knows what else. I told Nathan that Jake had been abducted and probably injected with drugs for four or five days to keep him sedated.

Nathan had taken care of Kitty Douglas, Jake's FBI agent girlfriend, until she died in Sunshine. Her death sent Jake to join David Dunne's group to dispense justice in a more timely and direct method, just as Susan's death and Jake's near-death had led me to do things I never thought possible.

I arrived in Sunshine that Friday morning as the sun began to rise. I parked the Nissan next to the Silverado and Dr. Clement's Suburban, and ran inside my house. Nathan was working on Jake on the downstairs sofa. Nathan had multiple IV tubes infusing Jake with fluids, antibiotics, and a Narcan cocktail. Nathan said Jake was seriously dehydrated. He was trying to get his kidneys kickstarted. The antibiotics and Narcan drips were preventive, Nathan said, because he couldn't find signs of an infection or a drug overdose.

Though Jake was still unconscious, Dr. Clement said based on his examination, he thought Jake would be weak for a while, but ultimately return to good health with no residual physical problems. I asked him where April was and he pointed upstairs. I walked up and found her in Susan's closet in the master bedroom.

"Oh, Willie Mitchell. I've never seen so many clothes and shoes."

"Those are old," April. "Susan hadn't worn them since we moved to Oxford full-time. You can have anything you want out of this closet, but I think you'll probably want to shop for clothes more suited to someone your age."

"You think I'll be able to?" she asked.

"I promise you will."

"What happened with Q-Man?"

"He won't be hurting anyone ever again."

"Good," she said. "Is A.G. going to be all right?"

"Jake," I said. "Dr. Clement said Jake is weak but will be fine." I paused. "I'm going to be staying here in Sunshine with Jake for a while, April. Not sure how long. You're welcome to stay, or go, or whatever you want to do. I wouldn't suggest returning to your trailer in Tallabusha."

"Like I told you over there, Willie Mitchell, I'm never going back. But I don't have anywhere else to go. Can I stay here and help take care of ...Jake?"

"That'd be great. It'll give us time to talk about what you want to do and where you want to go. You may want to go to school, maybe not. I'm going to keep my promise, April. I'm going to help you make a new start."

She hugged me tight, and whispered, "You are the angel I prayed for, Willie Mitchell."

I didn't feel like one. Maybe an avenging angel.

"Why don't you get some rest?" I said and led her into Scott's bedroom. "This can be your room while you're here. Make yourself at home."

I walked downstairs and out on the front porch to call Jimmy Gray. I told him I had found Jake and brought him to Sunshine, where we'd be for a few weeks. I promised to let him in on all the details if he would meet me at the Sardis marina at noon that day. I said I wanted to go out on his pontoon boat and clear my head. I asked him to drive there in my F-150 and we'd swap trucks. He was at our bank in Oxford and was happy to meet me because he said he had some news to share with me, too.

I was tired, but didn't want to rest until after I met Jimmy at the lake to take care of a final detail. I took a shower and changed into some old clothes I had in my closet, including my warmest coat. It was going to be chilly on Jimmy's party barge.

I emptied the Silverado of every vestige of the gear Jimmy and I had loaded into it in advance of my mission in the Tallabusha woods. Nathan said he would stay until Jake regained consciousness. I asked April to come downstairs, and asked Dr. Clement what April needed to do to help take care of Jake. I thanked Nathan, said I'd call him later in the day, and took off for the Sardis marina.

Jimmy called me when I was ten minutes out. He told me he was already on the pontoon boat warming the engine and sipping a beer.

I parked Jimmy's Silverado next to my F-150 in the marina parking lot and walked down the steep ramp to the first of four long boathouses and piers.

"I'm glad to see you in one piece, partner," Jimmy said.

"Glad to be seen," I said. "Let's cruise."

Jimmy backed his party barge out of his slip and headed out the marina inlet toward the middle of the lake. I sat on the plush, cushioned seat next to the captain's chair where Jimmy operated the outboard Evinrude 100 and steered the pontoon boat. The sun was out, but it was cold on the water.

I kept my hands jammed into the deep pockets of my coat, my left hand rolling the five spent brass rounds like Humphrey Bogart's Captain Queeg. My right hand cradled the Glock that had helped save Jake's life and get justice for Susan.

Ten minutes out, I dropped the first brass shell; ten minutes later, the second. After dropping the others at similar intervals, we had reached the middle of the lake. I asked Jimmy to cut off the engine so we could talk.

"I think I'm ready for a beer now," I said.

With his back to me, Jimmy reached into the ice chest on his port flank while I removed the Glock and threw it over the starboard side, coughing loudly to cover the splash.

"Here's what happened," I said after my first sip of Heineken, and told him about April, Flip-Flop, and James Lee Payne.

Jimmy raised his beer to mine.

"Here's to my bestest buddy, the bravest, toughest s.o.b. I know, and also one of the richest."

"Not hardly," I said.

"Oh, yes you are, if you give a thumbs up to the deal I've made."

Jimmy proceeded to explain why he had been spending so much time at our Jackson Avenue branch on weekends. He had been negotiating with our correspondent bank in Nashville for months. Yesterday, the day before our boat ride, he accepted their offer to buy the shares of stock he and I owned, and the shares of minority owners, too. He explained the details. The Nashville bank would pay $200 million in cash for one hundred percent of the stock in Sunshine Bank. Jimmy said he had polled the minority shareholders and they were all in favor of the deal.

"You own a little over twenty-five percent of the stock, so your payday will be $50 million before tax. And remember, we converted to an S Corporation a few years back, so there's no double taxation. You'll pay a capital gains tax on the sale of your stock, which should be a little north of $18 million to the IRS. If you say yes to the deal, you'll net about $30 million after federal and state taxes. What do you say? You'll have so much money it'll start backing up on you."

"I say what you're always saying when you hear good news. It ain't love, but it ain't bad."

We clinked bottles. When Jimmy cranked the engine and reached for the throttle, I pulled my burner phone and tossed it into the water. On the way back to the marina, Jimmy pumped me for more details about my long night in Tallabusha, so I told him what I could.

Jimmy's phone blasted "The Ride of the Valkyries" so loud I could hear it clearly over the roar of the hundred horsepower Evinrude.

"We're on the lake, David," he said. "Service is spotty out here. Let us call you when we dock."

"What did he want?" I asked.

"I don't know. Asked if I knew where you were. Then he said 'Reggie' and that's all I could make out."

"Reggie Barnes?"

"Maybe," Jimmy said, clinking Heineken bottles again. "I get five bars coverage in the marina."

Chapter Fifty-Nine

We tied up the barge in Jimmy's slip. Jimmy cracked open another Heineken. I passed because I was bone-tired and had a two-hour drive back to Sunshine. Jimmy grumbled about me being a pansy, and called Detective Burke, putting his phone on speaker.

"You got me and Willie Mitchell," Jimmy said. "What's up?"

"Reggie Barnes tried to kill himself last night," David said.

"No!" Jimmy said. "What happened?"

"Lana found him in their bathtub, unconscious. He had slit one of his wrists wide open. Taken a shitload of pills."

"Is he all right?" I asked.

"He's in the hospital, but he's going to make it."

"Thank God," Jimmy said.

"Have you talked to him?" I said.

"He's got a lawyer."

"Lawyer?" Jimmy said. "What the hell for?"

"He left a two-page note he wrote on his computer," Detective Burke said. "He says he didn't mean to kill El Ray, that it was self-defense, an accident."

I was sleep-deprived and my head ached from an adrenaline hangover, but what David said jolted me fully alert.

"He admitted in the note that he used a burner to talk to El Ray most of the time. He knew it was against the rules, but every recruiter in the SEC does it. Said he got a call on his burner from El Ray the night he went missing. Said El Ray was high, talking crazy, and told Reggie he was de-committing from Ole Miss because his old man was taking money from other schools without El Ray knowing about it. He said LSU had given his father so much cash he had to sign with them. Reggie said he never gave El Ray any money and to his knowledge, neither did any other Ole Miss coach or rich alum."

"He killed El Ray because he decommitted?" Jimmy asked.

"No. El Ray told him he was out in the county seeing a woman, and Reggie badgered him into meeting with him because Reggie was going to try to talk him out of de-committing. El Ray told him what time he'd be back at Sammy's, so Reggie drove out there and waited. He watched while El Ray got out of a Range Rover and into his Toyota. After the Range Rover left, Reggie says El Ray got into Reggie's car and they drove away from Sammy's. Reggie's coaching career was on the line. He was desperate to change El Ray's mind.

"In his note Reggie says he had never seen El Ray so agitated. He said El Ray was ranting about his father, slamming his fists on the dash, so Reggie pulled over to the side of the road to calm him down. Reggie said El Ray got really angry when Reggie said if he didn't honor his commitment to Ole Miss, Reggie was going to report the LSU payment to Coach Goodson and the NCAA, and it might be the end of El Ray's college career, maybe even his chances to play in the NFL.

"Reggie says El Ray went berserk, totally out of control, and hit Reggie in the face. Reggie said El Ray started choking him and that El Ray was so strong Reggie couldn't break his grip. Reggie says he felt like he was going to blackout, so he pulled his pen from his shirt pocket and stuck it in El Ray's side between his ribs. He said it didn't phase El Ray so he pushed it in further and harder until El Ray finally released his choke hold.

"Reggie said El Ray started crying, and after a few minutes El Ray broke into a cold sweat and couldn't catch his breath. Reggie said he wanted to take El Ray to the hospital but El Ray got upset again, saying he couldn't get treatment without the story going viral and ruining him. They sat there on the side of that dark country road, Reggie trying to help El Ray calm down and breathe normally, but after a while, Reggie says El Ray stopped breathing.

"Reggie tried to do CPR, pulled him out of the car onto the ground and did chest compressions and mouth-to-mouth, but it was no use. Reggie said he panicked, carried El Ray's body into the woods, saw the ravine and dumped El Ray into it."

"Holy shit," Jimmy Gray said. "Holy shit."

I was numb. As I sat next to Jimmy on his pontoon boat in the Sardis marina, I remembered interviewing Reggie in his house, watching him scribble notes on a pad while I talked to him. He wrote left-handed with a classic Cross pen. I pictured Reggie and El Ray parked on the side of the country road, El Ray leaning over from the passenger side to choke Reggie, and Reggie reaching in his pocket with his dominant left hand and stabbing El Ray under his right arm pit with the pen, pushing it into El Ray's chest.

I remember thinking that day in the marina that Reggie's slender, golden Cross pen may be the most elegant deadly weapon of all time.

Reggie's confession was an exact match with the physical evidence. The toxicology results showed alcohol with methamphetamine in El Ray's system, enough to achieve the desired result of enhancement of sexual intensity, but also enough to make El Ray go off on Reggie and try to choke him to death. El Ray left his jacket in his Toyota even though it was chilly that night, because he was amped up on alcohol and meth, and generating so much heat internally he didn't need the coat. Reggie Barnes, especially in his panicked state, was plenty strong enough to carry the big quarterback to the ravine.

"Hey, David," I said into Jimmy's phone. "Did Reggie say anything in his statement about what he did with his and El Ray's burner phones?"

"Yeah," Detective Burke said. "He said he took out the sim cards the next day, smashed them with a hammer, and put both burners and cards in different construction debris bins out near his home at Oxford Commons, where they're building all those new houses. And just in case you're wondering, they empty those bins every week, so that evidence is now buried deep in the landfill out in the county."

"When are you coming back to Oxford, Willie Mitchell?" Burke asked.

"I'm not sure," I said. "I've got things to do in my home town. I'll check in with you in a day or two."

"If that don't beat all," Jimmy Gray said after the call ended. "Can you believe that shit?"

"The older I get, partner," I said, "the more I'm willing to believe anything, no matter how crazy. Two months ago, if you had told me I was going to be sneaking through Tallabusha woods wearing NVGs, carrying a Glock in my holster and a Sig Sauer in my coveralls' pocket...."

"Ain't it the truth. I swore I'd never agree to sell our bank. Turned down offers from all over through the years."

"What changed?"

"I'm tired of watching the Delta go down the drain, I guess. Every year someone else throws in the towel and moves. Lots of these farms are owned by corporations or real estate investment trusts now. They ain't any fun to deal with. No loyalty, just who's got the best rate. I hope this Nashville bank knows what it's doing."

"I gotta get going and check on Jake," I said. "I'll call you later."

CHAPTER SIXTY

I spent the two-hour drive back to Sunshine digesting Reggie's combination suicide note and confession. It felt good to be back in my F-150. I dragged myself up the front porch steps and into the house, where April was spoon-feeding soup to Jake on the couch. The IV lines were continuing to drip, and Jake was awake, more or less.

"How're we feeling?" I asked him.

"Fuzzy," Jake mumbled.

"He's been drifting in and out all day," April said.

"Maybe you should go to nursing school," I said to her.

I sat in an uncomfortable, stuffed Victorian chair and watched Jake nod off after swallowing each spoonful of soup. April would wait a moment, tap Jake on the lip with the spoon, and feed him when he opened his mouth.

"You got this, April?"

"I do, Willie Mitchell. You go get some rest."

I walked slowly up the stairs and climbed into my bed. I fell asleep, my brain a simmering gumbo of the events surrounding the tragic deaths of Elston Raymond and Susan Woodfork Banks, and the well-deserved deaths I inflicted on Flip-Flop and James Lee Payne.

I woke up at midnight and walked quietly downstairs. Jake was sound asleep on the couch, his color much better. April was out, too, dozing in a chair she had pulled next to Jake. I watched them for a minute, turned and walked back up the steps to my room, back into my still warm bed.

Dr. Clement came by the following morning on his way to his office, checked Jake's vitals, and talked to him about his condition, giving him do's and don't's. Nathan removed the IVs, made recommendations for what Jake should eat, drink, and do for the next few days. After Dr. Clement left, April and I helped Jake up the steps and into his bed, where he promptly fell asleep.

Jimmy called and said I should check out the article in the Jackson paper about Detective Ronnie Tyler. I went online and read it. It wasn't an article, more like a blurb buried in the section on news around the State.

"Tallabusha Deputy Dies in Fiery Crash," was the title. It seems, according to Sheriff Burr, Deputy Tyler was in pursuit of a criminal on the winding county roads of southern Tallabusha County when he apparently lost control and ran off the road, flipping several times before crashing upside down into a tree and catching fire. The Sheriff said Tyler was probably dead from the crash before his body was almost totally consumed in the fire.

Sheriff Burr neglected to point out in the blurb that Tyler probably had a difficult time controlling his vehicle because his head had been blown apart earlier by Flip-Flop and his Draco.

"Damn," I said under my breath, "Tallabusha must be the Car and Driver Immolation Capital of the Deep South."

I scanned the paper in search of separate coverage of the discovery of two murder victims in Tallabusha County, but found nothing. I checked the Cedar Grove paper's online edition. Not a word about Flip-Flop or Q-Man. I decided April was spot on when she said people got killed out in the Tallabusha woods all the time and nobody ever did anything about it.

After a couple of days, I drove to Oxford. On the way, I called the Chancellor to see if she could meet with me at three that afternoon. I had already checked in with Aunt Bee the day after my Sardis Lake pontoon ride with Jimmy, and discussed with her the ramifications of Reggie's two-page confession. At that time, neither of us tried to predict what impact it would have on the NCAA's investigation.

Detective Burke and Jimmy Gray, as scheduled, showed up at my condo at noon. Jimmy picked up sandwiches from The Blind Pig and we sat around my little kitchen table eating and talking.

"Miss Hot Pants gets off scot-free," Jimmy said.

"Pretty much," David said. "She denies giving El Ray any meth or alcohol. Admits to sex with him that night but nothing else. She didn't see Reggie Barnes at Sammy's parking lot. Reggie knows nothing about her."

"With Tyler dead, there's no way to prove she's lying," I said.

"I'm fairly certain she got the meth for El Ray from Tyler," Burke said. "I haven't been able to dig up any other meth connections for her, and to tell the truth, I believe her when she says she doesn't do any drugs. Just alcohol."

"Who thinks Sheriff Burr was in on the meth trade at Sammy's?" Jimmy Gray asked. "Raise your hand."

Neither David nor I budged.

"Now," Jimmy continued, "who thinks Sheriff Burr was the one gave the order to Q-Man to kill Tyler after we found out Tyler was banging Reese Conklin and beat her up when he found out about her two-timing him with El Ray?"

David and I didn't bite.

"There's no way to know the answers," I said. "I believe Sheriff Burr was in on the meth trade with Tyler, and I believe it's likely Burr gave Q-Man the order to kill Tyler. But, there's no way to prove either allegation. Ronnie Tyler was the lynchpin. He could have insulated Burr from the trafficking, doing all the dirty work. It's easy for Burr to claim he knew nothing about it. He knows no one can prove otherwise. You could torture Sammy Kerry and he wouldn't give up a thing on the Sheriff or Tyler. It's probable, I think, that Burr ordered Tyler killed when he learned about him beating up the wife of his biggest campaign donor and then found out about our face-off with Tyler and Sammy in Sammy's parking lot. Sammy probably called Burr right afterward to tell him we were on to the Sheriff's office's participation in the drug trade at Sammy's."

"I don't want to have a Mossberg pointed at me ever again," Jimmy said. "I'll let you boys question Sammy without me next time."

"Won't be any next time. At least we now know that Ronnie Tyler, as big a scumbag as he was, didn't kill El Ray in a fit of jealous rage," I said. "His only involvement with El Ray's death was providing the meth to Reese. I'm sure he didn't know she was getting it for El Ray to use to enhance the thrill of his sexual encounters with her."

"Again I ask," Jimmy Gray said, "why the hell would the boy need it? He was eighteen, for Christ's sake."

"Maybe it was Reese's idea," Burke said. "But we'll never know. Her lawyer called me and said we can't speak to her about anything unless he's there with her. Same goes for her husband, the lawyer said."

"He's one strange cat, that Richard Conklin," Jimmy said.

"This old world is full of strange cats," I said.

"I feel sorry for Reggie," Burke said.

"Yeah," Jimmy said. "I wonder what they'll charge him with?"

"It'll be a tough case to prosecute," I said.

"If you were the Oxford D.A.," Jimmy said, "you could win it."

"Don't be so sure," I said. "Nobody's going to want the case against Reggie tried in open court. No one comes out looking good."

"Maybe a Grand Jury will say it was self-defense," Burke said.

"Maybe so," I said. "I believe it was. I think Reggie's deathbed confession is the truth."

Chapter Sixty-One

I walked into the Lyceum at three o'clock. James Braswell greeted me with a big smile and escorted me into Aunt Bee's office. She was all smiles, too.

"You look like the cat who ate the canary," I said.

"Jeffrey Blanchard just left here," she said. "The NCAA is leaving campus, closing the investigation."

"Hallelujah," I said.

"Reggie Barnes confirmed to Blanchard what he said in his note, that Ole Miss never gave El Ray a nickel."

"Is the NCAA going after LSU?" I asked.

"No. Blanchard said they didn't consider El Ray's father's allegations to be credible. Blanchard said the only thing Coach Barnes did against the rules was use a burner phone, and if they pursued us for that, they'd have to go after every university in the country."

"And all universities deny that their coaches use burners," I said. "Did Blanchard say they would issue a press release announcing the closure of the investigation of Ole Miss related to the El Ray signing?"

"I asked him, and he said they don't normally do that."

"That's b.s.," I said. "They leak like crazy so the sports media will do their dirty work for them. Everyone in the country knows the NCAA was investigating Ole Miss because of El Ray's commitment. I've seen it in USA Today, on ESPN, and the SEC Network."

"I knew it was b.s. when he said it, but I didn't want to engage him on the comment. I just wanted him to leave."

"I really regret not seeing Blanchard before he took off. There are a few things I wanted to say to the pompous jerk." I paused. "So, the NCAA investigation ends with a whimper, not a bang."

"My lawyer paraphrasing Eliot," Chancellor O'Donald said. "I like it. Willie Mitchell, I guess I am no longer in need of your services. Please send me a bill for your time and effort. You did a wonderful job for me."

"You know, Chancellor," I said "I enjoyed working with you so much on this investigation, I should pay you. Let's just end it on a handshake and say we're even. I'm not sending you a bill."

"Oh, Andy," she said in a very high-pitched trill, sounding exactly like Aunt Bee reacting to something Andy Griffith or Opie said on the black and white television screen I watched with my parents when I was a boy.

I searched for a tell on the Chancellor's face. Had I heard her right?

Beaming, she walked around her desk to give me a hug. I didn't know if Chancellor Clare O'Donald had become aware of the Aunt Bee moniker Jimmy Gray had bestowed upon her, and I was not about to ask. But if she did find out about it somehow, and was making fun of her caricatured persona to let me know she was in on it, it gave me great hope for the future of Ole Miss.

I drove back to Sunshine that afternoon with a lot on my mind.

I thought about Laura Raymond. Her worthless ex-husband set in motion the chain of events that led to El Ray's death. The only good thing to come out of their relationship for Laura was El Ray, and Sam Raymond had destroyed it.

Reggie Barnes was another victim, along with his wife Lana. I didn't think Reggie would go to prison, but his coaching career was forever tarnished. I was glad his children were too young to know what was going on.

Lynda Gianelli was collateral damage in James Lee Payne's vendetta. She made bad choices in her life, but didn't deserve to die like she did.

Sammy Kerry and Sheriff Burr would not miss a beat. No punishment for being up to their necks in the lucrative meth trade. They'd get away with involvement in Ronnie Tyler's death,too.

No big deal, I guess, in Tallabusha County.

Flip-Flop and James Lee Payne got what was coming to them. I did what I had to do. Taking the law into my own hands was antithetical to the way I had lived my professional and personal life. But James Lee was right—no one was going to convict him of anything in Tallabusha County. James Lee would have used his stroke with the Sheriff and his connection with potential jurors to exonerate Flip-Flop, too.

I was at the BP when Flip-Flop murdered Susan, and in Jake's trailer when Flip-Flop tried to kill him with a hot shot. I didn't need a jury to tell me he was guilty. I didn't need a judge to give him the death sentence he deserved.

I called Jimmy Gray as I neared Sunshine to tell him I would be at home with Jake for the foreseeable future.

"Good," Jimmy said. "I'll be in Sunshine, too, helping the Nashville bankers do their due diligence. Maybe you could teach me what you learned at Brass Tactical so I can be more help on our next case."

"All you have to know," I said, "is whoever makes the first move wins."

Chapter Sixty-Two

Two weeks later, I stood with Jake at Susan's grave inside what remained of the fence enclosing the Banks family cemetery on the edge of Sunshine. Vandals and thieves had made off with all four of the wrought iron gates and posts, and much of the ornate iron fence. Fortunately, over many decades, a copse of eastern red cedar trees had grown up in and around the Banks family graves. The cedars had become a natural demarcation, separating the cemetery from the rest of the 990 acres of cotton land I inherited from my father. So far, no thieves had made off with the cedars.

The weather was mild that day in Yaloquena County, temperature in the low sixties, overcast with a slight breeze out of the southwest that had traveled from the western Gulf of Mexico. Christmas was a few days away.

Jake was recovering, now strong enough to start a new diet, exercise, and strength regimen to undo some of the damage six months living as a deadender in the Tallabusha woods had done to his body, exacerbated by Q-Man and Flip-Flop keeping him tied, taped, gagged, and doped up in his trailer for five days.

Jake had told me Flip-Flop and Q-Man got to him while he slept after our Sunday morning meeting at the abandoned farm on CR 402. He asked me if I had checked the ownership of the farm. I said I hadn't, but would do so soon.

Over the course of Jake's two weeks in Sunshine, and only when April was not around, I filled Jake in on all the gory details of what I did that night in the Tallabusha woods. He was grateful to me for saving his life. I said if he hadn't risked his life going undercover, we would never have found out who killed Susan, and I would be forever thankful for what he did.

"What are you going to do when you're back to full strength?" I asked him at the grave.

"Head back to D.C. Get back to work. Billy Gillmon calls me just about every day. Says he needs me right now." Jake looked at me. "The bigger question is what are you going to do?"

"Go back to Oxford, play some golf. Get things back to normal."

"That might keep you happy for a week."

"What do you mean?" I said.

"Nothing's ever going to be the same for you. Mother's death, your near-death, what you did to those two guys to save me—you've crossed over."

"To where?"

"To the place I went when I took out those two assholes who killed Kitty. Nothing's been the same since. They deserved what they got from me. The law wasn't going to do a thing. All the FBI agents in the world, all the law enforcement, prosecutors—none of them could have produced the result I did. The world's a much better place without those murderers."

"I don't know, Jake," I said. "I'm no vigilante. I was just getting justice for Susan and looking after you."

"Right," he said. "That's what I said at first. But then Dunne talked to me, told me what he was doing. I've taken out a lot of dangerous people over the last six years, sometimes as part of a team, sometimes by myself. Our justice system in this country no longer works, Willie Mitchell. And it's worse in the rest of the world."

Jake walked out of the cemetery to the truck. I watched him, thinking about what he said. He was right. Something fundamental in me had changed. I was no longer the man I was before I ended the lives of James Lee Payne and Flip-Flop. I felt no remorse. I was glad I did it. I'd do it again.

I started off talking to you about having to play the hand you're dealt. Life has now given me an entirely new outlook on justice, and it's going to take me a while to see how I play it. Maybe Jake is right. I don't know.

My situation reminds me of the ancient Taoist story the late Philip Seymour Hoffman's character, CIA operative Gus Avrakotos, tells Tom Hanks' character, Congressman Charlie Wilson, in the last scene of the movie *Charlie Wilson's War*. The two men were at a party in D.C. celebrating the evacuation of Russian forces from Afghanistan due to the clandestine supplying of weapons and aid by the U.S. to the mujahideen fighters. Avrakotos warns Wilson not to celebrate so soon, predicting that those same weapons might one day be used against Americans.

"A boy is given a horse on his fourteenth birthday," Avrakotos tells Wilson. "Everyone in the village says, 'Oh, how wonderful'." But a Zen master who lives in the village says, 'We'll see.' The boy falls off the horse and breaks his foot. Everyone in the village says, 'Oh, how awful.' The Zen master says, 'We'll see.' The village is thrown into war and all the young men have to go to war. But, because of the broken foot, the boy stays behind. Everyone says, 'Oh, how wonderful.' The Zen master says, 'We'll see'."

So, I'm not sure what happens from here. We'll see.

Acknowledgements:

Thanks very much to family, friends, and fellow-travelers for their continued support for Willie Mitchell's exploits, including early readers and sounding boards: Gayle Henry, William Henry, Francine Luckett, Angelita Morris, David Fite, Lowry Lomax, Pat Austin, Charles Weatherford, Elizabeth Halford, and Mike Hourin.

Special thanks to the indefatigable Kaye Hooker Bryant for her suggestions and encouragement, and to June Goza for her insights and very sharp red pencil.

Author Biography

Michael Henry graduated from Tulane University and University of Virginia School of Law. 5 STAR is his tenth novel. He currently resides and writes in Oxford, Mississippi.

42356654R00157

Made in the USA
Middletown, DE
19 April 2019